ALL IN

ALL IN

GET UNSTUCK, ACCELERATE,
AND GO FURTHER FASTER

JEFFERSON K. ROGERS

ALL IN

Get Unstuck, Accelerate, and Go Further Faster

ISBN HARDCOVER: 978-1-5445-4195-2
      PAPERBACK: 978-1-5445-4193-8
      EBOOK: 978-1-5445-4194-5
      AUDIOBOOK: 978-1-5445-4196-9

CONTENTS

At a pivotal moment in my life, I found a book that was the right message, from the right person, with the right story that helped me believe different things were possible for my life.

This book is dedicated to all the people out there who are ready to start moving in a different direction.

You are meant to do great things.

FOREWORD

I AM HONORED TO write this foreword for a book that speaks to one of the most important qualities that a person can possess: going *ALL IN!*

The ability to be completely devoted to something, whether it be a goal, a dream, or a passion, is what sets apart the successful from the mediocre.

As someone who has spent my entire life studying and teaching systems of achievement, I can say with confidence that the distinctions in this book and the stories told throughout are the cornerstone of massive success.

I firmly believe that each and every person has the potential for greatness, and it is up to each one of us to cultivate and unleash that potential.

Creating greatness in life is not something that happens overnight. It requires a strong commitment to personal growth, a willingness to take risks, and a relentless pursuit of your goals and dreams.

And it also requires an honest look at oneself, a willingness to be completely vulnerable and the courage to reinvent yourself over and over again.

Although many people talk about creating greatness, and going *ALL IN*, this book is a powerful story of the full immersion of that distinction, and what kind of massive transformation can occur when you harness the power of your full commitment.

We learn through the journey of Jefferson that with the right mindset tools, strategies, and support, anything is possible.

In this book, you will find insights and strategies from a man who has achieved greatness in his life. From the lowest bottoms to incredible highs, all due to tapping into his own inner greatness.

But this book is so much more than that.

It is not just about some other person's success story—it is about humanity and how every human being creates a path to greatness and unleashes their full potential in every area of their life.

Throughout this book, you will learn how to develop a growth mindset, become a master over yourself, achieve compelling goals, and overcome obstacles that stand in your way. You will discover strategies for staying motivated, building resilience, and maintaining a positive attitude, even in the face of adversity.

And most importantly, you will learn how to cultivate a sense of purpose and meaning in your life, and channel your passions and talents into something that truly matters.

As you read this book, I encourage you to approach each chapter with an open mind and a willingness to learn. Take the insights and strategies presented here and apply them to your own life in a way that works for you.

Remember, greatness is not a destination—it is a journey. It is something that we all must constantly work toward, and something that we must never give up on. And as humanity evolves and we enter into new challenges and new complexities, it turns out there is a greater and greater need for the wisdom in this book.

Going *ALL IN* is more than just a behavior; it is a path to greatness, and an endless philosophy on how to never stop striving to become the best version of yourself.

It is the force that propels us forward when we are faced with obstacles, keeps us going when the going gets tough, and allows us to achieve things that we never thought possible.

But being *ALL IN* is more than just a state of mind—it is a way of life. It is a choice that we make every day to pursue our dreams and goals with unwavering focus and determination. And it is this choice that separates the winners from the losers, the doers from the dreamers.

In this book, you will find powerful stories and insights from a man who defied the odds and had set a course into a downward spiral. Yet, through determined awareness, he realized there needed to be another path forged—and went on a personal transformation only to discover the truest form of creation tools—the use of his mind and his will.

This book will inspire you and prepare you to take new actions and make new decisions about yourself to challenge yourself toward the highest level of greatness by being completely immersed in a story that was meant to be a demonstration of complete commitment. You will learn how an unlikely hero overcame obstacles, persevered in the face of adversity, and achieved to reach his dreams through sheer determination and complete focus.

This book is not just about someone else's success—it is about yours. It is about how you can harness the power of commitment to achieve your own goals and dreams, no matter how big or small they may be. It is about how you can transform yourself into a person who is fully committed to living life to the fullest, and who never gives up on their dreams.

I urge you to read this book with an open mind and an open heart. Let the stories and insights within inspire you to be the best that you can be, and to commit fully to your own journey of personal growth and success. And remember, you have greatness within you—let it out!

With love and admiration,
KANE MINKUS

INTRODUCTION

ABOUT FIVE YEARS ago, I finally started living halfway smart. These days, I'm the CEO of a business that has produced over $40 million in sales over the past four years. I'm pursuing success in my business, family, and personal goals. I work hard to take care of my body, and I've got an amazing relationship with my wife and kids. In fact, I regularly post coaching videos on my Instagram feed to help others on their own path to success. I've been blessed to experience a lot of highs at this stage in my life.

But I've also experienced a lot of literal highs. Most of my adolescence and early adulthood was spent getting drunk and high. I had everybody's number on speed dial who I knew was partying and had weed for me. I couch surfed instead of paying rent. I put in the minimal amount of work at my various jobs—most of which I got fired from. I blew up at people instead of responding like a mature adult. As successful as I've managed to become at this stage in my life, I used to be equally prolific in self-destruction.

I'm the kind of person who has an addictive nature—whatever I'm into, I go *ALL IN*. When I was a kid, I was addicted to video games. If nobody kept an eye on me or told me anything different, I'd play *Sonic* the *Hedgehog* and *Mario Bros* all day long. Later, it was BMX. As a ten-year-old, I'd ride my bike all the way across town to do jumps and ride with my friends—between six and ten miles. A lot of the time, I'd just go ride by myself, hoping that there would be somebody there I could ride with. When I was thirteen, I started hanging out with this fun group of kids who liked to party. I started drinking—that turned into my new obsession. The substances followed after that.

Fast forward into my thirties, and I'd had twenty years living on repeat, chasing the same old dopamine highs from doing questionable shit, living in the gray area with the law, doing drugs and alcohol, partying, and picking fights with people. For six and a half years, I drove my truck around without a driver's license. Every time I got in a car to drive, it was like, "I might go to jail today, but eff it. Here we go." Another shot of dopamine.

I liked the rush. I liked to go fast. But it took me years to wake up to the fact that my *ALL IN* addictive energy was getting me nowhere.

> My *ALL IN* addictive energy was getting me nowhere.

Here's just one of many, many examples of how this played out in my life.

One night about eight months after my youngest daughter was born in 2014, my wife, Shandell, and I went to a party in the Arizona desert. At the end of the night, Shandell told me we had to get home to the babysitter—it was time to go. Everyone was leaving.

But I was drunk and having a great time. I didn't want to go. So—in Shandell's words—I threw a fit.

I ran out to my truck and locked myself in. I must have been looking for my keys because I took my phone and wallet out of my pocket. I also assume I got hot at some point because I kicked off my flip-flops and took my shirt off. My friends and wife were trying to give me a pep talk through the window. Shandell was frustrated. "We have to get home!" she said. I was pissed off and didn't want to listen.

So, I threw open the door and ran off. I was shirtless, shoeless, and had no money or phone. I literally ran into the Arizona desert in the middle of the night with just a pair of jeans on.

But I was 100 percent committed. I was like, "I ain't going back. Fuck those guys." I figured I didn't need a truck, money, shoes, or other people's help—I had all the momentum I needed all by myself.

ALL IN.

I knew what general direction I had to head in to make it home—except I didn't realize how far it was. I walked through some cornfields on dirt roads and then past a couple of farm properties. After a few miles, my feet were really starting to hurt. I spotted some trucks at one property and tried all the doors to see if any had keys inside. If they did, I figured I would "borrow" the truck and drive myself home.

No one had left any keys inside, but I did find a pair of boots. They were size ten and a half. I wear a size thirteen. I shoved them on, like a drunk-ass Cinderella's stepsister.

I wore them for about half a mile until my feet hurt worse than when I was barefoot. I took the boots off and set them on a concrete culvert by the side of the road. The dirt roads had changed to gravel by then—not cute, little pea gravel but big, sharp construction gravel. I made it a little bit farther, but I was going slow. My feet were so sore.

I started tearing little pieces off my Buckle jeans and wrapped them around my feet to create a barrier. I tore a little off, then a little more, shredding my pants. I went higher and higher to get enough material to wrap around my feet until I had turned my jeans into Daisy Dukes. My pockets were literally hanging out below the fringe. The only thing left to indicate I had once been wearing jeans was the seams, which I hadn't been able to tear through, so they still hung all the way down the sides.

I looked like a complete idiot. The "moccasins" didn't even last that long—I tried retying them, again and again, but they just wouldn't stay together.

By daylight, I finally made it to some sidewalk and eventually started to get my bearings. Somehow, I had ended up way north of my house. I wasn't anywhere close to where I had wanted to go—but I *was* close to a Walmart.

I walked in, pants torn to shreds, no shirt, no shoes. Walmart's worst nightmare, basically. I walked straight over to the men's section. I found a pair of neon-green basketball shorts. I didn't even go to the changing room. I just dropped my pants and pulled on the neon-green shorts. Then I went over to the shoe section and put on some gray flip-flops.

I didn't bother with a shirt.

I walked to the front of the store and found the checkout aisle. I said to the lady, "I just want to give you a heads-up: I've got to take these, but I'm going to come back later and pay for it."

She said, "You can't do that, sir. We will have to call the police."

I shrugged. "Do whatever you need to do. If they want to know where to find me, I'm walking home. But I'll come back and pay for these later. I promise."

I walked the rest of the way home, about another two miles. When I made it to my driveway around eight or nine, I found Shandell backing out with all the kids in the car. She rolled down the window and said, "I was just coming to look for you!"

She paused and looked at me. Then she said, "What the hell are you wearing?"

I looked at my watch—I still had my watch—and gave Shandell a look like, "Why weren't you looking for me all night?" I think I was still drunk. I walked in the garage, chugged about a half-gallon of orange juice, and then went to bed.

That's how far my *ALL IN* attitude used to get me: I embarrassed myself. I hurt my relationships. I had to steal from effing Walmart. I was lost. I was stubborn. And I was too prideful to admit I didn't actually know what the hell I was doing.

I know what it means to be stuck. I know what it's like to get to the end of the day and wonder what the hell I accomplished. I'm an expert at dulling pain, shame, and the burden of responsibility with weed and alcohol. I have years of experience sponging off of other people's generosity. I'm a pro at acting like an asshole.

But not anymore. Somehow, I ended up going from a barefoot idiot in the desert to the CEO of a multimillion-dollar company. I saved my marriage. I've become a better father. I learned how to accelerate—in cars, in planes, on motorcycles, and in achieving explosive growth in my business.

I've figured out how to take the level of energy I used to channel into my addiction and instead channel it into areas of life that serve me: my business, my marriage, working out, getting healthy. I've been able to heal relationships. I've learned how to stop holding myself back and get focused, get disciplined. I've found people who've mentored me, coached me, helped me get past my destructive thought patterns. I've discovered principles of success that have launched me into incredible wealth, prominence, reputable leadership, and a whole lot more real happiness than I ever experienced when I was high.

> I've figured out how to take the level of energy I used to channel into my addiction and instead channel it into areas of life that serve me.

All of that started with the decision to get unstuck, manufacture change in my life, and start making choices I could feel proud of.

Then, I went *ALL IN*.

If you think you could probably be doing better than you are right now—if you wish you could get unstuck, accelerate, and start going further faster—I know exactly where you're at. I've only been living halfway smart for the last five years. But in that time, I've been able to experience more personal and financial growth than many people experience in a lifetime.

And I want to help you do the same.

DON'T ACCEPT THE UNACCEPTABLE

Let's get real for a second. If anything about my story resonates with your own, chances are, you've justified a lot of negative behavior in your life. Maybe, like me, you're dealing with alcohol and marijuana—and you may not perceive it as an addiction. You describe it as "more of a release," "just something I've gotten used to doing," or "a social thing"—for years and years and years. You've gotten good at making excuses for getting drunk and high instead of working toward your goals.

Or maybe you've come to accept what you see in the mirror, even though you're not in the best shape. You don't like what you see when you're naked, but you come up with excuses to avoid going to the gym, like I did for so long. For the first eight years of my marriage, I didn't make my health a priority. If you look at pictures of me in that eighth year of marriage, I've got a fluffy face, love handles, and a dad bod. I look older than I do now. But I ignored it for a long time. I *had* the urge to do something about it, but I came up with excuses to stay stuck. "I'm just going to hit the snooze button one more time," "My wife likes me the way I am," and "At least I have good genes—it's not that bad." All of it: a bullshit narrative.

Maybe the justifications are around your bank account: you've come to accept you're always going to have very little money. Early in my adulthood, I figured the only way to get more money was to work harder—but even when I finally did, I hit the ceiling. I capped out around $70,000, working seventy to eighty hours a week, and I had no further to go without developing more skills. I knew I was going to be stuck there, and I started coming up with reasons to justify accepting that reality.

> You've gotten good at making excuses for yourself instead of working toward your goals.

Why do we do that? Why do we accept the unacceptable?

Because the alternative is completely flipping your whole life on its head and looking at an entirely different way of living. Maybe that scares the hell out of you. It sure scared the hell out of me.

But what happens if you stay stuck?

Let me tell you where I was at: I was miserable. I knew I couldn't keep up that same way of living. My life was passing me by, seventy hours at a time. I was watching my kids grow up over cell phone pictures. I was irritable and tired when I got home. I had zero patience. The little time that I spent with my family wasn't quality. I got more excited about cracking open a beer than anything else.

And I got to a point where I decided I couldn't accept it anymore. I was wasting my life.

Listen: your life—your choices, your decisions, and the circumstances keeping you stuck—have become acceptable to you. *Until you decide* they're not acceptable anymore, you will continue to repeat the same patterns over and over and over. You will experience the same old shit. No matter how much you don't like it or how bad you wish you had more money in your bank account, nothing's going to change until you decide to refuse to accept it for one more minute.

> Nothing's going to change until you decide to refuse to accept it for one more minute.

That's when change becomes possible.

ALL IN.

PLANTED SEEDS

In this book, I'm going to share the principles that worked for me so that you can become the success story you're meant to be.

My own journey from being broke and addicted to millionaire CEO was a result of a lot of seeds that were planted along the way. Grant Cardone, author of *The 10X Rule*, was one big seed: like me, he used to be addicted and stuck. Now, he's a bestselling author, leadership coach, and billionaire. I read his book, watched his videos, and did what he told me to do. I took that example of somebody who had achieved the kind of life I wanted and started to emulate everything that he did. Then, I built on it. That's how I've been able to reach my level of success.

But Grant Cardone wasn't the only one who planted a seed. I had a lot of people who loved me and expected big things out of me. Every single time they had a conversation with me, it was a seed planted. They reminded me that I was capable of doing more—they saw great things in me. I saw people around me who were living the kind of lifestyle I wanted, and they helped show me the way.

That's what I want to be for you. This book is a roadmap to get you unstuck, help you accelerate, and then get you to go further, faster. You don't have to do things exactly the way that I did them, but I'm going to share the exact methodology I used, the commitments and sacrifices I made, and the timeline of what I did.

> This book is a roadmap to get you unstuck, help you accelerate, and then get you to go further, faster.

HERE'S HOW

Change starts with mindset. You've got to be willing to start looking at things differently—*believing* that good things are possible for you. I'm going to help you make the decision to get unstuck, find ways to manufacture change in your life, and learn to view even the worst experiences of your life as fuel for positive change. Most importantly, you're going to claim the truth that you are meant to do great things.

Then, I'm going to tell you how to start taking action in the direction of that different type of lifestyle and accelerate your progress. There's still all the work that has to be put in, the commitment that has to be made, the habits that have to change, and the discipline that has to be developed.

We're going to talk about getting focused and getting disciplined—

replacing habits that kept you stuck with habits that will help launch you into success. We're going to talk a lot about the importance of goals and identifying a vision for yourself. You're going to learn about the kind of people to surround yourself with and important ways to invest in your growth. I'm going to tell you some of the most important lessons I've learned about communicating well that have transformed my marriage and ability to lead. All these principles are going to help you go further, faster.

Don't go looking for some magic formula in all of this because there isn't one. Life is lived little bits at a time. You've got to do some tough inner work to get yourself off this cycle of repeat. Then, you've got to put in a lot of consistent daily activity to achieve success. It's going to be difficult. It was for me. It was hard. It was incredibly challenging.

> You've got to do some tough inner work to get yourself off this cycle of repeat. Then, you've got to put in a lot of consistent daily activity to achieve success.

But it also led to a complete, *literal* transformation of myself and my life. I used to be the guy on the couch, a guy with a fluffy bod and long, goofy hair that was all wispy on top and looked like shit. I drank any alcohol I could get my hands on, smoked weed every day, piled up debt, and fought with my wife. I was a shitty example for everyone who looked up to me, and I drank to suppress the burden of responsibility I failed to carry.

Now, I'm winning physique competitions and motocross tournaments. I'm leading a company I'm proud of, convincing some of the best people in the industry that they want to work with me, and watching explosive growth. I'm the example I want to be for my brothers, and I make my kids proud. I have an amazing relationship with my wife. I've completely transformed physically, mentally, financially, geographically, and relationally—basically in every way you can think of.

Yes, it's difficult—but with the mindset and discipline that you learn in this book, your journey will become a game of overcoming challenges. And every time you do, it's a win: you can trust and know that overcoming each challenge is another step that shapes the rest of your life for the better. If you're up for a challenge, then hang on for the ride. You'll learn about the mindset and discipline that will be necessary to overcome what once seemed to be insurmountable obstacles to get to the next level of your success.

And here's the proof: I'm not stumbling barefoot in the desert anymore. I'm accelerating my trajectory as fast as humanly possible and enjoying the ride along the way.

ALL IN.

That all happened because I finally started getting rid of my bad habits and trading them for good habits. I figured out how to manufacture change.

You can do the same. Instead of being stuck, you can be a person others admire. Instead of working seventy, eighty, ninety hours a week as an entrepreneur, you can find an alternative. You can show up to a crowded room, full of successful people, and be confident that you have something to contribute. The addictive tendencies that you have can be flipped and used toward progress and positivity. You can build a life you feel proud of. You can be a person others want to emulate.

> You can build a life you feel proud of. You can be a person others want to emulate.

I want to show you what's possible for you. You don't have to copy it or do it exactly my way. You're not going to be like me, but I'm going to share everything that I've done, in as much detail as I can possibly get in a book. Everything is in here: the thought patterns, your personal beliefs, the daily activities, the goals, your relationships, and your communication. I've spelled it out as clearly as I possibly can.

In fact, the main reason I wanted to write this book was because I'm emulating my own mentor. Grant Cardone was the right person at the right time with the right message for me. His book showed me a path out of self-destruction and helped me see what was possible for my life.

Now, I want to pay it forward. This book might be the planted seed in your life that helps you realize you're capable of great things. I've got an obligation to share some of the ways I've been able to reach this level of success in my life so that people like you can share in the success too.

Even if I get to be that person for just one reader—even if it's just *one* person who's ready for this message at the right time in their life—it will be worth putting in all the ridiculous hours this book required to come together.

Maybe that person is you.

GET READY

Are you ready?

You've got to be ready and committed to see this through. Because if you think that you're going to be able to stay in the same environment with the same people but make astronomical changes in your life, that's a complete fantasy.

If you're in a place where you recognize your same old habits are no longer serving you, you might be ready. If you can see that your current way of life isn't helping you get any closer to your goals and dreams or be the best version of yourself, you might be ready. If you're ready to put all the negative things in your life to death so that they're no longer acceptable to you, you might be ready.

What are you ready for? Let me give you a glimpse of your future.

You have completely transformed yourself and your life. You have new habits, disciplines, and daily activities, all of which serve you. You started with making small, small changes, but every one of those changes moved you a little closer to your goals. You've become a better version of yourself. You've healed your most important relationships. You're making good money. You're fit, strong, and confident. Everyone who knows you is proud of you, including you. You're living a life that reflects your true potential.

You want things to change? Don't accept the unacceptable. You are meant to do great things. Commit to the possibility of doing something great with your life.

Then—go *ALL IN*.

PART 1

Get Unstuck

CHAPTER 1

Unstuck Yourself

DECIDE YOU WANT SOMETHING DIFFERENT

GIVE ME A gas pedal, and I'll floor it. I love the adrenaline rush of speed. But here's something I've learned: if you want to *get* somewhere at top speed, your direction matters. Your vehicle matters. Your approach matters. If you're just into the rush, but you don't pay any attention to those other things, you're not going to get anywhere. You're going to end up *stuck*.

For example, like the time I drove off a cliff.

The truck I was driving was a piece of junk—dark brown, little 1983 Toyota single cab. I bought it when I was nineteen for 500 bucks. There was a bad oil leak out of the front cover which meant oil would get sprayed all over the front of the engine by the fan. The alternator would get so saturated in oil that it wouldn't charge the battery anymore. Whenever I started noticing that the battery seemed low, I would take the truck to the carwash, spray off all the oil on the alternator, and then it would start working again.

One night, me, a friend, and two other guys I had just met piled into that thing to drive to a party in Park City. My friend sat next to me in the cab, and the two other guys sat in the truck bed. I hadn't sprayed off the alternator in a while and I knew the alternator was on the fritz. We barely made it there.

Luckily, on the way back, it was mostly downhill. I'd had a couple of beers, but I wasn't drunk—just in the mood to be crazy.

I saw a truck full of some of my other friends—also with people in the truck bed—and I decided to try to pass them on the narrow dirt shoulder. I was doing around forty or fifty miles per hour as I raced past them on the mountain road. I could tell the battery of the truck was dying—the lights were terrible. And then, at the bottom of the canyon, a sharp right turn came out of nowhere. I spun the wheel as fast as I could, but I didn't even have time to hit the brakes.

We went right off the cliff.

The next thing I remember was being upside down. The roof of the truck was holding us up from the ground, but it was covered in shattered glass. Both my friend and I were held in by our seatbelts, suspended over the truck ceiling—we seemed to be okay. The passenger side of the cab had been smashed completely, so we were kind of crunched sideways, one on top of the other. We had to press against the roof of the truck to get enough slack in our belts to unbuckle. The shards of glass stuck into our hands and we both started bleeding like crazy. I had blood all over my hands.

There was a small space on the driver's side window that was just barely large enough for us to squeeze out. I got more glass in my face and my hair. I'm sure it should have hurt, pulling myself through that broken window, but I didn't really feel anything. I had so much adrenaline pounding through me.

I was kind of out of it—maybe from the adrenaline, maybe from the beer I'd drank or the weed I'd smoked, maybe because I hit my head. After crawling out of the truck, I walked straight up the thirty-some foot embankment to try and go catch the guys in the other truck, so they didn't go by and leave us there. Of course, they'd already pulled over. I stood there at the top of the cliff, feeling confused, bleeding all over myself, watching everybody else run down to the truck.

The two kids in the back were trapped underneath. I stared, feeling disoriented, watching the other guys lift up the pickup truck to let the trapped kids out. They were banged up pretty bad.

I didn't help. My thoughts were slow and fast, all at the same time. I was hit with the realization that I could have chosen *not to do that.* But I did it anyway—now it was too late, I couldn't take it back, and I was going to have to deal with the consequences. It takes a lot of words to explain, but the feeling hit me in a single moment. I'd made a decision, and now there was no going back.

Thank God, no one died.

I was pretty bloody by the time the cops showed up. They wanted to give me a blood-alcohol level test, which I refused. I wasn't sure I'd clear it after the beers I'd had—but I was even more worried that my marijuana habit of the past six years would show up on the test. My refusal resulted in an immediate license suspension for the next eighteen months. They also put me in jail.

I can still remember the shame I felt when my mom came to pick me up. I don't remember the specifics of what she said—but a lot of it would have been what she *always* told me in moments like this: "Think about the example you're being to your brothers. You're better than this. Are you finally going to learn your lesson so that you don't make this mistake again?"

I didn't. I went to jail several more times and didn't quit drinking for another fourteen years.

I wanted to go fast, but in all the wrong ways. I was focused on the adrenaline rush, but I had no discipline. I wasn't taking care of my vehicle. I'd lost sight of the road. As a result, going "fast" ended up taking me backward. I lost my license, I totaled my truck, and I wound up in a jail cell.

Stuck.

Here's a hard lesson I had to learn: it's a choice to get stuck. It's a choice to remain stuck. And it's a choice to get *unstuck*.

If you want to get unstuck, you need to recognize that your self-destructive habits are hurting you more than they're helping you, and *decide* to make a change. You deserve better.

> It's a choice to get stuck. It's a choice to remain stuck. And it's a choice to get *unstuck*. The choice is up to you.

ARE YOU HOLDING YOURSELF BACK?

Stuck: like you can't seem to get ahead or climb out of the rut you're in. You want to get unstuck, but you don't know how, and your head is full of negativity: not enough money. Not enough discipline. Not fast enough, not far enough.

There are many ways people get "stuck." For me, it was addiction. For others, it's getting stuck at a stagnant level in their business, ignoring opportunities for growth. Maybe you put up with a toxic relationship or maintain unhealthy habits. Staying stuck usually starts with your mindset: you have patterns of justifications to rationalize why you're not making progress in the ways you want. The most common reason people get stuck is because they're not ready to put in the time, energy, commitment, and work that will be required to accomplish getting to the next level—and there are some common symptoms. See if any of these descriptions fit the choices you're making.

YOU ESCAPE

Do you find yourself filling your time up with unproductive things, just to get through the day? One of the things that I used to do a lot is watch a ton of movies. I would go through one movie after another. These days, when I log onto Netflix with my wife, she gives me a hard time because

I've watched every good movie that was ever made. For so many years, that's how I filled up my time.

If you're wasting your day with time-fillers instead of being productive, you're choosing to hold yourself back. That includes wasting time on watching sports or movies, scrolling on your phone, or even doing bullshit hobbies. Maybe it looks fun, and maybe you see plenty of other people doing it around you, but when I was doing that stuff, I knew it was wasting my time. When I was watching all those movies, I could have been studying, or out working another job, or making money. Instead, I just sat in a dark living room, picking through the DVD shelf. I was choosing to keep myself stuck.

I'm in a very different place now. There are certain points during my week when I am faced with small decisions about how to use my time. I can continue being productive, or I can choose to waste valuable time on things that will not produce any results. This quote I heard years ago from author and speaker Tom Hopkins helps me stay on track, moving in the direction of my goals: "I MUST DO THE MOST PRODUCTIVE THING POSSIBLE AT EVERY GIVEN MOMENT."

There are a lot of different ways you can be productive—for me, that includes spending time with my family, putting in extra time preparing healthy meals, working out, pouring into my business, personal development, and so on. But I'm *always* asking myself, "Is what I'm doing right now productive?" Scrolling Instagram doesn't cut it.

Two of the things in this life that you have complete control over are your thoughts and what you do with your free time. How you manage these two things will determine the quality of life you have and the progress you are able to make in your personal and business life.

> Two of the things in this life that you have complete control over are your thoughts and what you do with your free time.

Sometimes, losing focus of your main priorities can be a form of escaping. If you're a business owner, you might be trying to escape by chasing after the next shiny thing, instead of staying focused on your business. You justify going after a new opportunity, like real estate or another investment, because you think you've earned it. You say it's worth the attention because it could turn into another revenue stream—but really, you're just losing focus on your main thing. Consider whether or not you're keeping yourself stuck by looking to escape.

YOU TAKE THE EASY ROAD

You're holding yourself back if you're always trying to get more for less, without putting in the work. Back in 2013, when I was still struggling with drugs and alcohol, I was working for my uncle. He had started paying me good money and was trying to lead me toward taking on more responsibility and becoming one of the leaders in his company. I wanted the money—but I didn't want to have to *do* more. I would try and justify my raises, thinking I deserved more money for other things I brought to the table. But my uncle could tell I wanted more, for less. It irritated him.

Now that I'm a business owner—and I see some of my employees trying to pull the same shit—I've realized that any employee's salary is a direct reflection on the amount of value they *offer* the marketplace. If you're not contributing value, you're not going to get value. Even if you manage to talk yourself into a position of leadership and higher income—if you're not continuing to back up the amount of value you give to support that income, it's going to be pretty apparent. Ultimately, you're going to go backwards.

If you want to get unstuck, you need to continue to *push* yourself. Develop yourself. Do extra and have less expectations. I have a couple of outstanding people on my staff that are an example of that. They can always handle more, and they want more, and they ask for more responsibility—and they're not necessarily asking for raises. They're just the type of people who want to prove their worth and value.

In my early adulthood, I always knew that I *could* turn up my effort and try something new. I *could* put myself out there, to go make more money. But I justified holding back: I wasn't ready for a big commitment yet. I didn't want to put in the work that would be required.

This stuck mindset can hold you back, no matter what level you've reached. One of my old mentors has stopped pushing for growth in his own business. He also continues to do much of the hands-on work himself, rather than delegating to his staff. Why? Because for him, that feels easier than learning how to train and develop other people. When I ask him why he doesn't push for more growth, he just tells me, "I'm tired." He's making a good income and things are still happening with his business—but he's not growing. And when you're not growing, you're dying.

If you're also looking to take the easy road—you're choosing to keep yourself stuck. You're training yourself to always be comfortable, which means you'll never get uncomfortable in the way that growth requires.

> If you want to get unstuck, you need to continue to *push* yourself. Growth requires discomfort.

YOU TAKE ADVANTAGE OF PEOPLE

You're not living into your full potential if you manipulate others to get what you want. Just out of high school, I went and lived with a couple of dudes I knew from school. They let me stay on the couch of their place while they were going to college. With the money their parents had given them to live, they supported me. I drank all their alcohol, smoked all their weed, ate all their food—and they still loved me.

Why? Because I got good at manipulating people. I don't even know if I was doing it intentionally—I think I was doing it innocently. I wanted to be there so bad, I learned how to read them and play a conversation so that I could stay in that cushy environment. It was manipulative, how good I was at it. I developed a strong sense for body language and tonality and sensing people's energy, because I was ultra, ultra, ultra aware of when things started getting a little bit tense. I'd sense that I was wearing out my welcome and shift tactics, to see how much I could get away with.

This tendency can apply in any context, any close relationship—and it can certainly happen at work. Especially when business owners hire people they have a close relationship with, that becomes a situation that is vulnerable to manipulation. The business owner might try to manipulate their friend to work harder for less. Or, the employee might try to manipulate their boss for more money, when they're attempting to skate by.

Manipulating others is another form of taking the easy road. If you take advantage of people to keep yourself comfortable, then you're not a contributor. You're not pushing yourself to grow or learn. You're not making a positive impact on others—you're a drain. And that's going to keep you stuck.

YOU'RE KEEPING YOURSELF IN A DEAD END

But what if you're letting other people take advantage of *you*? Then, you're keeping yourself in a dead end—and that's just one variation. Maybe you're settling for an unhealthy relationship when you know it's not a good situation. Maybe you're settling for a dead-end job. Maybe you continue to say you don't have time to eat healthy or work out, so you never feel any better about your physical appearance. Maybe you're tolerating the presence of a toxic employee because of the preexisting relationship you have.

If you're keeping yourself in a place that's not optimal—you're holding yourself back.

> If you're keeping yourself in a dead-end situation—you're holding yourself back.

Many people do this because they don't have the confidence to get out of their bad situation. If that's you, we're going to work on that confidence over the next few chapters.

But another big reason people stay in a dead end is because they're coming up with reasons to stay there. It's very similar to the lines of justification you hear from people that deal with alcohol and weed. Alcoholics and addicts say things like, "I can quit anytime I want to." "I take care of my body in a way that I can drink hard on the weekend and recover quickly." "I only do it socially." They're all the same lines of justification that I used to feed myself and the people around me. These days, when I tell people I don't drink and then they immediately go to justifying their drinking habit, I get a smile on my face, listening to them. I know exactly what they're doing.

You'll hear the same kind of thing, just on a different subject, about people's shitty situations at work. They *know* they don't like it. They know it's not going to lead them anywhere. They know there's very little chance of growth, or making a six-figure income. But they come up with justifications like benefits and security: "I could never quit on them; they've been so loyal to me." That's a bullshit line of justification to make yourself feel better about staying in a shitty situation.

YOU'RE ALWAYS RIGHT

When someone refuses to hear any kind of feedback, they're working themselves into a dead end. Mentors don't want to work with people like that. Team members are going to get sick of working with someone like that too. You will terminate your possibility for growth when you choose pride over humility.

This kind of pride can be common among young entrepreneurs. As soon as anyone challenges their way of thinking, they get defensive. They're not open to criticism or willing to apply it. They're convinced that whatever they've been doing is working for them—and they're not interested in whatever perspective other people might want to give them, even if it's clear that they need to develop in some key ways.

I used to operate with that mindset. In the early years of my marriage, when I was still addicted, I had to always be right. I didn't want my wife to challenge my way of thinking. And Shandell is stubborn as hell, too, so guess how that worked out? I finally realized I was driving a wedge between us by trying to convince her that her truth and experiences weren't valid. The only way we were going to make progress is if I took her seriously and listened. She also had a unique and valuable perspective to offer me—and once I started actually listening to her, I started growing a lot as a husband.

The same is true in the workplace. You will alienate your staff if your opinion always has to be the right one and no one else can be trusted to share any decent ideas. In my early days as an entrepreneur, I was short with people. I didn't ask other people questions. I had this perception that—because I was in a position of power—I didn't need outside perspectives. But I started to pick up on people's negative energy around me. Once I started realizing how valuable other people's perspectives were, along with their experience and expertise, it opened my eyes to what they could bring to the challenges we were dealing with. I started asking more questions. I opened up. The change in my attitude caused people to engage more, which led to more innovation and growth.

Once you're willing to own the fact that you don't have all the answers, you can grow. Don't ever stall out on your emotional and professional development. Once you assume that your current level of maturity is good and you have nothing more to learn—heads up. You're stuck.

> Don't ever stall out on your emotional and professional development.

STOP BELIEVING YOUR OWN BULLSHIT

Some people are stuck, and they will never get unstuck. There's nothing

I could say to those people that would ever change their minds. They're convinced that their situation is all they're capable of, all they're made for—all they're meant for. If I were to try to tell them they're holding themselves back, I'd only make things worse. They'd get riled up and double down on their situation, because they believe so strongly in the story they're telling themselves. They've convinced themselves that their justifications are correct and true, and that's the only reality to them.

But if you can *hear* your own bullshit—you've got a chance. When you're explaining to other people about your job, or your bad habits, or your toxic relationship, there may be a part of you in the back of your brain that doesn't believe your own justifications. You don't truly buy into the narrative you're telling. *That* part of you is telling the truth.

You know you're settling for less than what you're meant for. And because you recognize it—you can get out of it.

> If you can *recognize* your own bullshit, you've got a chance.

Think about the narrative you're telling yourself. It's the narrative that constantly plays in your head. It's the narrative that comes out in your conversations. You play this narrative over and over and over, and that's what you're drawing from to tell somebody about why you keep that toxic employee, or half ass your job, or smoke weed: "It helps me sleep. It helps my anxiety. It helps me unwind at the end of the day."

And it's not just people in an addiction or working a dead-end job making these justifications. Even people at a high level, even me, still, sometimes—I justify stupid things I do. I'll think to myself, "What the fuck are you saying?" I say it anyway because I'm trying to convince myself it's okay. But I know it's bullshit—and once I get a second to register that I'm being an idiot again, I can make a different decision.

I've had hundreds of people reach out to me after seeing some of my podcasts and hearing me talk about overcoming addiction and reaching a high level of success. They ask me how I did it. I'll write back and ask, "What do you feel like you're struggling with the most?" Immediately, they want to write me an entire paragraph full of their narrative: all the justifications they've been telling themselves over and over, for who knows how long. It's like clockwork.

The people who are starting to climb *out* of their rut are the ones who can smell their own bullshit. They have started to take some steps forward. Seeds have been planted in their own minds and they're reaching out because they *know* they want something different—but they're not quite done justifying the choices that are holding them back. I could ask them the same question I'm going to ask you:

Do you *want* to get unstuck? Do you truly want something different?

If the answer is yes, then make the choice to call bullshit on your stuck narrative. You know you're justifying choices that are holding you back. You can smell the odor when you're writing that paragraph to me, when you're telling those stories, when you're feeding yourself the same lies as you crack open a beer. If *I* can pick up on that bullshit when you're talking to me, I know you feel it too.

Stop justifying choices that are holding you back.

Now, start paying closer attention to the narrative you're telling yourself. Ask yourself a few key questions:

- Is my narrative truly aligned with who I want to be? Put differently, do I really want my life to look like this in five years' time?
- Is my narrative going to help me accomplish what I want to do? In other words, are my actions propelling me forward toward my goals and dreams?
- Is my narrative helping me become the very best version of

myself and reach the next level—personally, professionally, and with my family?

- Am I excited to get out of bed in the morning?

If the answer to any of those statements is no, then it's time to start telling yourself a new story. Decide you want something different bad enough that you're willing to do something about it. Stop ignoring your instincts, or your conscience, or your intuition telling you that you're capable of doing more. You don't have to settle for this situation.

So, ask yourself one final question:

- Do I want to get unstuck? Do I truly want something different?

TOO COMFORTABLE

Driving off a cliff got me stuck in a jail cell, with no truck or license. But I was stuck in many, many other ways—for a good twenty years.

For most of my adulthood, I've been the guy on the couch. I did a lot of nothing. And I hated myself for it.

I got kicked out of my mom's house because of a bad relationship with my stepdad. Then, I got kicked out of my dad's house because of a bad relationship with my stepmom. I started couch surfing at my friends! Most of the time, I didn't pay rent. Like I shared earlier in the chapter, my friends let me eat their food, drink their booze, and get high under their roof. Sometimes I would contribute a case of beer, but other than that, I didn't bring anything to the table. Eventually though, my friends got tired of my freeloading, too, and it was time for me to find a new place to crash.

In 2008, I had a decent job and moved into a house with my brothers. Then, in April, I broke my leg bad in a motorcycle accident. Now, I didn't have any way to support myself or contribute rent. Guess where I ended up?

Back on the couch.

I got *really* familiar with that mustard-colored corduroy couch. I had a lot of time to think about my situation and where I was at in my life. I thought about what kind of example I was setting to my younger brothers, at twenty-four years old.

A lot of memories came up. I remembered the time in high school when I went to a local drive thru restaurant with a couple of friends when I was high. Some cute girls from school came up to say hi—and I couldn't even talk to them. At school, I was never that stoned, so those girls probably thought of me as a good-looking guy who could have a conversation. But that night, I was so awkward and paranoid—I thought they were going to see my red eyes, and I could not get a single word out to those girls because I was ashamed of myself. I hated that.

I remembered one time I was doing construction in east LA, staying at a seedy Motel 6. I partied with some guys who were smoking meth out of a bong. Their pupils were as big as the color of their eyes. They were so strung out—their energy felt evil. I remember them telling me all the sketchy things they did to make money, and then they offered me a hit. How many times had I smoked out of a bong? I'd never done hard drugs, but in that moment, I was *so* close.

I tried *not* to think of all the other accidents I'd been in. The time I drove off the cliff and nearly killed the two kids in the back. The time I almost killed my brother when my car got T-boned because I ran a red light. Tried not to think of my mom bailing me out of jail— and all the times she told me to be a better example to my younger brothers. Tried not to think of all the times people had told me I was better than this.

Instead, I'd prop another pillow under my busted leg, swig my beer, and change the channel.

One night, after recuperating for about four months, I was sitting on that corduroy couch after watching Supercross. It was the middle of the night and a commercial came on for Motorcycle Mechanics Institute. I sat forward and zeroed in. The next day, I called the number. I don't know what it was about that commercial, but I knew I had to figure out a way to get myself to that school.

I knew if I stayed in that house, on that couch, nothing was going to change. I didn't have the discipline to kick my addictions. I didn't have an alternative. I'd burned most of my bridges.

If I kept going down the same path, I was never going to be able to tap into that version of myself that I knew I was capable of being. I was sick and tired of justifying my behavior. I was sick and tired of doing the same shit over and over, and that being the sum total of who I was.

I don't even know that I realized what I was doing for myself in calling that school. I wasn't smart enough or aware enough then to think through it like I am now. It was just an instinct.

I had to get the fuck out. And I decided to do something about it.

COMMIT TO ACTION

What about you? Is enough, enough? Are you ready to make a change? Ready to be done with the excuses and mediocrity? Are you ready to be a success story?

If so, then make a decision to do something about it. If you don't decide, you're never going to take any of the steps you need to take to make progress. And *action* is what's ultimately going to get you unstuck.

Action will not feel like a comfortable corduroy couch. Change starts with doing difficult things. For a lot of us, that's going to be a painful shift. Most people get out of high school and think they're going to go out and accomplish some big things. But then, they get knocked down a couple of pegs. They get their teeth kicked in a little bit. They get complacent with their dreams because it's difficult. It's challenging. It's daunting. So, they revert to doing what's comfortable, and they get stuck. Just like I did.

I just did a podcast the other day with a guy who is in this exact place right now. He's stuck. And he's trying to justify to me why he's still hanging out with the same people, drinking socially, and doing all the same shit that I did. I was thinking, "You're not fooling me, buddy." He already knows the answer to why he's still stuck. But he's not ready to do the hard work to change.

That was the funny thing about all the years I kept myself stuck—I knew what I needed to do the whole time. I just hadn't come to terms with the work it was going to require. I wasn't ready to commit to the different habits, different thinking, and different group of people I would need if I wanted to come out better on the other side. I had always been ALL IN, but I finally made a shift to channel that energy in a direction that was positive and productive.

Honestly, manufacturing that change scared me to death. When I was trying to change my life, I didn't know what the outcome was going to be. I didn't know if it was going to work. There were no guarantees.

There are *still* no guarantees. I can remember that fear in my distant past because I feel it again with each new opportunity I commit to. Right now, I'm working on raising twelve million dollars for a real estate investment and prepping for several big speaking gigs. Guess what? I still feel that fear. I'm a long way from where I used to be, but I still feel a level of uncertainty and insecurity with every new challenge. It's there at each new stage and every new opportunity for growth.

But you've got to get used to living with the anxiety that comes with change, because that's the sign that you're pushing the edge of the envelope. It's *important* to feel that anxiety. If you're not feeling it, then you're not growing or progressing.

You'll get better at taking on challenges with time. You'll build more confidence in your ability to overcome them and get to the other side. But the fear never goes away. That's why you've got to get comfortable being uncomfortable.

Years ago, I got through that discomfort by claiming a positive narrative for my life and then committing to action. I was scared and uncertain when I started up my business, but I believed it was possible, and then kept putting in the work. Every day—day in, day out—I put in the work. Progress never happened as fast as I wanted it to. Honestly, I still feel like I have a long way to go. Shit does not happen as fast as I want it to, it never will. But I never stopped making progress.

If you're justifying doing whatever is the most comfortable thing and finding yourself repeating the same old patterns—listen to the voice that's telling you, "You're meant for bigger things. You're meant to do great things with your life. But you're going to have to get through some difficult times to see it through."

So, practice discomfort. Start implementing some difficult shit into your life, even something as simple as a cold shower. I've been able to reach some incredible success at this point in my life, but I still try to put myself in an uncomfortable situation any chance I get. I know that if I want to keep taking it to the next level, it's not going to be from my comfort zone. I'm always on the lookout for something hard—something that can help me adapt and evolve into the next best version of myself. That's one reason why I'm training to become a pilot and spending six figures a year on Mastermind conferences and working with advisers: I want to keep learning. I want to keep pushing myself. Change does not happen from the couch.

> Change does not happen from the couch.

Want to join me? Stop trying to justify your stuck choices. Stop making excuses for not following your dreams. Stop brushing it off if things are going badly, or even if they're average.

Decide you're done giving in. Decide you've had enough with the bullshit narrative. Decide you're not going to let life keep *happening to you* from a cushy place of comfort and complacency.

Instead, do the scary thing, the hard thing, the better thing. Let's talk about how to manufacture change in your life to get you unstuck, and get you accelerating in the direction you want.

ACTION STEPS

Get honest with yourself. Are you holding yourself back? Challenge your thoughts:

- Is my narrative truly aligned with who I want to be? Put differently, do I really want my life to look like this in five years' time?
- Is my narrative going to help me accomplish what I want to do? In other words, are my actions propelling me forward toward my goals and dreams?
- Is my narrative helping me become the very best version of myself and reach the next level—personally, professionally, and with my family?
- Am I excited to get out of bed in the morning?
- Do I *want* to get unstuck? Do I truly want something different?

If you realize you really want to get unstuck—bad enough that you're willing to experience the discomfort of doing something different—you're ready. Make the decision today to start making concrete changes in your life that will put to death your negative patterns and build healthy momentum into your life.

How can you do that? Keep reading.

CHAPTER 2

Manufacture Change

PUT YOURSELF IN A POSITION WHERE
CHANGE IS ALL THAT CAN HAPPEN

YOU WANT CHANGE? Then put yourself in a place—physically, emotionally, mentally—where change is *all that can happen*. Take concrete steps to change your environment—ones that won't allow for easy backsliding. Even baby steps can be huge in shifting your trajectory. Be deliberate about crafting an environment that will facilitate the change you're looking for and optimize your chances of success.

For me, that meant moving from Utah to Arizona in October 2008 to enroll in the Motorcycle Mechanics Institute. By the time I was ready to move, I'd gotten the hardware out of my leg and had been able to start working again—but I still didn't have a driver's license. The night before I left, my brother threw a party for me. I've got a picture from that night of me and my brother. We'd just gotten done smoking some weed, and we were partying our asses off.

If I'd stayed there, I would have kept doing the exact same thing. Instead, I chose to get out.

I'll be honest: I got my ass kicked those first couple weeks. When I moved to Arizona, my aunt and uncle were good enough to let me live with them, but my Uncle Craig—a cop—laid down some ground rules: I had to agree to stop drinking and smoking weed for as long as I was under their roof. I'd also decided on my own to give up smoking cigarettes.

I had always gone from one parent's house to the other, or had stayed with people I knew well, in a familiar environment. In all those other contexts, I'd been able to use drugs and alcohol to suppress all my negative emotions. Any time I felt any uncertainty, all I needed to do was get another bag of weed.

Now—in a new place, outside of my comfort zone—I couldn't ignore my anxiety. For the first time in a long time, I had to deal with my emotions. The first week after I got to Arizona, I cried basically the entire week. There were *years* of negative emotions catching up with me. I also felt like I had the plague, with no substances in my system. But even though I felt scared to death and sick as a dog, crying felt good somehow. It was like purging—it was a release to get all those emotions off my chest. I was on the phone with my mom multiple times a day, and she was giving me tons of love and support. My family members were all making me feel good about my decision.

But holy shit, it was rough. I was in this uncomfortable new place, with nothing to dull the pain.

And there was a ton of uncertainty. I had to figure out how to get from Mesa, Arizona, to north Phoenix—forty miles away—without a car. The challenge took a lot of my mental capacity that I'd never had to use before when I was just doing construction. In my couch days, when I was keeping things comfortable, I was doing work I didn't have to think hard about. I could smoke weed all day long and use nail guns and Skil saws and walk on two-by-four walls, but never talk to anybody. I didn't have to answer to anyone. I knew my job well enough that I never had to communicate about anything challenging or take on extra responsibility.

Now, I was going to be going to school, learning a new trade. I had to find somebody to give me a ride to campus and back every day—which was going to mean talking to strangers, something I hated doing. I had to get a job, which meant finding someone to hire me who wasn't my own family member. And I had to do all of it sober, without anything to dull my anxiety or the pressure I felt from all these new responsibilities.

No wonder I bawled my eyes out for the first week.

I thought about moving back—but I knew if I stayed in Utah, nothing was going to change. I didn't have the self-discipline. I also didn't have any alternatives. If I moved back, I'd be right back in the shitty place I was trying to get out of.

Somehow, I made headway. I chewed a ton of sunflower seeds to take the place of the cigarettes, weed, and booze. I found a guy who agreed to give me a ride to class—so long as I could get myself to his house, which was about five miles away from my aunt and uncle's. I began making that ride on my bike. I found a gym to work out at. I got a job at a little restaurant, running food out to customers' tables.

But it was in class when things really started clicking. I had some mechanic experience already and a lot of natural ability, so the material came easy to me. But I also had no distractions. Other than riding my bike, working out at the gym, and doing stints at the restaurant, I had nothing to do other than study. I'd get home after riding twenty-five miles on my bike over the course of the day, and be ready to stay up late, studying more.

I ended up being head and shoulders above everybody in that school. I aced every single class. They gave out these little achievement pins that were different colors, like red, blue, yellow, and white. I got a pin for every single class. For the first little while, I would wear them on my shirt. But then I had so many, it was kind of geeky. Still—it felt good to be recognized for something other than being the party guy.

I was getting my shit together. I was working out. I was accomplishing something. I had found a way to manufacture change in my life.

MANUFACTURING CHANGE

Some people decide they need change because a crisis occurs, and they're forced into it. Other people hit a different kind of rock bottom that forces change. They get divorced, or have to declare bankruptcy, or end up in jail. A major "rock bottom" experience can shake up your world so much that you have to move forward in a different way.

But sometimes—maybe most of the time—change doesn't force your hand. You need to manufacture that change yourself. That was the story with one of my heroes, Grant Cardone, author of *The 10X Rule*.

> Most of the time, change doesn't force your hand. You need to manufacture that change yourself.

When Grant Cardone was in his twenties, he was dealing with a drug addiction. Eventually he went to rehab and made some progress. But when he got out of rehab, one of the guys working there told him, "You'll be back." The guy shrugged and said he was just speaking statistically. "These drug problems don't just go away for the majority of people. You'll be back."

When that guy told Grant Cardone he couldn't do it, and he'd be back in rehab eventually after repeating the same destructive patterns—that planted a seed in his mind. He decided he was going to change his life. He was going to prove this guy was wrong about him.

One reason that I relate to Grant Cardone so much—besides the fact that we both used to be addicts who have now achieved a lot of success in life—is because neither of us like people telling us what we can or can't do. We feel a natural resistance to authority. If someone tells me I can't do something, my reaction is "Oh yeah? I'll show you." We've got something to prove.

Grant is in his sixties now and he's got a net worth close to $2.6 *billion* dollars, from what I could find. When that rehab worker told him he'd be stuck for the rest of his life, he made the decision to manufacture change. That started with getting clean, but then he just kept moving the target to go after more, and more, and more. He's still working just as hard as a billionaire as he was when he first had a net worth of a million dollars. He keeps increasing his activity, and increasing his skills, and increasing his team, and his ability to produce more.

See, once you get unstuck, there's like a motor inside you that keeps wanting more. More progress, more speed. In the last five years since I got clean, I've done a lot. Like Grant, I've fought against ever being still. I keep moving the target and evolving my goals. I always remind myself that I'm capable of more and I can do more. I keep telling myself that I'm still just scratching the surface of what my potential is. I never want to feel stuck again, so I *keep* looking for ways to manufacture change.

So, how do you start the process of manufacturing change? You change your environment.

CHANGE YOUR ENVIRONMENT

If you're anything like me, sheer willpower isn't going to get you very far. You can't make astronomical changes in your life while staying around the same people, in the same environment, in the same circumstances.

Think about Albert Einstein's definition of insanity: it's doing the same thing over and over, but expecting different results. If you've been in a certain environment that's giving you a certain result—a *stuck* result—it's delusional to expect anything different. Small changes to your lifestyle will only lead to very small variations of what you've already been getting this whole time.

> You can't make astronomical changes in your life while staying in the same circumstances.

I used to watch a ton of TV every day. I'd get home and plop down onto the couch, grab a beer, and turn on the TV—still wearing my greasy-ass clothes from work. It would get my wife fired-up mad. She was ready for me to spend time with her and the kids. The habit was hurting my marriage and leading to more guilt and shame. So, I finally decided I had to go *ALL IN* on a change and announced I was getting rid of the effing TV.

For the next few years, we didn't have a TV. And that was a good thing.

Maybe you're not doing anything as extreme as moving states, but for big change to happen, you have to *change your environment*. That might mean changing your group of friends, making hard staffing changes, or rethinking your career. You might have to change your daily habits so that you're learning new skills, doing new tasks, and developing your staff in ways you haven't needed to before. If you want to level up, your day-to-day routine is going to require change: what got you this far won't get you much further. You're going to have to manufacture change and stretch yourself to get to the next level of success. Or, maybe the first step is something straightforward, like getting rid of your TV. Basically, you're looking to cut out anything that's bringing negative energy into your life. In fact, "cut out" is putting it gently. You want to put to death the sources of negativity in your life.

Let's talk about some of the specific areas that deserve your attention.

PEOPLE

You may have people in your life who have been there for a long time— close friends, family members, early hires. It's easy to wear blinders with people you're close to, even if their track record shows they're having a negative impact on your life or business. You might not want to recognize that these people are holding you back because of the nature of your close relationship. You might even be inclined to protect those people. But look closer. Ask yourself: Are some of those people keeping you in negative patterns and activities? Are they pressuring you to go out to the bar and party, after you've said you need to get home to your family or study? Are they telling you to blow off that potential client so that you can play a round of golf instead? Are they calling you up for a binge night of video gaming when you're trying to start up a new early morning workout routine?

These kinds of people can keep you stuck. As you try to create space for new relationships, habits, and activities, you might discover that the people around you aren't ready for that kind of positive change yet. You may need to take time away from those relationships. That doesn't mean quitting the relationships forever—but you might want to take a break until you get stable and grounded in the new changes you want to manufacture in your life.

If I had stayed in Utah, I would have kept partying with the same group of friends. I knew exactly who to get weed from, I knew who'd want to get wasted with me, I knew who to call to find out where the party was. In order to manufacture change in my life, I had to completely remove myself from that group and find new people to be around.

The same concept applies in a business environment. A lot of entrepreneurs start out by hiring close friends and family members— I'm no exception. If those people are working out, that's ideal. But if they're consistently slacking off or talking shit, you've got to make some tough decisions. It's dangerous to keep a low-performing or toxic person around, just because the two of you have a history together. Their negativity could tank your entire culture, not to mention compromise the success of your business. You've got to consider: Is their presence on your staff helping your relationship? Is it helping your business? If the answer to both questions is no, it might be time to cut them loose.

People will show you if they're the kind of person you want to be around. Look for signals of negativity—for example:

- **Avoid drama.** If someone's always talking about drama, I try to steer clear. There are tons of people on social media who try to stir up conflict, or people who want to talk shit about someone else. I don't need that in my life. It's unnecessary and negative.

- **Avoid the downers.** I know this guy at my gym who's reached a level of success that most people will never reach. But whenever I share something I'm excited about with him, he always plays devil's advocate and shuts me down. He meets my positivity with negativity. That's not someone I want to be around.
- **Steer clear of people who lack integrity.** There are a lot of monetarily successful people who have questionable character. They make great money, but behind the scenes, they're up to their knees in partying, drinking, drugs—you name it. They put out to the world this perception that they have it all together, but when you actually talk to them, you can pick up on their insecurities. You can see the holes in their integrity. Stay alert for any signs that a person is giving you a false perception about their character—you don't want to be around that.
- **News junkies: no thanks.** I can't hang out with people who obsess over the news. When a lot of people watch the news, that's all they talk about: politics, gun rights, LGBTQ issues... Guys: there's better stuff to talk about. Don't get stuck worrying about other people's lives. Put your energy into how you can improve your own life in areas you have direct control over.
- **Avoid enablers.** After high school, I used to stay rent free with some friends who let me eat their food and drink their beer. For a while, their tolerance of my behavior enabled me to continue in my unhealthy habits. But eventually, they told me, "We don't want to continue to be your crutch." That tore me up a little. I wanted to continue down the easy path. But being forced to move on meant I had to pull myself together—I had to get a decent job, start paying rent, develop more discipline. Their refusal to enable me any longer was a good thing. But there are plenty of well-meaning enablers out there who will help keep you stuck. Think of parents who let their kids live with them for entirely too long, enabling them to avoid responsibility. The same attitude can show up in the workplace. Some people in your network will be happy to

make you feel good about yourself and the current state of your company. They encourage you to maintain the status quo, instead of pushing you, challenging you, and asking the hard questions like, "What's next? What else is possible?" Those people might feel good to be around, but they're keeping you from innovating, doing more for your customers, and creating more value. They're keeping you stuck.

- **Avoid people who live for short-term pleasure.** Watch out for people who have an attitude of complacency with their lives too. I see some people take off early on Fridays, take long weekends, skip work for concerts or professional sports games, or go on yet another vacation. Time off is not always a bad thing, but when this is done repeatedly with never a concern about the lost production or loss of momentum, those are choices that create a huge drag on forward acceleration. Being around those sorts of people will keep you stuck. When you live for pleasure only, you will prevent any significant progress in your life. People like this are focused on instant gratification, excitement, and adrenaline. I want to create opportunities for other people and add value to their lives, everywhere I go. And I want to be around people who are protective of their time, who are consistently doing something productive, whether that's for the benefit of family relationships, their work, or personal development.

Honestly, I could go on. Avoid the complainers. Avoid the people with a victim mentality who don't recognize their own agency to make positive changes. Avoid the energy vampires—people who suck all the positive energy out of you. Basically, avoid anyone who's generally miserable to be around. You don't need those kinds of people dragging you down. You may not even be able to recognize that certain people are a force of negativity in your life yet because their presence feels so normal. But until you start to consciously recognize the effects of these types of people in your life, the negative patterns will continue.

> Surround yourself with people who will challenge you to become the best version of yourself. Avoid people who are a source of negativity.

And, a heads up: as you get further and further along, making progress, you're going to have people who want to try to take you back down to their level. They're going to puke all of their insecurities on you, but don't listen. These people may try to encourage you to maintain a level of mediocrity because it makes them feel better about their *own* mediocre lives.

Think of the "crabs in a bucket" mentality. If you put a bunch of crabs in a bucket, they *could* all team up to help each other get out. Instead, as soon as one crab figures out it can climb on top of another one to get out, the others drag that crab back down. Misery loves company. Some people will encourage you to continue in your same stuck behaviors because it keeps you on the same level as them. The more you start to talk about goal setting and increasing your productivity, the more you'll hear criticism and sarcastic jokes about your attempts to change. Those crabs want to pull you back down into the bucket. They don't want to look at themselves in the mirror and admit they could do more to level up. Instead, they want to drag you down.

I remember hearing from a guy on Facebook that I hadn't talked to in four years. This is before my business had even started, and I was just starting to turn it up with my daily activity and commitment to take it to the next level for myself and my family. He could see some of the progress I was posting about. He messaged me and wrote, "Slow down, man. Take it easy. You only live once, so spend more time with your family." Maybe that was well intentioned, but I don't need anyone telling me to slow down or take it easy. I want people around me who believe in my goals and support me doing the work required to make them happen.

Sometimes it's the people you're closest to that are keeping you the most stuck, and they might be people you love and deeply care about. For years, my brothers were my favorite people to party with. When I wanted to get clean, I knew I had to step away from those relationships for a time. I wasn't sure for how long, but I knew that if I stayed around them, I was going to continue to justify my behavior, just like they were. In fact, that was another reason why I moved completely out of state. There was no move across town that would get me away from that.

If you have family members who you can't cut out of your life, limit the time you're around them. You don't have to burn those bridges, but you may need to step away for a time. Be very, very honest with yourself about whether or not the people in your life are bringing you down—and then, make a change.

In Chapter 7, I'm going to talk about how to build a community around yourself that will help you accelerate in all areas of growth, but I'll give you a preview of that right here. You want to surround yourself with positive, successful people. When I was in Arizona, I met other guys going through my same mechanics program—they were all motivated and looking to learn. Try volunteering, join a professional network group, or reconnect with old acquaintances that are doing well. I'm not a big fan of church or religion, but there are some great people that go to church. You could find some new buddies lifting weights at the gym, or by joining a workout class.

Don't go back to the old crowd simply because they make you feel better about yourself. Hold onto the burning desire to do something great with your life. Find people who will challenge you to become the best version of yourself.

> Hold onto the burning desire to do something great with your life. Find people who will challenge you to become the best version of yourself.

You hate your job? Quit. You're comfortable at your job, but it's not getting you anywhere? Quit.

"But I can't, I've got bills to pay."

Fair enough. Let's get realistic about what this would take. If you're serious about making a change, you have to set it up. There's no excuse why you can't change your job or your environment—you just need to do some planning ahead of time so that the change becomes possible.

I have a friend right now who has gotten himself stuck financially. Even though his income puts him in the top 1 percent in the nation, he's overextended, overcommitted, and overleveraged. Every last penny that comes in is already accounted for. Because he's so reliant on the income from his job, he can't take advantage of an incredible investment opportunity. Long term, the investment could put him in an entirely different financial sphere, but if he steps away from his job for even a week—it throws a wrench into everything he's got going on.

There's an excuse for everything. Even people at a high level are going to make excuses about why they can't go on to the next level because they've gotten themselves stuck. They don't want to face the discomfort and uncertainty of the unknown.

Yes, it's challenging. But remember what I said at the end of the last chapter? Change isn't comfortable.

Stop making excuses for yourself.

Instead, do some preparing. Save up a little buffer if you need to, or cut down your expenses. Line up the new job before you quit your old job. Bottom line, if you know you're stuck professionally, take the steps you need to in order to manufacture change.

MEDIA CONSUMPTION

The effect of negativity on your life is toxic. When you're changing your environment, you've got to think about negative media, social media, news, TV, music—there was a time when I cut *all* of those things out of my life. In every category, I was taking in negativity. I had to slowly bring them back into my life after I'd figured out how to make them a more positive source.

How do you know if something is negative or not? You've got to develop some self-awareness about what you're taking in. You might enjoy a certain kind of music or podcast, but ask yourself—is it serving you? Something can be enjoyable but still be negative, like music that pumps you up but leaves you feeling angry.

> Something can be enjoyable but still be negative—and the effect of negativity on your life is toxic.

I grew up listening to rap music all through high school. I used to have this big-ass CD case—hundreds of CDs, all with the raunchiest, nastiest, most hardcore rap music. It wasn't until I started paying attention to the words that I began registering what they were portraying as a lifestyle and belief system. It was like I started hearing the negativity for the first time—and I knew it wasn't aligned with the kind of person I wanted to be.

Social media also was a source of negativity. Especially during certain political seasons, there was a lot of drama on my Facebook feed. My dad had gotten interested in politics, which spiked my curiosity. I started following some of the same guys he was listening to—people like Glenn Beck and Rush Limbaugh. But over time, their shows started to wear on me. I don't think they're bad people, but they talk about a bunch of negative bullshit, *all the time*. I also had a bunch of family members—people that I love—but the only way they knew how to post on Facebook was to publish all their drama.

I started cutting it all out. If someone posted something negative—no matter what it was, or how minuscule—I immediately unfollowed them. Instead, I started following a bunch of pages that posted motivational quotes and tended to be consistently positive.

I quit listening to music altogether for a while. These days, when I listen to music, I choose stuff that helps me feel regulated and calm. I've got a Spotify playlist called "Flow State." I also listen to classical music.

Later in my life, I started getting into reading books too. Pretty much every book that I've ever read has been a recommendation—which is another reason it's been so important for me to be surrounded with positive, successful people. If you're hanging out with the right people, they're going to recommend good books for you that align with where you're at in life. With every book I picked up, I was looking for a nugget to take away—even just one new thought that aligned with my mission and the ways I was looking to grow.

Some books didn't align whatsoever, even if they came highly recommended. Either because of the author, the message, or the basic energy, they just wouldn't resonate. Eventually, I learned to just stop reading those and picked up something else. That used to be hard for me. Once I pick something up, I want to *completely commit* to go all the way through it. But honestly, life is too short for bad books. Now, if I don't like the message or I find out the author hasn't actually done shit, I don't want to bother with that book.

BOOK RECOMMENDATIONS

Looking for suggestions to get started? Here's a list of recommended books that I personally found life changing and compelling—even for someone like myself who used to be a "nonreader."

- *The Traveler's Gift*, Andy Andrews
- *The Alchemist*, Paulo Coelho
- *177 Mental Toughness Secrets of the World Class*, Steve Siebold

- *How to Win Friends and Influence People*, Dale Carnegie
- *The 10X Rule*, Grant Cardone
- *The Five Love Languages*, Gary Chapman
- *Today I Begin a New Life*, Dave Blanchard
- *The Greatest Salesman in the World*, Og Mandino
- *The Success Principles*, Jack Canfield
- *Outwitting the Devil*, Napoleon Hill
- *Can't Hurt Me*, David Goggins
- *The Four Agreements*, Don Miguel Ruiz
- *Extreme Ownership*, Jocko Willink and Leif Babin
- *The Obstacle Is the Way*, Ryan Holiday
- *Twelve Pillars*, Jim Rohn and Chris Widener
- *The Power of One More*, Ed Mylett
- *The Power of Moments*, Chip Heath and Dan Heath
- *The Miracle Morning*, Hal Elrod

In all these areas—music, social media, books, podcasts—think about what is going to accelerate your forward momentum, versus hold you back. What's going to be a source of positivity? What's a source of negativity? What media is *aligned* with the kind of person you want to become?

> Think about what is going to accelerate your forward momentum, versus hold you back.

When I started proactively changing my environment, I started thinking more about the way that I dressed, talked, the music I listened to—I wanted *everything* to be in alignment with the kind of person I would respect. I didn't want there to be any alternative versions of me.

That's not to say I was going to act like a saint. I was still going to fart, burp, cuss, and do all the things that I would do normally, whether I was around other people or by myself. But I was also going to make sure my life reflected my core values. I decided that every decision I made should be in alignment with the person I was aspiring to be, along with every influence I chose in my life.

THE IMPORTANCE OF DELIBERATE INTENT

You've got to be *deliberate* in crafting your environment. It's easy to wind up in a negative space because that's where life is going to take you if you're not actively working against it. When you're just drifting through life and going through the motions, you can easily get stuck in negativity.

The author Napoleon Hill talks about this concept of drifting in his book *Outwitting the Devil*. He basically says, "Listen—if you don't have a plan, you're just letting things happen to you. You're not being intentional about what your days look like, or the people you hang out with, or the activities you do and how your time is spent. You're just drifting." That's the way 95 percent of people live their lives.

> If you want to get unstuck, you need deliberate intent.

Look, sometimes life just deals you a shitty hand, and then you have to decide what you're going to do with that. Take Hal Elrod, for example, bestselling author of *The Miracle Morning*. I met Hal about a year ago and got to hear more of his story in person. Before writing his bestseller, Hal got in a car accident and ended up in a coma. After waking up, doctors told him he'd never walk again. For a while, he just lay in bed, feeling sorry for himself.

But then, he decided he had a choice about how he responded to it: he could stay stuck and depressed in bed. Or, he could use the accident as fuel to make something of himself and make a comeback. He could prove the doctors wrong. He could choose to get unstuck.

He fully committed to that mindset and regained his mobility and strength. Around thirteen years later, he wrote his bestseller, *The Miracle Morning*, which has sold over two million copies.

But then, in 2016, Elrod ended up getting cancer and had to fight through a cancer battle. He could have let that defeat him, but he didn't. He kept fighting, kept using the challenges as fuel to get better. Circumstances forced change into his life, but Hal Elrod chose the mindset to get through them in the best possible way.

I can't overstate how important your mindset is in establishing a positive trajectory—and that's something you *choose*. Early in my marriage, there were a few months when my wife and I did food stamps when we ran into some tough times. I hated the feeling of showing up to the same place with a lot of other people who seemed like they had accepted poverty. Most of them seemed like they had just settled for it. They had low energy and a victim mentality—like they were just waiting for somebody to come to the rescue.

It would have been so easy for me to go down that same road. But I remember thinking to myself, "I never want to come back here. I never want to feel this energy again. I'm going to do whatever it takes to change my direction so that I go down a different road."

In some of the chapters coming up, I'm going to talk about goal setting and identifying a mission for yourself. That's how you're *really* going to accelerate your growth. But before you can get there, you've got to start by shifting your focus away from whatever is keeping you stuck. Stop focusing on how tough things are all the time, and how expensive things are, and how you can't afford everything you want: "This job is terrible. I hate my roommate. The people I hang out with are a drag."

It's helpful to identify that—you're starting to get some awareness about sources of negativity in your life. But then, *stop focusing on it*. If you stay focused on negativity, you're just going to attract more negativity into your life because that's what you're putting all your energy into.

> If you stay focused on negativity, you're just going to attract more negativity into your life.

So, here's what you do instead. Build the habit of becoming *aware* of the negativity when it pops up in your thoughts, conversations, posts, and so on. Once you're aware, push it to the side. Delete the post. Correct your thoughts.

Then, focus on positivity. Remind yourself that there are *good possibilities* for you. Be deliberate about expressing gratitude throughout your day. Focus on your goals: find a target to go for, then take intentional steps to move toward that target.

I'm not trying to be delusional or anything, but I'm much more successful in every area of life when I'm focused on positivity, being optimistic, and believing in myself. So, be deliberate about choosing the good. Inevitably, you're going to end up with some version of whatever you're focusing on.

MARRIAGE

This same concept applies to your marriage, by the way. You can either feed yourself negative thoughts about your partner, or you can deliberately try to believe they're coming from a good place and remind yourself why you love your spouse. If you're in a committed relationship or married, then you've made a promise to see it through. It's on you to practice deliberate intent so that you can heal your relationship and help it thrive.

Shandell and I have gotten to some low points in our marriage. We've been in some knock-down, drag-out fights. God knows, I've put her through some shit. I've gone to a really dark place at times, thinking about whether or not we were going to make it.

But when my mind starts to go there, I reel my negative thoughts back in. If I let the bad times go further, it's only going to get worse—

but I know that I can get things better quickly if I'm *intentional* about it. I start by thinking of all the reasons I'm grateful for her. I remember what the good times have been like and prepare to swallow my pride. I make up my mind that I'm going to be the one who fixes it. I'm going to be willing to apologize first. After all, even in the hardest times—I committed to this woman. She's the mother of my kids. And I'm not going to let us become a statistic.

> Don't ever let the relationship deteriorate because of you.

If you've conditioned yourself to believe that your relationship isn't going to work, and it's not a good fit, and you don't love your partner anymore—guess what? You're not going to work it out. When you tell yourself they want to fight you every step of the way or there's no chance to save the marriage, that negativity taints everything. It fills your head with blame and makes you too prideful to initiate any kind of positive change.

Instead, tell yourself you're committed to getting it back on track. Apologize. Initiate those difficult conversations. Tell each other, "There's no question, we're going to work this thing out." Wherever you're at in your marriage—commit, today, to making it work. Take responsibility for whatever might be your fault, *apologize,* and stop acting like you're always right. Most relationships fail because nobody was willing to go back and just apologize.

Don't ever let the relationship deteriorate because of you—always be the one to communicate and take the time to work things out. Put deliberate intent into saving the most important relationship in your life. Read books. Seek out coaching and mentorship from people whose relationships you respect. Learn your partner's love language. Do everything in your power to fulfill the commitment you made to your partner.

Every step of the way, you're going to encounter people who are not quite as far along in their journey as you. So, another way you can be intentional about manufacturing change is by taking the opportunity to mentor someone else or offer advice. That's one of the most powerful ways to accelerate your own growth. There's no better way to solidify concepts or strengthen good habits in your own life than to be around other people who would benefit from hearing about your experience and perspective.

> Sharing about your experience and perspective with others is one of the best ways to solidify new concepts and strengthen good habits in your life.

That's true, even if you're still *in the process* of manufacturing change—even if it still looks messy. In one of the first classes I took at the Motorcycle Mechanics Institute, I met this kid who was struggling a little bit. I mentored him through most of the rest of our classes together. The content wasn't as easy for him—he needed things to be broken down into more simple concepts than I did. He sometimes got frustrated with me because of my inexperience as a mentor or coach—and I would get irritated at him for how little he was picking up. His favorite thing to ask me was "How? How? How??" And I'd say things like, "You should just *know!*" Or, "What do you mean, '*How?*' Are you serious?"

We didn't always make much headway. But we became friends, and both of us helped each other along in becoming better versions of ourselves.

Rather than trying to force your new choices onto other people, I recommend you try to embody the change instead. Let people see the proof in your life. I had to learn the hard way with this one. Early on, I wanted people like my brothers to make similar changes in their lifestyle. I saw the benefits in my life, and I felt like I could offer value—but I didn't really know how to approach the topic in a way that was going to sink in. Basically, I shoved it down their throats. I was pretty abrasive. I've learned how to be more tactful now—I just focus on being the best example I can and embody the principles I talk about.

Remember what's gotten *you* this far along your own journey. If you're like me, it was a lot of little conversations, planted seeds, and seeing other people be an example that you wanted to emulate. There was never one groundbreaking conversation for me that changed my whole trajectory. I had to come to the conclusion over time—after all those planted seeds—that I was ready to do the work and make the changes.

Now that I'm in a position to be a leader to others, I want to be able to offer positivity and inspiration. I don't try to change someone's life in one conversation—I just focus on planting seeds. Eventually, someone might look back on something I said and realize it changed the way they thought about their relationship, or job, or the way they show up for people, or the energy they have when they walk into a room. Planting seeds for others may not look like much in the moment, but it can lead to big changes down the road.

> Planting seeds for others may not look like much in the moment, but it can lead to big changes down the road.

CHOOSE THE GOOD

It sounds tough—doesn't it? I'm telling you to potentially cut out relationships, take a critical look at your job, rethink all of your media consumption...It's a lot. This is why I told you in chapter one that you had to be ready to *commit* to getting unstuck. You've got to start pursuing a different way of life by going *ALL IN*. Change is hard, and discomfort is part of it. Expect that.

But remember: on the other side of this discomfort, you're going to find accomplishment.

> Change is hard. Discomfort is part of it. But there's *accomplishment* on the other side.

One of the reasons I loved being a carpenter for so many years was because I was naturally good at it. I could take a piece of paper with a drawing on it and build whatever you told me to build. When I had a finished product, it felt like a huge accomplishment. Sometimes there was recognition that came along with it.

What gives you that good feeling of accomplishment? You can trick your mind to think positively about the discomfort of all these changes by focusing on the sense of accomplishment you're going to feel on the other side. Yes, there's uncertainty. Yes, you're going to completely change your environment and get out of your comfort zone—but on the other side, there's a better version of yourself. In fact, pushing through these changes is the *only* way to get yourself unstuck and level up.

> Pushing through these changes is the *only* way to get yourself unstuck and level up.

Pressure is what turns coal into diamonds. The most successful people you've heard of went through a period of time in their lives where they experienced extreme pressure, discomfort, and uncertainty. But just about every one of those people will tell you that pressure helped mold them into a success story.

The transformation doesn't happen all at once—it happens incrementally. When I first arrived in Arizona, the pressure and discomfort hit me like a sledgehammer. I had to feel all the pain and emotion and self-doubt I'd been avoiding for so long. But that pressure also began to create incremental change. I started slowly, *slowly* believing that I could do it. I began racking up little wins—and then I'd get another, and then another. I started to believe I could be a success story, and that on the other side of all the discomfort, there would be accomplishment.

I started getting myself unstuck.

So, don't give up. Keep looking for the good, keep searching, keep calling. Being resourceful means being persistent. Even if it doesn't seem like a lot is happening, keep going.

Especially if you find yourself stuck...again.

THE PAYOFF AFTER THE PAIN

By the time I finished the program at the Motorcycle Mechanics Institute, I was high on life. I was super healthy. All my daily twenty-five-mile bike rides and hours in the gym had made me super cut—two hundred pounds of lean, solid muscle. I'd aced my classes, graduated with honors, and gotten my driver's license back.

I'd also married my dream girl.

I still remember the night I met Shandell. I was back in Utah, at the restaurant where my brother used to work. A couple hours after the dinner service was over, the restaurant had shut off some of the lights, turned on some music, pushed the tables out of the way, and created a little bar setting. Someone had invited Shandell to come on by.

She was wearing a white skirt that showed off her long legs, with a jean jacket. She looked incredible. I knew her from before because she was friends with one of my brothers. But that night, I fell completely head over heels for her.

I was showing her all my interest—and doing my best to flex my muscles, trying to get that to work in my favor. Thankfully, it did. I'd known and liked a lot of girls, but it was different with her. I felt this instinct with Shandell. I could tell she was loyal, which is one of my most important values—that really struck me. I loved her demeanor. I loved how well we got along.

I had to go back to Arizona after that weekend, but I started calling her every day, asking her what she was doing and who she was hanging out with. I knew I had to find some way to sell her on me, even if I was 450 miles away. My way of doing that was showing *my* loyalty by spending hours and hours talking to her on the phone—sometimes until 4:00 a.m.

We were just such a great fit. I was having conversations with Shandell that I'd never been able to have with anyone else, even my family members and closest friends. I'd never been in love like this before—but I knew this was the real deal.

I asked her to marry me on October 9, 2009. Her family was going out to dinner for her brother's birthday and while they were out, I set up this cool little seat in her backyard, surrounded by candles and roses. I planned the whole thing with her mom.

When they got back from dinner, her mom texted that she was trying to get Shandell to go out into the backyard, without giving away the reason why. I expected Shandell to come out from the sliding door in the house, but then she came out from around the corner. We both caught each other off guard.

She's so funny. She thought I was one of *her dad's friends*. So, the first thing she says when she sees me is "What are you doing here, Jerry?" Granted, we'd been doing long distance and it was dark outside, but I still give her a hard time for not recognizing me right away.

Once she realized it was *me*—thanks, babe—I popped the question. Over the next few weeks, we started planning to move in together and made plans for a wedding.

Then, reality started to hit. I'd been single, living by myself. Every morning when I woke up, I had very simple responsibilities for my day: I needed to eat, get myself to school, get my homework done, make some money, and then go to bed. It was all about me. I didn't have to worry about anybody else.

Shandell and I moved in together a couple months before we got married. Now, I had a rental payment for the first time in my life—for a nasty-ass rental house, no less; I'll never forget that fucking green carpet with all the pet urine stains. I was preparing to take care of a wife. And Shandell also had a three-year-old son, so I was going to become a dad. The responsibilities felt like they were piling up.

I felt a lot of pressure. A *lot* of anxiety. And that's when I turned back to drinking.

Near the tail end of my classes, I started hanging out with some new friends. School was so easy for me by that time, I didn't have to spend as much time on schoolwork to get good grades. So, I started spending a little more time taking lunch breaks at a friend's house. We'd have a beer, maybe two. It was almost like I was rewarding myself for doing well for so long.

The same thing happened when I would go back to visit in Utah. I'd smoke and drink and hang out a bit with some of my old friends—and then I'd go back to Arizona and refocus on school. I wasn't falling back into my addiction—yet—because I wasn't around it all the time. I figured I had changed my environment *enough*. I could start cutting myself some slack, cutting loose a little more.

I was drawn right back into it again. I started asking to go to lunch and to So-and-So's house and asking certain people what they were doing on the weekends—just like I used to.

I knew I was doing the wrong thing. I knew I didn't have enough control, and now I had a whole new set of responsibilities. Suddenly stepping into the role of husband and father was hard. I didn't know how to handle it, and I hadn't developed much patience for a little three-year-old. Hayden loved to ask questions and be involved in whatever I was doing. He wanted support and acknowledgment—but I didn't know how to give it to him. I don't know how many times I told him, "I'm busy right now," or, "Just *do* what I'm telling you to do."

Before we got married, Shandell never really saw me under the influence. I had never smoked weed or gotten super drunk around her. But now we were in our own little ecosystem, and there were all these stressors of marriage, and responsibility, and having to make money. It started bringing out the "Rogers' rage" in me. I would blow up sometimes—once, I smashed a bookshelf. Completely destroyed it.

I began reaching more and more often for a glass of booze or a joint to suppress the pressure of responsibilities when I was winding down.

The first time I brought home a thirty-pack, I dumped it out into the bottom shelf of the fridge. I was ready with my justifications if Shandell said anything—"I'm twenty-six years old, I'm an adult, I can have a couple when I get home from work." We'd always had a good relationship, but it got rocky when I started drinking again.

Changing my environment took me leaps and bounds forward. It got me unstuck. It helped me make progress in every area of my life. All the gifts that came out of it—my health, confidence, new skills, my wife, my son—none of those would have come into my life if I hadn't pushed through the pain and gone through with manufacturing needed change. I'm thankful for every single one of those things, and I don't regret for a second what I had to give up in order to get them.

But it wasn't a summit. It was only a plateau.

And I still had a ways to go.

ACTION STEPS

How serious are you about changing the trajectory of your life? I had to go as far as moving to a different state to change my environment. What steps do you need to take to manufacture change? Think about the areas of:

- Location
- People
- Profession
- Media Consumption

Also, how do you need to practice deliberate intent in your life? In your marriage? In mentoring others and planting seeds?

Remember: if you keep doing the same things with the same people, you're going to get the same results. Commit to the hard work of manufacturing change in your life, and don't give up when it gets hard. The pressure of discomfort will make you stronger in the end.

CHAPTER 3

Find Your Fuel

YOUR LOWEST LOWS CAN FUEL YOUR CHANGE

TURNS OUT, THE words "rock bottom" can mean a lot of things. I thought I'd bottomed out when I was sitting on that mustard-yellow couch with a broken leg, wondering what the hell I was going to do with my life. I thought getting clean, marrying Shandell, and acing my program in Arizona was the start of a new life—that it was only forward and upward from there.

But I had a few more rock bottoms to go. And each one got harder to bounce back from.

Here's something I've learned, though: your lowest lows can drive you into paralyzing shame, or they can be your fuel to make *bigger life changes*. The lows can teach you about who you really want to be, help you understand your destructive habits, and ultimately help you rewrite your narrative. Mistakes are great opportunities for growth if you use them to learn. It's crucial to *study* them to become aware of the impact of your decisions. Then, adjust along the way to do it better next time. Never make the same mistake twice.

Although there's a ton of value in learning from books, mentors, coaches, and other people's mistakes—there's nothing that can compare to going through something difficult yourself and learning how to navigate it differently the next time. Even your worst experiences can teach you lessons about yourself that can propel you forward and change the way you think.

> Even your worst experiences can teach you lessons about yourself that can propel you forward and change the way you think.

Even an experience that causes you to almost lose your marriage.

I can still remember that long, hot drive home through the Arizona desert. Both Shandell and I were feeling sick.

Not only was I hung over from all the drinking and weed from the day before—I was pretty sure I had done some coke as well—but more than that, I just felt like a dirtbag. I didn't even want to look over at my wife. Everything we had worked so hard to build together over the last few years—in one stupid, drunken moment, I had almost thrown it all away.

As a new husband, father, and rent-paying tenant, I had decided alcohol and weed were once again a great idea. There was a lot of pressure. A lot of anxiety. For most of my life, I had suppressed the burden of responsibility by getting drunk and high. Those habits also helped me dull the feelings of shame and guilt I felt over disappointing my new bride. I started seeking out other friends who would make me feel better about my habits. They were easy to find—and Shandell came along for the ride.

We hooked up with a new group. They appealed to me because they seemed very successful. The guys were fit, and they had nice trucks and owned boats. The women were gorgeous. We started partying a lot with this group. Most of the time, the parties were in a somewhat controlled environment—it was at someone's house, or there were kids around. But one weekend, we decided to get babysitters for the kids, rent out some suites in a hotel in Scottsdale, and really go hard.

That was when I almost ruined everything good in my life.

The day had started by the pool. One of the wives owned her own swimsuit business and all the women were wearing the skimpiest little "scrunchy butt" swimsuits. We started drinking early, out in the sun. The girls were letting loose—we were all letting loose. Everyone got wasted, fast. Even though we were used to drinking, there was something about the drinks that weekend that took us all to another level.

It's hard for me to remember the details of what happened next— we were following each other from room to room, getting drinks for ourselves. At one point, I was in the room with my friend's wife. Everybody started leaving to get ready to go out for the night. Somehow, I ended up being the last one in there.

The woman started taking off her swimsuit to get in the shower. She smiled at me.

Then she invited me to get in with her.

I was close. I was so fucking close. It still scares the shit out of me to think of how easy it would have been for me to get in the shower with that woman. Honestly, I don't know how I had the willpower to resist it.

Downstairs—probably at the exact same time—the woman's husband was putting his hands on Shandell. I considered that guy to be a mentor. He was super successful and had given me a lot of advice. I'd seen him flirt with my wife, but I always found ways to justify his behavior because I looked up to him. Somehow, Shandell booted the guy out of her room, and I managed to get myself out of the room I was in.

Now, on our drive home—both feeling sick in more ways than one— we finally started talking about it.

I told my wife about what had happened when I'd been alone in the hotel room with the other woman. She told me what had happened downstairs. Eventually, we got it all out there.

"I don't ever, ever want to be in that position again," I said. "We were all so drunk. It just would have been *so easy* to go there."

After that time, we almost never hung out with that group again. The experience changed our dynamic with everyone. I couldn't trust myself in that situation again. I knew—if I continued in that environment—I would inevitably make a choice that would completely destroy my marriage. It was scary how close I'd come to throwing everything away.

STUDY YOUR SELF-DESTRUCTION

That was a major low for me. It was an experience that I still hate thinking about.

But I didn't waste it.

I could have let that party convince me that I was nothing more than a dirtbag. I could have chosen to believe that my marriage was a lost cause. I could have accepted the identity of addict. Unfaithful husband. Bad example.

But I didn't. Instead, that low lit a fire under me. It became fuel for change and sharpened my awareness of who I wanted to be.

Number one: I learned that I didn't want my relationship to look like those other couples' relationships. Both Shandell and I could see the other couples' marriages deteriorating. The husband and wife who had made passes on the two of us got divorced not long afterward. I didn't want that. I wanted to fight for my marriage—even if, at that point, I still didn't really know how.

Two: I knew I couldn't hang out with that group anymore and I needed to change my environment, yet again. I loved those people—and they all loved me. They encouraged me and gave me so much support. It was easy for me to feel at home with those people. But I could see things going south. I had already started to justify my own bad choices and the shitty behavior I saw around me. I didn't cheat on my wife, but what if I *had* made that choice? Most likely, I would find a way to justify it and do it again. Then, that would probably turn into a whole slew of bad decisions where I was doing stuff behind people's backs and betraying the people I loved the most. That scared the shit out of me.

Three: We're human. Shandell and I are influenced by our environment. I'd learned this lesson before, but I had to learn it again. I didn't have the willpower or the discipline to be around those people and not go down that path. I drank every day because I was around a bunch of people who drank every day. If I was in a positive environment around positive people, I would be influenced in positive ways. A negative environment with negative people influenced me in negative ways. This was a simple concept—but it took a lot for it to get through to me. Somehow, I had to get rid of the negativity in my life, again.

Four: I wanted to be a good husband. So far in my marriage, I'd been defensive and angry way more often than I'd wanted to be. When Shandell and I fought, I acted like I didn't care about her as much as I did, to try to get some control over the situation. But that was all bullshit. I never wanted to lose her.

Five: I wanted to be a good example. I still felt the pressure to be a good example to my brothers, and now I had my own boy looking up to me, along with my two young daughters. I'd been a pretty shitty role model to my kids. I didn't want to be a deadbeat dad. I wanted to be a *good* dad.

I didn't have any strategies at that point. All of the discipline that ultimately got me out of my addictions and self-destruction was still years away. All I had was a growing awareness about who I wanted to be—or, more accurately, who I *didn't* want to be. That was something.

Can you relate? You might have a list of stories about people you've hurt, times you've embarrassed yourself, instances when you've fallen short of where you want to be. Maybe you have more memories than you can count, defined by your mistakes. You've failed to be intentional with your time. You've set targets for yourself and then haven't followed through. You've been undisciplined, you've self-sabotaged. You've fallen short. You've gotten unstuck, only to mess it up again.

I'm not telling you to ignore any of that. I'm telling you to *use* it. Study the shit out of those bad experiences. Learn more about who you want to be and who you *don't* want to be. Let your lowest points become fuel to propel you forward.

> Let your lowest points become fuel to propel you forward.

CORE VALUES: WHO DO YOU WANT TO BE?

Take a hard look at some of your lows—the experiences that make you feel ashamed or guilty. Why do those memories bother you? What *weren't* you doing that you *wish* you were doing? What *were* you doing that you want to *stop* doing? The answers to these questions can shed light on your core values. Write out a description of the kind of person you genuinely want to be:

- What do you want your relationships to look like? How do you want to *contribute* to those relationships?
- What kind of people do you want to be influenced by? Are the people you're around right now helping you or hurting you?
- How is your environment currently influencing you?
- What kind of role do you want to play in your family?
- What are some of the qualities you value most, that you'd like to be known for?

Sure, your great, happy memories can help teach you the answers to these questions too. But often, it's the gut-punch experiences that can shed the clearest light on *your core values.* That's why the pain points can be fuel to get you moving forward.

I can remember an experience I had as a teenager when I realized how important the value of integrity was to me. I had agreed to help this woman move—I didn't know her all that well, but I had made a commitment to show up and help. My license was suspended at the time, so I recruited my friend with a pickup truck to help out too.

But then my friend just ghosted. We had *both* told this woman, "Yeah, we'll come help you move," and she was relying on us—but he bailed. I called him over and over and over. He finally sent me a text—"Hangin with the GF. Can't make it. Sorry bro."

I was so fired up that he had let me down. I had to try to find a ride just to get to the woman's house. Then, instead of having a big pickup truck to move furniture in, we had to try cramming the furniture into her small Honda Civic.

I wanted to kick that guy's ass. The whole time moving furniture, I was doing my best to keep down my rage. I never wanted anybody to look at me or feel the same way that I felt about that guy. I'd made a commitment. I was relying on this guy to help me fulfill that commitment, and he'd promised me he'd be there. But then he went against his word. He let me down, and he let this woman down.

That disgusted me. I don't think I talked to him for a couple years after that.

Maybe I shouldn't have had such high expectations for this guy. After all, our main connection was that we partied together. But, in my mind, if I tell somebody I'm going to do something—even if I don't have a driver's license or a truck or money to help out—there's nothing that's going to stand between me and doing what I said I was going to do. It's incredibly important to me that I keep my word.

You know what's crazy? That experience happened almost twenty years ago, but I still remember it like it was yesterday. I have lived a very active life and have plenty of good memories, but I wouldn't be able to draw on those good memories as clearly as I remember this one. That's because of the emotion that was tied to it. This guy's blatant disregard for some of my most tightly held values—integrity and trust—made an incredibly strong impression on me. In fact, that's a reason I've tried to focus on practicing integrity consistently in my own life—I don't want to be anyone else's bad memory of letting them down. The good times will fade from memory, but these moments when you show them your dark side will stick with them forever. Keep your dark side in check.

I didn't realize that integrity was one of my strong personal core values until I hit these pain points. I saw how these qualities like integrity and follow-through were lacking in other people's lives, and it made me realize just how important those values were to me.

You know what else it made me realize? It's hard to be much of a contributor without any resources. At that time, without a vehicle or license or much of an income, I couldn't do much for anybody. That was a terrible feeling that I had throughout my teens and early twenties. I usually spent most of my money before I even cashed my paycheck. I began to wake up to the fact that I hated not being able to offer much value to anyone. All those shitty moments made me realize that, eventually, I wanted to be in a position to offer real resources to other people.

Small moments that reveal your values are important. They help shape who you are and how people view you. Your life's journey should take you closer and closer to living up to those values—strengthening your ability to live in alignment with the kind of person you want to be. *Identifying* your values is the first step in living *up to them.*

Identifying your values is the first step in living *up to them.*

What's the second step? You've got to get away from the habits that keep you stuck in a place you don't want to be. You've got to take a hard look at the choices that pull you down. Understand your destructive habits so you can get free from them.

ANALYZE YOUR HABITS

Maybe, like me, it's drugs or alcohol. Maybe you're addicted to your phone. Maybe you habitually overeat. You might waste valuable hours in your day watching TV or playing video games. You might seek out exhilarating experiences that will take your mind off reality for a short period of time.

Or maybe your stuck habits are something more abstract—like a familiar situation that you can't bring yourself to get out of because of the discomfort it would require, or worrying about what people think of you. You might react in a damaging way to your spouse or your kids when you're emotionally triggered. Maybe you have some other negative thought pattern that you struggle to get out of: overanalyzing, gossiping, complaining, second-guessing yourself.

There's some habit you're hanging onto that isn't serving you anymore, but you're making excuses to keep it around. If you want to unstuck yourself—you've got to recognize the appeal of what's keeping you stuck and confront it.

Early on, I drank because I wanted a tribe. The group of people I was most comfortable around liked to party. I had my first beer when I was thirteen—I remember I was at a house across the street from my grandma's and I was nervous the whole time, thinking she might find out I was there partying. Then, I smoked weed for the first time at a good friend of mine's house. His dad owned the local skate shop and we were getting in his stash. We were fourteen years old. At first, getting buzzed and high were just ways to spend time with my friends.

But all the time, I knew I was doing something stupid. I felt some guilt and shame over it. That's why my motivation to smoke and drink changed. I started leaning on getting drunk and high because it took away my sense of responsibility to live up to my potential and the expectations that people had for me. I'm named after my dad—one of the most badass dudes I've ever come into contact with—but I wasn't living *up* to his name. Later on, I knew I wasn't being a good example to my kids, or a loving, reliable husband to Shandell. I also felt pressure from the responsibility of being the oldest of four brothers, and even pressure to pay my monthly bills. Alcohol and weed were my crutch—they helped mask my guilt, shame, and stress.

I got to a point where I was so sick of my same negative patterns, it literally gave me a stomachache. I wasn't proud of who I was as a brother, and later, as a husband and father. But I didn't know how to be anyone else. Everyone around town knew me as being a personality—somebody fun to hang out with, who knew where the parties were. They loved me. Even my brothers admired me for how hard I could party. But that identity—that reputation—became its own trap. I didn't know who I would be if I couldn't regularly get drunk or high.

The circumstances I'd built around my addiction made me feel good, even though the pleasure only lasted a little while. Then, it was followed by guilt. And I would drown out the guilt with more of the pleasure, which would just repeat itself over and over. That's why I never went long without substances for twenty years.

People cope and self-medicate for a lot of reasons, but most of the time, I think it's to suppress negative feelings. A lot of people have trauma in their backgrounds. Some people are lonely, or anxious. We want to suppress the negative thought patterns and emotions, drown them out, quiet our minds. Other people want a way to let go—feel free from whatever is weighing them down.

For a lot of years, I would always say that I didn't regret anything that I'd ever done. But that wasn't true. I felt shame and guilt from going against my core values—from undermining my integrity as a person. I was saying certain things, but doing other things. It was that shame that kept me in my addiction for so long. Before I could get myself unstuck for good, I had to figure out *why* I kept making excuses to continue these destructive habits.

MAKE A PLAN TO OVERCOME YOUR TRIGGERS

My addiction gave me community. It gave me an identity as the fun party guy. It gave me a way to deal with my anxiety, guilt, and shame.

Guess what happened right before I finally got clean? I found a new, positive *community* to be around by joining a mentoring program. (I'll share more about that program in the next two chapters.) The program helped me form a new *identity* as a productive, successful contributor. And it helped me form new habits that made me feel *less guilt and shame*, and deal with my anxiety.

You think that was a coincidence? Hell, no. It was because those pieces were in place that I finally was able to kick my bad habits for good. I was feeding the needs in my life with new, healthier alternatives. That meant I had options when I was triggered, other than weed or alcohol.

It didn't stop there, though—I also had to start dealing with some of my pain. Triggers have deep roots and long memories. If you want to turn those triggers off, you have to look at what they're connected to.

I had to work through some pain and confront the anxiety that I felt whenever I was sober. Stress and anxiety were probably my biggest triggers. Before I got clean, those triggers led immediately to drinking or using. I knew that just a couple of beers or drags off the pipe would suppress those feelings to a level where I could go have some fun and let loose. For a long time, my environment facilitated that response to those triggers: I was around a bunch of people that drank every day. Even if I wasn't drinking, my neighbor would walk over with a couple of beers and get me started. I didn't have the willpower or discipline to be around that and not go down my same path. I had to learn how to recognize my triggers and form a game plan to do something different when they hit.

I'll bet 90 percent of the people who are reading this are trying to suppress those same two emotions—stress and anxiety. Maybe it's stress with your spouse or kids; the responsibility of providing for a family; making the rent, the car payments, the bills—and when those triggers hit, you reach for something that will suppress all those negative feelings with some sort of dopamine hit, to put off dealing with them until tomorrow morning.

That thing is familiar and enjoyable: turning on a movie, lighting a joint. You've done these things enough times that you know they'll help you deal with the stress. Now, it's habitual. You don't even have to think about it anymore. You just divert your attention to whatever that thing is to help you avoid dealing with reality.

But listen—how much worse are you going to feel tomorrow morning after giving in to those triggers? Ask yourself: do you have literally *any* other alternative to coping with those emotions, other than the self-destructive things you're doing? Get yourself a plan so that you can prepare for those triggers and make a different choice when they come.

Imagine yourself one year from now, putting that plan into action when the trigger hits. Picture yourself recognizing the trigger, responding to it thoughtfully, looking at it with curiosity. You've gone from being *unaware* of your triggers and responding reactively with destructive habits, to now, doing something different when you feel stress and pain and fear. You've learned to ask: "Where is this coming from? Why do I have it?" You still feel stress in your life, but these days, it's mostly from the opportunities you've taken on that make you feel proud, not ashamed. You remind yourself, "I've signed up for this. All of these responsibilities are a result of good things I've brought into my life. I'm stressed because I'm investing in good things and I care about the outcome—it's a package deal." When your emotions get intense because you're feeling overwhelmed, you don't try to escape them—you let them out with a laugh.

This is possible for you. It starts by simply paying attention to when you get triggered and why.

> Identify what you're getting out of your addiction. Then, make a plan to replace bad habits with good habits that will feed those needs.

When you analyze your addiction, you can start planning to replace the bad habits with good habits that will feed your needs—like having good people around who can help you work through some of that pain, or working out to get dopamine highs through exercise, rather than drugs. I'm going to talk about some of these new habits in future chapters.

REWRITE YOUR NARRATIVE

In Chapter 1, I talked about the narrative you tell yourself—a narrative that might be the reason you stay stuck. Some people get so used to justifying their self-destruction that they start believing the false narrative they're giving to everyone else: "I can stop anytime I want." "My habits aren't that bad. I'm still functioning." "I could never leave my current job. I need the money."

You're going to stop that bullshit narrative right now.

I was finally able to recognize my own bullshit justifications because my energy was all wrong. Words would be coming out of my mouth about why I needed to drink, but none of it felt right. It wasn't true. It didn't align with who I knew I wanted to be.

I wanted positivity in my life. I wanted to be proud of who I was and what I did. I wanted to be intentional about producing less guilt in my life. I didn't want to hide stuff anymore or be a bad example. All the ways I was coping with my pain were bringing me temporary moments of pleasure, but more powerfully driving my life in a negative direction. I wanted to stop my bullshit narrative—enough that I was ready to deal with the pain and discomfort of making a change.

You might have feelings of guilt from saying or doing things that go against your core values. I've been there. You might feel shame from all the ways you constantly diminish your sense of integrity. I get it. But don't let your guilt and shame feed a bullshit story about who you are.

Listen to me: your current patterns are *not* the only option. There are healthier ways to cope. There are resources to deal with pain and shame. Challenge your current habits and change them.

So, what's the truth, to counteract the lies you're telling yourself? Here are a few ideas.

YOU HAVE THE ABILITY TO CHANGE YOUR SITUATION

No matter how shitty your current circumstances may be, you have some power over your attitude and your approach to your circumstances. You don't have to crack open a beer as soon as you get home from work. You don't have to fill your mind with negativity about how much you hate your boss and bring that negativity home to your spouse. You don't have to accept getting that shit salary and feeling poor for the rest of your life.

Stop playing the victim. You have power over your attitude and your approach to your circumstances.

If you're regularly complaining about your current circumstances, then *do* something to change your circumstances. Take stock of your options. Talk to someone who might have an idea of where you could go that would be better. Tell yourself a story that paints you as the hero—someone capable of making changes—instead of a story that paints you as a helpless victim.

Remember how I told Shandell I was throwing away the TV? I didn't even want to be tempted to watch it, and I recognized I had the power to change my situation. So, I literally just went home and sold it one day. What's your TV? If something in your life is preventing you from becoming the person you want to be, take action to change your situation.

YOUR BRAIN IS FINE

Sometimes, you might justify destructive habits because you don't like what's in your head. Maybe your brain works in a way that makes you self-conscious—like, you have a learning disability or a mental health disorder, which makes you self-medicate in unhealthy ways. But you can learn to work with your negative feelings. You can embrace your unique mind.

I'm pretty sure I have ADHD and I've experienced somewhere between ten and fifteen concussions in my life, which has made me pretty self-conscious over the years about my capacity to retain information. My younger brother was always able to retain a huge amount of information, and my Uncle Darren, who was like another brother to me, has an incredible vocabulary. He would call me out when I would use simple words. Compared to them, my way of thinking seemed so simple. I couldn't remember things the way they did or think of the right word. But none of that bothered me when I was drunk.

I also sometimes got high just to slow my brain down. One of the reasons I struggled to stay sober was because my thoughts jumped around so much—I'd leave the room to get something, and by the time I got there, my mind would have thought of a million other things to do, and I'd forget why I came in the room in the first place. That was frustrating.

I didn't like what was in my head. And I justified a lot of my stuck choices because I wanted to shut off my mind. If it wasn't weed and alcohol, it was TV or some other distraction.

In order to get unstuck, I had to accept that my brain works the way it does. Once I got sober, it took me a long time to learn how to focus, and build my memory, and learn how to emotionally regulate myself. But without pushing myself to go there, I would never have reached the level of success I have now.

Even the "simple" way I think has helped serve me in its own way. I've realized that many of the most intelligent people I know sometimes get stuck by overanalyzing things to death. In order to take action, things have to be lined up just right. My approach has been to jump out of the plane and build the parachute on the way down—learning to perfect the process midair. As I've learned from my mistakes and my experiences, those risks have translated into incredible growth and success. Some people want to perfect the process before they begin, without the benefit of learning from experience. That can keep them from moving forward. There are things I'm capable of that others are not, because of how I learn and vice versa. We each have our own strengths.

Now—I've totally embraced the way my brain works. One of my favorite things to do is go for a long drive in silence and just let my mind go. I don't turn on music—I just let my mind run from one thought to another. I get some of my best ideas that way.

You may have a weird brain, like mine. Don't tell yourself a bullshit story about how that disqualifies you from success or happiness. Instead of ignoring it or suppressing it, face it. Do the hard, painful work of dealing with what's in your head. Then—use it as fuel.

> Do the hard, painful work of dealing with what's in your head. Then—use it as fuel.

YOU CAN CHALLENGE YOUR PATTERNS

My mom is always trying to tell me, "You're fine as you are. Don't change. You've done enough. " She says that from a place of love and support because she's proud of me, but I finally told her she's not allowed to tell me that anymore—I *always* want to keep getting better.

Don't settle for the status quo. Pay attention to the things that repeat in your life and challenge them. In the early stages of my adulthood, I felt shame and guilt repeat over and over again. Those emotions *kept* coming up. Finally, I started becoming more aware of them and decided I didn't want to accept that pattern anymore. I could challenge it. I could change it.

In this stage of life, I've got a lot of good things going—I go to the gym every morning, I'm reading, I'm eating well and taking care of my body. But I still challenge my patterns. I'm always asking myself, "Is there a different variation of this discipline and these great habits that could produce even better results?"

One concept that I'm currently challenging my thinking on is the idea of balance. I used to be so one-sided on balance, probably because in *The 10X Rule,* Grant Cardone talks about "balance" as a fantasy. He makes the point that if you're ever going to do anything significant in your life, you will always have things out of balance—you're either focused on your business and your family is sacrificing, or you're focusing back on your family and something else is sacrificed. I decided "balance" was total bullshit. But then, well-intentioned people like my mom would say things like, "You need more balance in your life, between work and play and with your family..." And I would have an extremely abrasive response. Anytime somebody brought up the word, it was triggering to me—and I don't want to keep reacting that way. I've read a lot more about balance and harmonizing your life's priorities in other books. It's something I want to be less black and white about. This is the belief I'm currently challenging because I sense I can develop more in this area.

There's always another level you can reach. Don't hold yourself back from growth by believing the lie that things are "good enough" where they are.

> Don't hold yourself back from growth by believing the lie that things are "good enough" where they are.

YOU HAVE RESPONSIBILITIES

Maybe you want to believe the lie that the people around you don't need you to be sober or healthy or successful. Maybe you want to forget the fact that you have responsibilities.

Listen: you need to come to terms with the fact that you have responsibilities—like every other human being. I used to feel crushed under the weight of being a father, husband, business owner, and brother. That weight made me want to dull that burden of responsibility any way I could.

But we've all got responsibilities. That's just a fact. Even if you're not a spouse, parent, or business leader—you're still responsible for being a good person. Everyone has responsibilities to deal with. And you *can* deal with those responsibilities productively. I finally realized I didn't have to run from my responsibilities. I could *live up* to them instead.

> Everyone has responsibilities to deal with. You can deal
> with those responsibilities productively.

And on that note—you're not alone in dealing with these inner battles. Lift your head up from your lows long enough to look around and identify other resources that can help you.

YOU HAVE RESOURCES

Remember: staying stuck is a choice. But as soon as you choose to change your situation and commit to that choice, you'll be able to recognize the resources out there that can help you.

What got me off the couch and into the Motorcycle Mechanics Institute? It was a commercial on TV that I followed up on. What got me into a healthy living situation in Arizona? Calling up my family members who were willing to house me, love me, and hold me to a higher standard of life. One of the best moves I ever made was to follow my younger brother who got me plugged into a Primerica Insurance sales group for a time. I was terrible at selling insurance, but I was surrounded by a new network of people who were all positive and highly motivated. They completely changed my perspective on what was possible in my life. In the next chapter, I'm going to share a story about a Facebook ad that changed my life—literally, a fucking Facebook ad. These were resources I had at my disposal. A lot of them were nothing more than good marketing. But I went after the ones I saw real value in and committed myself to what they could offer.

I saw the opportunity and went *ALL IN*.

In many cases, you don't even need to leave your room to start taking advantage of the resources out there to help you. Wherever you're at, somebody else has been through something similar. Find those stories. Between YouTube, and social media, and books—you can tap into the possibilities that are available to you, in your own context. The experiences of others can add value to you and give clarity about where you're at, where you want to go, and what life looks like on the other side. Wherever you are on your journey, someone else has been there before—and moved past it. The same kind of success is possible for you.

> Wherever you are on your journey, someone else has been there before—and moved past it. The same kind of success is possible for you.

There are other resources you can use to help you stay on course. A healthy diet is a big help. Eating the wrong things can create mental blocks and hormonal imbalances. A good, clean diet can help you focus on your mindset and connections with others. Physical activity can also be a game changer, because it naturally helps your body produce a lot of the same hormones you may have gotten through an addiction. Getting fit will also help you feel stronger and more confident—again, helping you rewrite a more positive narrative for yourself.

You have other options to cope with your stress—and you can commit to those better options. Use your network. Use your skills and connections. Lean on the people who believe in your potential and *get yourself a new story.*

I want to acknowledge that these methods worked for me, but many people have layers of trauma in their background that make forward momentum harder than just mustering up grit and willpower to do the hard, necessary thing. You may need more resources than what I can provide in these pages, telling you my own story of what worked. I am actively looking into building my own awareness of how emotional pain needs to be acknowledged in order to get unstuck, especially when it comes to trauma. Reach out to me in a year—I hope to have more understanding to share with you then.

INTERROGATE THE LOWS UNTIL THEY STOP HAPPENING

As you learn how to use your lows for fuel to move forward, stay alert and self-aware. Recognize when you might need to make even bigger environmental changes—like when Shandell and I realized we needed to move away from our new group in Arizona. You've got to recognize the signs of falling back into old patterns. If and when you do—that's a sign you need to develop more self-discipline.

It happens. And there was one more major low for me. One more experience that had to shake me awake and scare me into permanent life change.

September 29, 2017: it was my son's birthday, which meant I felt entitled to start celebrating early. I drank my first few beers around 10:00 a.m. and kept the party going throughout the day as we did birthday festivities, presents, and so on. That night, there were more celebrations planned. My brother and sister-in-law were going to a Florida Georgia Line concert for their anniversary, and had invited my wife and me along. I'd been drinking all day, so I had someone else drive my truck. I kept right on drinking in the backseat.

I'd brought a water bottle full of vodka—planning to share. But I didn't like having two drinks to hold, so I ended up pouring the entire bottle into my beer. My wife took one drink of it and made a face. "What did you do to your beer?" she asked, disgusted. I shrugged. Then, I polished the rest off myself.

By the time Nelly wrapped up and Florida Georgia Line took the stage, I was absolutely hammered. I could barely talk or comprehend what people were saying around me. I started getting irritable—it seemed like everybody else was having fun except for me, because everybody else had it together. I could hear the words coming out of my mouth and they didn't sound all that intelligent anymore—they were slurry. Stuck in cursive. I started getting self-conscious, which meant it was a very short amount of time before I got fired up. I can't remember what I said to my wife, but I stormed away from my group in a rage and decided I was going to walk back to my truck. I don't know what I was planning to do—maybe ride out the rest of the concert and try to sober up.

But my next action took things in a very different direction.

A random guy and his girlfriend approached me from the parking lot, walking down toward the concert area. I was angry and irritable—I decided I didn't like the look of him. I don't remember why I did what I did. Maybe he said something, or maybe I was just looking for a fight. I walked right up to him and headbutted him as hard as I could.

His eyes rolled back into his head. His arms flew out in front of him and his whole body got stiff before he fell to the ground, unconscious—it was like something from a UFC fight.

My first thought was, "Shit—did I just kill him?"

His girlfriend screamed at the top of her lungs, which scared the heck out of me and attracted a whole lot of attention from others in the area.

Very quickly, people from the parking lot started surrounding us. Many people saw what happened—they started getting loud, yelling profanities, asking what was going on. His girlfriend was going berserk—she thought he was dead too. I started to panic.

I could see my truck and ran for it. I punched in the lock code, grabbed the keys that had been left on the seat, and peeled out of the parking lot, swerving around the people that were trying to get me to come answer for what I'd just done. I'm surprised I didn't run anybody over. Crazy shit. I was so drunk.

Security had obviously been alerted to what had just happened, because I could see them hurriedly closing the gates. I saw little golf cart security vehicles chasing after me—I was swerving and speeding up, trying to lose them. I had almost made it out of there—if there hadn't been one last turn to make, I might have just blown through the gates and tried to get away. But in that last turn, I spotted a little industrial maintenance building with a small parking lot that looked out of the way. I turned in there, skidded to a stop, and parked the truck, leaving the keys inside.

Then, I just ran.

I was too drunk to be strategic. I ended up running back to the same exact parking lot I had just fled from. In fact, I walked right behind the police as they were interviewing the girlfriend and—I was relieved to see—the guy, who had woken up.

I thought, "This is way too close."

I walked faster, trying to get away from there, when I ran into my brother—he must have come looking for me. We look a lot alike, so I hissed at him, "Switch me shirts!"—hoping maybe they wouldn't recognize me. He did what I told him to do and then ran to get the rest of the group to tell them we had to leave.

So much for the concert or anniversary celebrations.

Most of us had come in the truck, but we couldn't all go back in the truck. The authorities had my license plate number—they were looking for me. So instead, we crammed nine people into my sister-in-law's six-seater car. I insisted on sitting in the front.

My sister-in-law was in med school at the time. She's intelligent and very sweet. In the presence of this smart, decent woman—I felt like a huge asshole. So, I acted confident—trying to compensate for what I'd just done. I started talking shit about doctors and the medical industry. "You're just book-smart," I sneered at her. "You don't have to think for yourself." We weren't that close to begin with, but that night, I ruined whatever relationship we did have.

The next morning was my son's birthday party. His friends showed up at our house, and the plan was to drive them all in my truck to a play center. But obviously, we didn't have my truck. My wife—who was, understandably, super irritated and frustrated with me—ended up having to call an Uber to get everybody over there. She insisted I come along.

I was too sick to participate. I laid on a bench and felt like shit—in many more ways than one. Several weeks later, I was summoned to court to answer for what I'd done. It was not my first court appearance, but thankfully it ended up being my last.

During those two days, there wasn't a whole lot of clear self-awareness happening. But I knew the way I'd acted was the opposite—in every way—of the kind of man I wanted to be. If there was one thought that made it through my physical sickness and humiliation, it was "Enough."

I knew I could be better than this. I knew I was *meant* to be better than this.

You've got to listen to that little voice inside you saying, "Enough." That guilt is a message from your conscience. Every time you get done doing something that you know doesn't align with your true nature and core values—you get that little shot of guilt. The more you ignore that voice, the quieter it gets. Before it gets too far down the road, or your beliefs just completely go away—*listen* to it. While that voice is still strong and present, let it plant a seed in your life to start making some changes.

> You've got to listen to that little voice inside you saying, "Enough." While that voice is still strong and present, let it plant a seed in your life to start making some changes.

I chose to use my shame as fuel. I never wanted to treat anybody like that again. I want to feel good about every interaction I have. I want the people I interact with to feel good as well. So, rather than wallowing in shame, I kept learning from my lows.

We've all had failures. Instead of commiserating about them, look for the lessons they offer. Stop suppressing those painful memories and feelings and wake up to how your actions affect other people. There is enormous value that can come from failure if you choose to learn from it. That's true of all levels of failure—whether it's a minor conversation that didn't go well or a business venture you didn't take as seriously as you should have. They all have lessons to offer.

You can choose to let these awful experiences be your excuse to stay where you are. Honestly, that's probably what 95 percent of people choose to do. But 5 percent of people will use them as fuel to change.

That's you. You're going to grow from this. You'll try something different. You're going to tell yourself a new narrative.

I chose to use my lowest lows as fuel. Now, you're going to do the same.

Napoleon Hill, author of *Think and Grow Rich,* said, "Every failure has the seed of an equivalent benefit." All of these experiences—these failures—can benefit you, if you choose to learn from them. Take the little seeds planted from each failure and use them to remind yourself that you'll never make those mistakes again—or at least you won't fail as badly as the last time. Tell yourself, "My mistakes will not define me."

We're all put here on this earth to make a difference and to help people. Don't believe the lie that your mistakes will keep you down. Your purpose is to make a positive impact on the people around you.

You are meant to do great things.

ACTION STEPS

Your lows can teach you about who you really want to be, help you understand your destructive habits, and ultimately help you rewrite your narrative.

- Take a hard look at the experiences that make you feel ashamed or guilty. Why do those memories bother you? What *weren't* you doing, that you *wish* you were doing? What *were* you doing, that you want to *stop* doing? Write out a description of the kind of person you genuinely want to be, focusing on your core values.
- Analyze your stuck habits. What are you getting out of these unhealthy coping habits? What else could you do to meet those needs?
- Identify your triggers. Do you have literally *any* other alternative to cope with your negative emotions, other than self-destructive choices? Get yourself a plan so that you can prepare for those triggers and make a different choice when they come.

- How do you need to rewrite the narrative you're telling yourself? What truths can you grab onto, to get yourself unstuck?

Choose to use your lowest lows as fuel for change. Grow from this. Try something different. Tell yourself a new narrative. Listen to the voice inside you saying, "Enough" so that you can become the person you are meant to be.

CHAPTER 4

Believe You Are
Meant for Greatness

MAKE A POSITIVE IMPACT ON THE WORLD

I F YOU WANT to achieve greatness, you need to get greatness in your head. Get your thoughts out of negative patterns, pessimism, and a scarcity mentality. Instead, fill your thoughts with dreams of what *could* be. Tell yourself it's possible—and that you can achieve it.

As a kid, I remember riding my bike to a neighborhood full of huge houses. Now, I look at those houses and they seem pretty average, but back then—they looked like mansions to me. I felt so curious about how all the people in that neighborhood made enough money to live in those big houses.

That idea stuck in my mind. *I* wanted to eventually have a family and be able to buy a big house. I wanted to be one of those people who lived in a nice neighborhood. I wanted to live a great life—and even then, I knew I was capable of doing more.

But thirty years later, I was driving around drunk every single day. I was leaving work early to go home and get high. I was hiding my weed and my bottles of liquor from Shandell. We lived in a rental house that I hated. My head was full of guilt and shame.

Something changed though, after the terrible experience at the concert and being hungover at my son's birthday party. I felt more sure than ever that my behavior went against who I wanted to be. I knew if I continued down that path, I was either going to kill myself, kill somebody else, or go to jail. I decided it was unacceptable for me to do those things anymore.

For years, my family had tried to convince me I was meant for greater things. Both my mom and my uncle would lecture me after every stupid accident or jail stint: "You need to be a better example to your brothers. You need to live up to your responsibilities. *You are meant to do great things with your life.*"

Meant for greater things.

I wasn't ready to hear that yet. At that time, I couldn't imagine how I could achieve a better life for myself. I only knew how to be the party guy. After I got married, I wasn't ready either. Throughout the first eight years of my marriage, I had been introduced to a dozen or so people that could have made an impact in my life, but—even when it was the right person with the right message—it was the wrong time. Their advice went right over my head. I wasn't ready yet to make the decision on my own.

Well, now I was ready. I was hungry for new realizations and new awareness—something that could help me permanently make the change.

When I got to that point, the right person just happened to be Grant Cardone and the message was his book: *The 10X Rule.* My uncle Darren turned me on to Grant Cardone. Darren is my mom's younger brother, and he's actually only three months older than me. He's more like a brother than anything else, but I still look up to him a lot. I remember asking Darren questions about his company and what had inspired him to go into business for himself. He mentioned that he had just finished listening to *The 10X Rule* on Audible. "You should listen to it!" he said. "It's narrated by Grant Cardone himself. He has such amazing energy! I know you're going to love it."

I reactivated my dormant Audible account and downloaded the book. I was struck by the fact that Grant had overcome addiction and completely changed his life. He talked about being focused on personal growth and development, making progress in his life, promoting his brand, and becoming a better version of himself. He had a wife, a family, a business, and became well known on social media.

Grant Cardone started off in a similar place *to me*. Now, he was living the kind of life I had only ever dreamed of.

His book made me wonder: What if I started to *believe* different things were possible for me? What if I believed I was capable of living a better life, that I could be a better leader and example to my family? The book planted an idea in my mind that was different from all my usual negative thought patterns. It was a little bit of hope in the midst of all the mental shit that was keeping me stuck.

> What could happen if you start to *believe* different things are possible for you? What if you believe you are capable of living a better life?

My thought patterns started to change—and it was like the universe aligned to meet me there.

Six weeks after I'd headbutted the guy at the concert, I was sitting in my car in a neighborhood full of nice houses—a neighborhood that was a lot like the one I used to ride my bike through. I was supposed to be knocking on doors, but I wasn't. I was scrolling through Facebook on my phone. And that's when I saw an ad from Grant Cardone. He was offering a mentor program leading up to his 10X Growth Conference in Vegas.

And I knew: *That's it.* That's my ticket out.

I signed up for the program and, within weeks, was meeting every week with a group of other people being mentored by Grant Cardone. We were coached in developing new, positive habits. A huge part of the program involved changing the way we thought—identifying goals for ourselves and believing that we were meant for greatness. I had taken a baby step in that direction by signing up for the program. Now, I was accelerating. I was going faster and further than I ever had before.

My decision to enroll in that mentoring program wouldn't have happened unless I believed in my ability to change my life and accomplish good things. It was because of that *belief* that I started looking for a way out. It was because of that *belief* that I was ready to take advantage of the opportunity when it presented itself—and go *ALL IN*.

This message is as true for you as it was for me. *You* can change your life. You are capable of huge accomplishments. You are meant for greater things.

BELIEVE YOU CAN CHANGE

Never, ever say you can't change. "I can't" is a very powerful, self-defeating phrase. It only serves to reinforce the belief that you're incapable and that you don't have the talent or the willingness to figure out how to change.

One of my mentors once told me that whenever his kids would say, "I can't," he would have them do ten push-ups. I started that with my own children. It's gotten to the point now that my kids call each other out when someone says, "I can't." No one gets away with saying that in our house.

I know my kids can do whatever they set their mind to, but sometimes *they* don't know that. When they're struggling, I ask them a series of questions: "How many times did you try? How do you know you can't do it if you didn't try two or three times? Let's figure this out."

Do you get stuck in the lie of "I can't"? Well, how many times have you tried?

Instead of a pattern of believing that you can't, how would it feel to have enough confidence in yourself to think that you can? And then—after trying a few times—how would it feel to get some wins under your belt so that you know with absolute *certainty* that you can? Your success is less about how many times you've tried and more about how many things you ultimately accomplish. Trying leads to succeeding, and succeeding leads to more confidence. Imagine yourself in that place: the things you set out to do, you get done. You keep fulfilling your promises. You keep racking up wins.

You may not be there yet, but there's no reason why you can't get there, with consistent work and focus in the direction of being this person. *That* can be your reality.

Refuse to accept that you can't do something. Actually, you have an amazing ability to figure out your own problems and become more resourceful. Reinforce the idea that you can do anything you put your mind to.

> Refuse to accept that you can't do something. Actually, you have an amazing ability to figure out your own problems and become more resourceful.

You want to know something silly? One of the things that held me back from getting clean was the fear that I wouldn't be good at country dancing and karaoke anymore. Before getting sober, I had tried karaoke a couple times. I freaking loved karaoke. I'm not very good at it—which was why I only ever did it after having some drinks—but I loved just getting out there, having a good time, dancing and singing karaoke. I had come to rely on alcohol in so many different situations in my life, I was afraid that if I gave up that crutch, I wouldn't be able to do some of my favorite things anymore.

Well, guess what? A few years after I got sober, I bought my own karaoke setup for my house. My girls and I love to sing together. And

I'm not afraid to take my performance public either—I was out with some friends recently and went out to a local bar so they could get some drinks after dinner on date night. There was a small dance floor with a bunch of people dancing who were clearly letting loose. I was almost certainly the only sober person there. But in spite of that, my wife and I showed everyone there how to "dance like no one's watching." Turns out I'm pretty damn good at dancing and karaoke without the alcohol. It just took me a while to get the nerve to do it again without the liquid courage.

But let's say I never did karaoke again. The choice still would have been worth it! Between drunk-karaoke-Jefferson and sober-successful-Jefferson—guess which guy she'd prefer to be married to? The people I love the most want me to be more than just the fun party guy. And *I* want to be more than that guy. I want to be proud of who I am and what I'm doing with my life.

Have you tried to change already? How many times?

Remember: even if you end up reverting back to your old, destructive habits, even if you feel shame, even if you question whether you can ever change—there's fuel there. You can use the energy from those feelings to drive needed changes in your relationships and in your future. Claim your self-worth as your true identity, change your negative thought patterns, and start living as the person you are meant to be.

> Claim your self-worth as your true identity, change your negative thought patterns, and start living as the person you are meant to be.

THE IMPORTANCE OF CHANGING YOUR THINKING

When I was still drinking, it was like an adrenaline rush to know I was about to get home, have a beer, and smoke some weed. I knew the guilt and shame I felt nearly all the time were about to go away, silenced by the booze. Soon after that first sip, I would begin to feel calm and relaxed. I would watch a movie or work on my motorcycle and feel good—for a little while.

Then, the booze would wear off. And I'd be stuck in the same old shit.

I knew I wasn't making enough to achieve the quality of life I wanted for my family. I was broke, stressed out, and stuck in a place of uncertainty. I couldn't figure out how to get past that. Why? Primarily, because I suffered from a lack of self-worth. My head was full of negative thoughts.

Negative thought patterns fuel your addictions, because you rely on self-medicating to suppress the feelings of shame and guilt. Keeping those feelings suppressed feels all-important when you're in a "stuck" mentality—and for a long time, that's exactly where I was.

It was my negative feelings and self-doubt that had primarily led me to hit a ceiling with my income level—I didn't believe I could possibly do more than what I was doing then. Those negative feelings began to inform every interaction I had. I began to get irritated with my wife and kids whenever they asked for something we couldn't afford. My negative thoughts weren't just keeping me stuck—my family was stuck right there with me.

> My negative thoughts weren't just keeping me stuck—my family was stuck right there with me.

What was I afraid of? I was afraid of change. But I was also afraid that I *wouldn't* change—that I'd be stuck where I was for the rest of my life. I was afraid of uncertainty—I'd been regularly getting high and drunk since age fourteen. Who would I even be, sober? I was afraid of the discomfort involved to get clean, deal with my negative emotions, and put in the work to get to a higher income level. I was afraid of my weakness: I didn't know if I had what it took to find another job or really make it.

It was those doubts and fears that led me into my last experience getting high...But it was the belief that I *could* change that ultimately took me out of my addiction.

THE LAST HIGH

The last time I hit rock bottom was in January 2018. I had been enrolled in the Grant Cardone program for two months. I'd made a lot of progress, but I was still regularly getting drunk and high.

On January 7, my brother and I went on a bender. We'd begun drinking during the middle of the day and kept going all night. We drank all the whiskey, we drank all the beer, we smoked all the weed. After we finished every last drop of booze and smoked all the weed, we were still so desperate for more that we spent forty-five minutes scraping out the resin that had accumulated in the pipe. Then, we lit that tarry crap and smoked it.

Late that night, after we finished the last dregs of resin, my wife took me home. I was belligerent, ignorant, acting like an asshole. I treated her like shit that night.

The next morning when I woke up, I knew I had to be done. All the years of planted seeds, my changed thinking, and my desire for a better life culminated in that moment. I turned to Shandell and finally admitted out loud what she had known for years: "I have a problem. I need help." I started crying. "I want to change," I told her. "I'm scared. But I want to be a better husband and father and communicator. I want to make something good for our family."

Shandell held me. She said, "I've got your back every step of the way. I'm going to support you, whatever it takes. I'll do whatever I can to help you stay accountable to it."

She never gave up on me. She always believed I could do it. And I finally started to believe it too.

PEOPLE ARE COUNTING ON YOU

I was thirty-three when I finally decided to get clean. My fear of failure had kept me from making this decision for a long time—but ultimately,

I realized I wanted to be a better role model to the people who loved me.

Here's the thing: I was *already* a role model to the people around me. I was just a really shitty one. Growing up, I never planned to become such a shitty example to my brothers. In fact, the very first time that I smoked weed with one of them, I felt so guilty that I ratted us both out to my mom. I bawled my eyes out as she lectured us and demanded to know why we did it. I didn't have a good answer for her. And I did it again. My guilt didn't stop me from pulling my brothers into my own addictive cycle for the next fifteen years.

But the combination of all the events in my past—the way I treated my wife and the terrible example I was to my brothers—led to my decision to finally make changes.

Everyone has people who count on them. In my case, I'm a husband, father, and the oldest of four brothers. I always knew deep inside that all of them were counting on me. But it wasn't until I committed to sobriety that I was able to admit that to myself and own up to the responsibilities I had to them.

Listen: it doesn't matter who you are or where you're at in life, people are counting on you. Even if you're single with no kids, there are people who depend on you—your siblings, your friends, your coworkers... Hell, even your dog. They believe in you. And you can believe in yourself. Trust that people are watching you. You make an impact on them in everything you say and do.

Whether that's a negative or positive impact is up to you.

> You make an impact on the people around you in everything you say and do. Whether that's a negative or positive impact is up to you.

And here's some advice, from someone who's had a lot of low points: even if you are at your lowest low, you can still make a positive impact by showing the people in your life that you love them. Your love will help them accept you, and may even help you believe the truth of the words that changed me forever:

You're meant to do great things with your life.

GET UNSTUCK

Do you believe that yet? Are you still stuck believing the lie that you can't change? Are you stuck in your fears and your doubts?

I want you to read some words out loud. Doesn't matter if you're on an airplane or at the library. Say these words out loud and claim them for yourself: "I am meant for greater things."

You've got to challenge your beliefs. I know how easy it is to get stuck in your own narrative. You can fail to realize good things are right there for you—like, *right there*. But you can't see them when you're stuck in a negative way of thinking.

Let this book start to shift your paradigm. Somebody else has gone through it and found success on the other side.

So: why not you?

I've spoken with dozens of people over the past couple years on Instagram and Facebook Messenger. They tell me some of the things that they're dealing with—relationships, business, habits—and ask for my advice. I share very, very simple concepts with them. I'll ask questions as basic as, "What are you dealing with? What do you feel like is the biggest issue that's holding you back from making the changes? Why would it be important for you to make these changes? Who else would you be doing it for?"

> Why is it important for you to make these changes? Who else would you be doing it for?

The process of answering some of those questions helps them come to realizations that were right there in front of them—but they'd never taken the time to go through that exercise and confront their own assumptions. By the end of it, they're like, "I can't believe I didn't think of these things myself. They're so simple—it was right there for me to see, and I was just overlooking it."

Ask *yourself* these questions. Why is it important that you make changes in your life? Who would you be making them for?

Look at your answers. Use those pieces of information to stop the negative narratives going on in your own head. If you need to, find someone who can talk through the process with you. The simple process of truthfully answering those questions is a powerful first step and one that will help you plant the seeds of change.

CLAIM POSITIVE THOUGHTS AS TRUTH

When I started with the Grant Cardone mentorship group, I was with people who were able to think past their current situation. This new group of people got together to share industry secrets and success principles with each other. They all wanted to win—and they wanted me to win as well.

As I began to observe this new group, I realized that, before I met them, I never thought on a big scale. I just concentrated on getting by. Most of the other people I had worked with in the past reinforced that limited thinking. Growing up, my thinking had been shaped by a scarcity mentality: there wasn't enough. We couldn't afford it. I could only go so far.

Bullshit.

I wanted to emulate this new group. Listening to them, I began to believe that I could be successful too—the only thing these people had on me was time and experience. And once I *believed* that, I began to *act* accordingly. I started to do things that I had never done before: I worked harder than I ever had and put in longer hours. I started pushing myself to get better at sales calls: I practiced my smile in the rearview mirror of my car and sought out coaching from the best salespeople. I threw myself into my work with conviction and enthusiasm, and started feeling genuine excitement about my possibilities.

I was also deliberate about training my thinking in a new way. I started journaling daily and described myself as the person I wanted to be, only in the present tense—as though it had already happened: "I am a loving husband and father. I live in my dream home. I am debt free." I'll talk about goal setting a lot more in Chapter 6, but this was a big step for me in deliberately reshaping how I thought about myself.

It paid off. Thanks to a new combination of belief, activity, and additional training, I made great progress with my sales job. I made $18,000 in just one month—which, at the time, felt like an unbelievable amount of money. I was more excited about my prospects than I'd ever been in my life—and that was only the beginning.

Listen: this can be *your* story. When you get to a place of confidence and belief in yourself, you help create an environment that is conducive to growth and positivity. You start to *act* differently. When you believe you're a highly successful person, you put in the hours of a highly successful person. You seek out advice from other highly successful people. You interact with your loved ones from a place of confidence, not shame.

> When you get to a place of confidence and belief in yourself, you help create an environment that is conducive to growth and positivity.

In fact, you may get so pumped about thinking positively, you become a maniac about it. In my case, I went from one extreme to the other. I became *ultra* aware of negativity in my life and how it was affecting me. I would walk into a room and see people watching some negative TV show and I'd tell them, "You need to turn this shit off. This is garbage." Admittedly, I was pretty abrasive at first. But it's because I realized how powerfully my thinking affected everything else in my life. Once I identified a negative pattern or behavior, I cut it out completely. I wanted to fill my brain, life, and schedule with positivity, improvement, and healthy changes *only*.

What about you? If you don't feel confident about your own inner worth yet, you can take concrete steps toward changing your negative thought patterns and internalizing the belief that you are meant for greatness:

- **Build awareness about your negative thinking.** Notice when you're having a negative thought, or when you're taking in negative messages. When you become more aware of your negative thinking, you're better equipped to change it to positive thinking.
- **Learn to look at your own thoughts from a place of curiosity.** It's easy to view negative thoughts with judgment, but that only compounds the negativity. Ask yourself *why* these thoughts happen. Where did they come from? Why do they feel so powerful? Be curious, and then let them go. Don't get too down on yourself, don't stew on anything, and do not let negative thoughts take up your energy. Just be aware of them and keep changing your paradigms.
- **Switch your scarcity thinking for thoughts of abundance.** This means you start thinking about possibilities, rather than limitations: "I'm not worth a billion right now, but I could get there. So, *how* do I get there?" I'm living proof that if you want something and you're willing to put in the work, you can get it. Anything is possible.
- **Give yourself time.** Changing your thought patterns won't happen overnight. It may prove to be hard work. Even now, I still catch myself thinking in terms of limitations or about the "what ifs." I'll make a note of it and ask myself, "Isn't it interesting how I just went to that place of thinking?" Then I balance that negativity with some positive reinforcement: "I don't have to think that way. I can think in a more positive way. So, how can I go there?"
- **Strengthen your skills.** Sometimes, getting better in *external* ways can help you build more *internal* confidence. Get new training in your job, or start watching YouTube videos of highly successful people and follow their advice.

- **Start taking your personal integrity seriously if you're not already.** If you make a promise, keep it—especially the ones you make to yourself. Don't look for shortcuts, or cheats, or the easy way out. Do the right thing. When people have low integrity, it changes how they show up. They may try to project confidence, but you can see through it. Real integrity means you can show up with true confidence.
- **Stop justifying and making excuses for your bad choices.** I've talked about this already: don't believe your own bullshit.
- **Describe the life you want and yourself as the person you want to be.** Do it in the present tense—"I am an amazing provider"—as though it's already happened. This will help trick your subconscious into believing you are meant for greatness, rather than staying stuck in negativity.
- **Start working out.** Exercise produces the same hormones (endorphins and dopamine) that an addiction does, so, not only will this help you kick your bad habits, but you'll also start to feel more confident about your strength and appearance.

Also, never underestimate the power of your loved ones in reinforcing a message of greatness in your life. Remember: they believe in you. Let their love fuel your positive changes. You're not just doing this for yourself. You're doing it for them.

> You're not just doing this for yourself. You're doing it for them.

MAKE IT HAPPEN

On the morning on January 8, 2018, I committed to Shandell that I was going to change. We cried together. Then, we made plans. We spent the day together as a family. It was a quiet, mellow sort of day.

It would have been nice if that was all it took: some crying, some planning, some hanging out. But change is hard. That's why you have to believe you can follow through with it.

The next morning—more than thirty-two hours after my last high—I got in my car and headed back to St. George. I started feeling sick on the drive. I made it to work and started to go out and knock on doors to set up appointments—but that's when I really started feeling like shit. It felt like flu symptoms were coming on strong.

After eight hours of work, I decided I didn't want to spend the night in St. George, like I'd planned—I wanted to get home to my wife. I drove the four hours back to Salt Lake City, feeling like hell the whole way. Once I got home, I crawled into bed and laid there for five days straight. I was sick as a dog. At some points, I could barely make it to the bathroom. I thought for years that I had come down with the flu, but looking back on that illness now, I think I was probably detoxing from sixteen years of almost daily alcohol abuse.

I'll be honest: my brain was not full of positivity that week. I was not thinking about how I was meant for greatness. I spent most of those five days feeling really fucking sorry for myself.

But I also spent that time thinking hard about my life. By the time I was feeling well enough to get up, I had made the major decision to leave the window company I had been working for to start up my own business. Two months later, I started JKR Windows.

My decision to get clean was one of the most pivotal moments of my life. Thanks to the support I had from my wife and family, and the faith they had in me, I was able to make the healthy changes necessary. But the commitment I made to Shandell was more than just a promise to her—it was also a promise to myself. And it was more than just a commitment to get clean. It was the moment when I decided to stop just "getting by" in life—and start succeeding.

Make a promise to yourself and the people you love. Make a *commitment* to yourself and the people you love. Believe you are meant for greatness—and then, start acting like it.

> Believe you are meant for greatness—and then, start
> acting like it.

Changes need to come from within. There's a big difference between someone telling you what you have to do, versus sitting down and deciding for yourself, "I want this. I can do this. I want it bad enough to put in the hard work to make it happen." You need to claim those beliefs for yourself.

And it *will* require a hell of a lot of work. You can't just imagine a Ferrari and make a Ferrari appear. Put all these goals and dreams into your mind—then, take *action* in that direction.

That's what we're talking about next.

ACTION STEPS

Your beliefs translate into action. When you *believe* you're meant to do great things with your life, you start making the choices of a successful person. Work through some of the points below to help you claim self-worth as your true identity and start living as the person you are meant to be.

- What's happening in your life that you wish was different? What do you feel like is the biggest issue that's holding you back from making necessary changes?
- Why would it be important for you to make these changes? Who else would you be doing it for?
- Describe yourself as the person you want to be, only in the present tense: "I am _____."

- Identify some of the "Train Your Brain" strategies that you want to implement. Make a plan to start changing your negative thought patterns for positive ones.

Remember: you're not just making hard changes for yourself—you're also making them for all the people who depend on you and look to you as an example. Love can be one of the biggest motivators in getting you unstuck and driving your success story.

Now—let's start accelerating.

PART 2

Accelerate

CHAPTER 5

Get Focus | Get Discipline

BUILD MOMENTUM, ONE WIN AT A TIME

FIRST STEP: BELIEVE you are meant for greatness.

Second step: go *ALL IN*—and fucking *do* something about it.

There's a reason "Believe You Are Meant for Greatness" is the last chapter of Part 1. Changing your thought patterns is a critical step in getting unstuck. But if you don't follow up with focused *action*, you'll never be able to start living like a success story.

How you do anything is how you'll do everything. That's why the key to transforming your life is to *focus* in one intentional direction and develop *disciplined habits*. A lot of people talk a big game, but never get around to taking real action. You want to accelerate your progress? Then show up for yourself. Get focused, get disciplined, and build momentum—one win at a time—until you're consistently making progress on your goals.

> You want to live like a success? Then show up for yourself. Get focused, get disciplined, and build momentum—one win at a time—until you're consistently making progress on your goals.

Focus came first for me. After I started the Grant Cardone mentorship program—but before I got clean—I started to change my thinking. I wanted to change my behavior too. So, I developed one clear focus: to add as much value as I possibly could to the window business where I had been working for the last three years. I'll call it "ABC Windows."

During December, January, and February, I ramped up my activity. I went as hard as I could in selling windows and was more consistent than I'd ever been. In those three months, I made more money than I'd ever made before. My focused effort completely transformed my ability to generate value.

But all that value was ultimately profiting another company. I'd had a lot of frustrations about ABC Windows for a while. It bothered me that the founders hadn't made me a partner after telling me they would, and every time I raised an idea to innovate and improve their processes, it got shut down.

Granted, I had been pretty irresponsible during those first three years in the window business—something I can recognize now, which I couldn't then. I wanted to believe that I had everything it took to be a great partner and was positive that ABC Windows would have been more successful with me as one of the primary decision-makers. But looking back now, I can see that the leaders had a number of good reasons to not include me. I don't blame them for the decision they made, and we're still friends. That's the wisdom of hindsight.

But at the time? ABC Windows pissed me off. I had a chip on my shoulder and a lot of complaints. But as long as I was regularly getting drunk and stoned, I put up with those frustrations and self-medicated them away.

Once I got clean, I was clear headed. That made it harder to ignore those problems. I began to question whether or not this company was where I wanted to direct all my energy.

I started looking for a *new* focus. Being a part of this mentor program, I was on weekly calls with all these other high-level entrepreneurs. Each of them was talking about their different field of business and sharing about the wins they were getting. My ADD kicked in big time. I was like, "What if I did roofing? What if I did solar? What if I did real estate?" I even went out to Las Vegas to meet with a guy doing real estate at a high level, who was looking for partners.

My uncle Darren went with me to Las Vegas to vet out that real estate company. In Chapter 4, I shared about how Darren had introduced me to Grant Cardone and *The 10X Rule*. He was an incredibly important part of my change in trajectory. Honestly, I think I was trying to impress him with all the new opportunities I was lining up for myself. On the drive there, I was all over the place. I talked about dabbling in real estate. Then, I talked about selling windows. Then, I pulled up my Spanish language app, because I was also trying to study Spanish at the time. Darren was overwhelmed by how many different things I was trying to do at once.

We met with the Las Vegas guy, which was pretty disappointing. He was doing some shady business and was super condescending. He made me feel like shit.

After meeting with him over a couple days, we ended up at Panera Bread to talk about it. Darren and I both ruled out the Vegas option—that much was clear. But I was still fired up. I was just barely three weeks sober and had all this new, clear focus. I was desperate to find the vehicle where I could *channel* all my energy.

I talked with Darren about the Spanish language app and doing Cardone University. I'd bought a real estate tracking app and said to Darren, "Listen, we can do it on our own, without this guy!"

He said to me, "Dude, you're doing so many things right now—you're not going to do *any* of them very well. Have you ever heard the phrase, 'If you chase two rabbits, you get none'?"

He was spot-on. My lack of focus was preventing me from doing anything well.

I knew he was right, but I felt overwhelmed by the pressure of figuring out what to do. I told him, "I want to win *so bad*. I'm scared. I'm nervous I'm going to go back to drugs and alcohol if I don't find something soon. I have all this passion and enthusiasm to do something better, but I don't even know what game I should play." All the strong emotions I'd been suppressing for years started rising up, and I was completely unprepared to deal with them. I started bawling hysterically—in the middle of the restaurant, during lunch rush hour.

That was pretty awkward for Uncle Darren.

But his advice stuck. And once I got home and had a little time to process, I got focused.

If you chase two rabbits, you get none.

Not long after that trip, I made the decision to cut out *all* the other distractions in my life—no more dabbling in real estate, learning Spanish, or exploring other industries. Instead, I was going to focus all my attention on becoming an expert in the window industry. Real estate could come later. For now, I was going to go ALL IN, selling windows. And in the days after I finally quit drinking and smoking, I made one of the biggest decisions of my life: I was going to open my own window company.

For the next two years, I ate, slept, and breathed JKR Windows. Other than my family and working out, the business got every bit of my focused attention. And that laser focus was key to accelerating as fast as we did.

CHOOSE ONE MAIN THING

There are plenty of average, ordinary people out there, and they're average and ordinary at their jobs. If you want to live like a *success story*, you need a way to separate yourself from the crowd. How do you do that? You choose one main thing to focus on.

> Separate yourself from the crowd by choosing one main thing to focus on.

Just look at what I was doing before Uncle Darren set me straight: I was distracted. My attention was split between a ton of different ideas and directions. Because of that, I wasn't allowing myself to become an expert in any one thing.

And I'm not the only one. The majority of entrepreneurs and business owners I know have some level of ADD. They've always got a lot going on—there's a lot of processing, a lot of opportunities, a lot of juggling. But if you're not focused in *one* direction, you're going to be doing lots of little things and be mediocre at all of them.

You can easily separate yourself from the crowd—no matter what industry you're in—by focusing on *one thing* and becoming an expert in that area. Here's an example. Let's say you're Joe Roofer and you own a roofing company. You're doing pretty well for yourself. The only problem is, you're doing *everything* in your business: the sales, the marketing, the ordering, the actual labor—you're a one-man band. And you're exhausted.

You hire a consultant to come in and help you scale your business. You want to hire, train, and develop people so that you can separate from the day-to-day grind. Your consultant says, "Okay, in order to do that, you're going to need to put in a lot of work up front. It's going to take all of your focus, time, and attention for at least a year. We've got to get you a good hiring model. You're going to need to take some time to train and develop your team and get them aligned behind your vision. Maybe, after a year or two, you can start scaling back. If you stay focused and put in the work, you're going to find the freedom you want."

This doesn't sound good to you. You want an easy way out. "I can't give it *all* my time and attention," you say. "I'm working on a real estate deal to set up another income stream. That's taking some time. And I've got the bowling league—I'm not giving that up. I hired you to figure this out for me. Why can't you do all that?"

The consultant pushes back. "There's no magic formula or button to press or consultant to hire that will make this transition for you. YOU have to put in the work."

You fire the consultant. You line up another real estate deal. You go out and hustle more roofing jobs. And ten years later, you're still doing the exact same thing: pounding the pavement, doing your one-man act, and feeling more exhausted than ever.

But what if you were to *focus* instead? What if you took the consultant's advice and put in the hard work to hire people, develop systems, train and develop a team, and delegate your responsibilities? Not only could you get yourself the freedom you want—after a couple years of focused, hard work—you could actually grow and scale your business. You could go from three million in sales, to six million, or ten million, or thirty million.

How do I know this? Because I did it.

That's the momentum that comes from focusing on one thing and going ALL IN.

And I have to *keep* refocusing. As my success has grown, so have the possible distractions. There are a lot of new opportunities coming my way right now. I've said yes to some, but no to most. To help guide my decisions, I reference a series of questions to evaluate whether or not a new opportunity is going to take too much of my focus away from my main business—or ultimately serve it:

- Does this serve my current business?
- What time commitment is this going to take away from my current business and my family?
- Is it possible to acquire a company or service that does this, rather than build it from scratch?
- If I were to put the same amount of time and effort into my main business that would be required for this new thing to take off, what would be the return on investment (ROI)? Would it be higher than the potential ROI I could get from the other thing?

Those questions help me determine if an opportunity is going to be *worth* my time, investment, and divided focus—or if it's actually an unhelpful distraction.

Why is it worth focusing on your main thing? Think about the work that went into building your business to the place it is now. Think about all the time that was spent to develop yourself into the polished expert you have become today after years of experience and reps. A very similar amount of effort is going to have to be spent building anything of significance up to the same level that your current business produces. Let those factors give you a gut-check when you're thinking about starting something brand-new. That new thing might seem really seductive right now, or maybe you saw someone else doing it at a high level who made it look easy and you could see yourself enjoying that line of work. Take a good, hard look at what you're doing and remind yourself what you're dealing with: DISTRACTIONS! Keep the main thing the main thing. If what you really want is more freedom, then go hard for a period of time to build toward an exit or to get a CEO in place who will allow you to step away without having the company fall apart. *Then* you could explore some of those other shiny distractions.

But until then, stop half-assing it. Think about what you want to achieve and identify the best trajectory to take you there. Then, focus on that *one* area, and focus hard. When you divide your attention, you also divide the results. You want big results? Devote big, focused attention.

Once you identify your focus, start taking consistent, disciplined *action*.

Sometimes, I hear from someone on Instagram or run into somebody at a conference. They'll say something like, "I want to take all these concepts and run with them!" They talk a big game.

But when I start asking them about their habits, their tune changes. I'll say, "So, what are you doing now to make that happen? What books are you reading?" They start to go off on a tangent. They give me justifications to explain why they're not doing more. And it becomes obvious: they're not doing anything productive with their lives.

I get it, honestly. Until I had consistently built the discipline to make daily progress toward my goals, I was coming up with justifications to keep myself stuck. I had spent years and years justifying my drinking habit, making excuses for my addiction. Once I got clean, the addiction wasn't there anymore—but I still found ways to justify my stuck habits. I'd sleep in and wake up with half the morning already wasted. But I'd tell myself, "I need energy, it's important for me to get eight hours of sleep." I conditioned myself with stories to make me feel better about failing to keep a commitment I'd made to myself.

Once again, I had to decide I was sick of my own excuses. I had to decide to show up for myself, consistently, and put in the work required to change my life.

> Zero in on where you want to go, start channeling all your energy in that direction, and give yourself momentum on the way by building discipline.

You may have made some progress—and that's no small thing—but if you continue to make excuses for unproductive behavior, you're not going to accelerate the way you want. Sure, sleeping in was less destructive for me than getting high, but it was still a habit that was slowing me down. Don't enable stuck habits with your excuses. Break those patterns. No more excuses. Get organized with your day so that you can build the habits you want and practice them consistently.

Before I got plugged into the Grant Cardone mentorship program, I wasn't organized with my day. I didn't have consistency either. I'd go to the gym every once in a while. I'd manage to get through a book, but then I wouldn't read again for months. I'd think about my goals, but I wouldn't write them down. No surprise, I was not making progress anywhere close to the speed I wanted.

What changed things for me? Getting laser focused on one thing—and then, building disciplined habits. I started replacing all my bad habits with good ones. Ultimately, that led to me starting my own business.

Starting a business won't be the outcome for everyone, but no matter what your goals are—if you combine focus with disciplined habits, you're going to turn up the gas. It might take you months or even years to develop consistency in your habits. Changing habits doesn't happen overnight. But that's not slow—that's *progress*. Every time you keep a promise to yourself by practicing a new habit, you shift from talking a big game to *walking* a big game.

That's how you change your life.

So, let's talk about how to make it happen.

BUILD DISCIPLINE: REPLACE BAD HABITS WITH GOOD ONES

This message is for everyone. I don't care if you have zero discipline in your life, or if you're practicing ten good habits a day: you will never get to a place where you're able to coast. You will *always* need to be intentional about building new disciplines to take you to your next goal.

> You will *always* need to be intentional about building new disciplines to take you to your next goal.

I've made a ton of progress now, but still, I'm always asking, "What's the next level for me? What's the next big commitment that will help me get closer to a better version of myself? How can I become more disciplined, more regulated, more organized? What's the next thing I need to do to go further faster?"

Ironically, the more success I get, the *harder* it is to maintain habits of discipline. When success is rolling in, it's easy to get sloppy. You *have* to be intentional about continuously moving the target and then matching your effort with the goal.

Right now, my new discipline is opening up time in my day to be creative and fully present. I'm such a go-go-go type of personality, that unless I literally book time in my calendar for creative thinking, it won't happen. I have to be *that* intentional about it. When I'm deliberate about making that time, I'm able to let my mind stop. I can give it permission to wander and start thinking about new ideas. That's been important for me to strengthen my abilities as a leader and continuously evolve the vision for JKR Windows.

But that's not where I started. When I was just getting clean, I almost scared myself out of having any downtime or white space on the calendar. If there was any space, I was afraid I'd find ways to feed the addiction negatively, instead of positively. So, to feed my addictive personality with something positive, I chose relentless productivity.

For the first two years of my business, I worked around eighteen hours a day. I ate, slept, and breathed JKR Windows. Besides that, I spent just enough time with my family to keep that part of my life healthy.

I avoided alcohol like the plague. I didn't want to be around any drinking. I didn't have time for it, didn't want to be close to it. I was scared to death that just one decision would cause me to fall back into all my old justifications. So, I just completely removed myself from any type of circumstance where I was going to be around it. I made a deliberate choice to replace my bad habits with good ones.

I was pretty extreme—that's my *ALL IN* personality. You don't have to go to the extremes I did, like getting up at 4:00 a.m. or working eighteen-hour days—but if you want to cut out your bad habits keeping you stuck, you need to replace them. Fill your day with good habits. Building healthy disciplines in the direction of your goals doesn't just get you momentum—it gets you confidence. You'll realize that you live and embody the life you want. You're not living a life you feel guilt or shame about anymore—you can be proud of the way you're spending your days.

> Building healthy disciplines in the direction of your goals doesn't just get you momentum—it gets you confidence.

What kinds of habits can help you specifically? I'll take you back to my Grant Cardone mentorship program days. These were the habits that got me out of my addiction, got me accelerating in a healthy direction, and ultimately changed my life.

BEAT THE SUN UP

Grant Cardone told us, "If you're going to take your professional life seriously, you've got to get up before the sun comes up." We called it BTSU—beat the sun up—and we all committed to make that a daily goal for ourselves.

That was the very first habit I tried to change. I struggled with it for a couple months. At the time, I was working in St. George while the rest of my family was in Salt Lake City. I'd come home on the weekends, but during the week, I was waking up by myself. Nobody knew if I woke up late—Shandell wasn't there to give me shit about it.

Those should have been the easy months, too, because it was winter. The sun didn't come up until around eight o'clock. Still—way too often, my alarm would go off around 7:30 and I'd hit the snooze button. The next time I woke up, the sun would already be out.

I started to let it really bother me. I remember waking up on those days and looking over to where I'd written my goals down on a notepad next to the bed—one of which said "BTSU." I'd see the clock—9:00

a.m.—and I'd think, "Fuck, I did it again. The sun's out. I could have had a couple hours of productivity already." My day would start off like shit because I didn't keep that little promise to myself.

So, I kept working at it. I *kept* working at it. Eventually, I started getting more consistent—and that felt damn good.

The morning is such an important time to gain momentum and build in other daily rituals that will feed into your day. It's *worth it* to rise early. Start building the discipline by getting up thirty minutes earlier than you normally do. After a week or so, try sixty minutes. Keep moving that alarm earlier in thirty-minute increments until you're waking up at the time you want to wake up.

Now, six days a week, I get up at 4:41. It's got to be 4:41 because Shandell gets up at 4:40, and if I set my alarm for 4:39, she'd kill me. Every day, we get up before the sun and go to the gym together. On Sunday, we take it slow with the family. "BTSU" has become a mantra— that's how ingrained it is now.

It's powerful to start building a discipline like BTSU—there's a power that comes when you keep those little promises to yourself. You build confidence and momentum from building a streak of kept promises that nobody knows about, except you. The longer and more consistently you do it, the more belief you have in yourself—not only to keep practicing that new habit, but also to now add new things. You know that building a new habit may not go perfectly for a while, but you've done it before— you *know* how to add a new discipline in your life.

So, let's talk about a few more.

WORK OUT

In the summer and early fall of 2019, I started going back to the gym. Before that, I'd only gone sporadically, and I had a list of justifications to keep me home. "I need more sleep. I have a lot going on. I'm running a business. I have to make time for the family. My schedule isn't aligning with Shandell's." Finally, halfway through 2019, I decided I had to quit my excuses. It was time to get my ass back to the gym on a consistent basis.

My routine at that point was pretty sad—I wasn't doing any of the stuff I'm doing now. I barely even picked up a weight, even though I'd lifted a lot in high school with a great weightlifting coach. I had just read *Can't Hurt Me*, by David Goggins, and in that book, he talks about how important stretching had become in his life after so many years of power lifting and carrying heavy shit. He used to joke, "I'm a lion! You ever see a lion in the jungle stretch before he goes and kills his prey?!" But all of his joints and his hips and back had started to deteriorate because he never stretched. Now, he can't shut up about stretching.

My joints were pretty stiff after all my motorcycle injuries—especially my hips, legs, and back. I figured if stretching was cool for David Goggins, it was cool for me. So, for those first three months, I never even entered the gym area with the weights and machines. Right by the entrance, there was an area of green turf with bouncy balls and yoga mats. I would go lay on the turf for thirty minutes and do my stretching.

That was it. Then I'd go home.

I didn't feel much like a lion. In fact, I found a picture from one of the first days I started going back to the gym. I'd gotten quite a bit out of shape—narrow shoulders, love handles, wider middle. Your classic dad bod.

But even if my workouts were pretty tame at that point, I was gaining wins in consistency. I was building the discipline of showing up for myself: getting out the door, going to the gym, *keeping the promise I'd made to myself.*

I didn't even like being there. Honestly, it was so hard for me to even *stay* there—that's why it was only thirty minutes. I would think, "I don't know what the fuck I'm even doing here. I'm just stretching. Am I even getting anything out of this?" I would think about doing something else. Then I would just say, "Fuck it, I'm going home." I didn't enjoy myself.

But I just kept showing up, kept showing up.

Eventually, Shandell started coming with me too. I loved that—it was so much more fun going with her. But she got irritated with me because

I was still in my stretching phase. She'd say, "You just sit here and lay on the grass all the time! Let's go do something else."

Eventually, we did. But by then, my habit of getting daily workouts in was established—and I started accelerating.

Maybe it's shallow, but there's a lot to be said about the confidence that comes when you show up somewhere and you feel good about your appearance. At this stage in my life, being physically fit is something people associate with me. When people comment about the energy I bring into a room, it's not just because I've got a positive vibe or because I'm smiling. It's also because I show up with the guns out. In a room full of corporate leaders, I'm usually the fittest person in the room. And there's a confidence I feel, knowing that I put in the consistent work to take care of my body.

> There's a lot to be said about the confidence that comes when you show up somewhere and feel good about your appearance.

Being physically fit and eating healthy gives you more energy, it's going to add longevity to your life, it helps your mood, and it can jumpstart your day. It's also one of the best good habits a former addict can use to replace their bad habits, because it produces a lot of the same hormones you get from an addiction, like dopamine.

I always work out first thing in the morning. It gets my blood flowing and makes me feel good. Now, working out is a nonnegotiable—it's become a consistent discipline in my life.

BLOCK OUT THE NEGATIVITY

In some of the previous chapters, I talked about getting negativity out of your head. Rather than telling yourself you're a loser, you have to retrain your brain to think positively. You need to internalize the belief that you're meant for greatness.

Unfortunately, negative thought patterns die hard. You've got to *continuously* work to block out negativity in your life and especially in your mind. That's another discipline I've had to develop.

> Negative thought patterns die hard. You've got to *continuously* work to block out negativity in your life, especially in your mind.

Even after I was making serious progress with JKR Windows—doubling our revenue from the first year to the second—I still had to battle self-doubt. I'd wonder whether or not my activity was really productive, whether it was truly driving the business forward. I still get impostor syndrome sometimes. Now, JKR Windows has brought in over forty million in just over four years, but especially as I take on bigger goals, bigger numbers, bigger challenges than I ever have—the negative self-talk is still there. My belief that I'm capable of accomplishing these huge things is challenged.

And ironically, success can make it easier to get lazy, too, which can be another source of negativity. When you're making good money and you've built up your business to operate as a successful team rather than a one-person show, it gets easier to wake up late. You don't have to put in the same hours you did when you first started. Your actions don't have as big of an impact on your ability to make money, because you're already making good money. That allows a new level of negativity to creep in.

I've tried to build up resiliency to negativity. I can feel when the self-doubt starts to creep in, and I *notice it*. I examine it: "Isn't this interesting?" I'll say to myself. "This negativity has made its way back into my life."

Being *aware* of your negative thoughts is the first aspect of this discipline. Ignoring it or pretending it doesn't exist doesn't help—you can't just block it out. Instead, you ask, "What has given me the most fuel to overcome the negativity in the past? What's helped me build momentum against negative thoughts and reinforce positivity?"

> Build awareness of your negative thoughts. Then, ask yourself what's given you fuel in the past to overcome negativity and reinforce a positive narrative.

Here's an example of how I intentionally try to block out negativity. One of the things that helps me get out of bed so early in the morning is deliberate positive thinking. When I set my alarm every night, it tells me how much time I have before it goes off. Sometimes I'll see something like, "Three hours and thirty-seven minutes." I could go right toward negativity and focus on how tired I'm going to be. But if I do that, I'm going to hit the snooze button when my alarm goes off.

Instead, no matter what that number is, I'm always trying to frame it in a positive way. I'll be like, "Three-and-a-half hours? That's going to be plenty of sleep! Holy cow, this has been such a productive day. Tomorrow's going to be amazing. I've got a lot of stuff to accomplish."

When you deliberately frame it in a positive way—telling yourself that no matter how much sleep you're getting, you're going to wake up with as much enthusiasm and energy as you need to get through the next day, 100 percent committed—it changes the way the alarm goes off in the morning. You wake up feeling ready, feeling pumped. There's never any question about what's happening when that alarm goes off.

I learned this from the book *The Miracle Morning* by Hal Elrod. He talks about re-creating the "Christmas morning feeling" when you think about waking up. I knew exactly what kind of feeling he was talking about. When I was a kid, I could barely sleep on Christmas Eve. I was counting down the minutes until I could wake up. I was always up before the alarm and I had to keep checking the clock, because if I got up too early, my mom and dad would be pissed. I couldn't wait for the day to start!

That's the kind of feeling Elrod encourages you to re-create when you're setting your alarm. It's easy to dread getting up in the morning, like you did in high school—"Ugh, I have to wake up early." Those habits get carried into adulthood. Normally, you wake up with just enough time to drag your ass out of bed, wash your face, and get yourself to work. That's a negative way to start the day.

Instead, shift the way you think about it. However many hours of sleep I'm going to get, I try to think of that Christmas morning excitement. I hype myself up the night before and think positive thoughts. "I know I've got to go to sleep, but I've got this nervous excitement—I don't know what I'm going to get tomorrow! I can't wait to get up." You can't re-create the feeling completely, but you can tap into the positivity it represents.

Your mind is capable of some incredible things if you condition it in a way that is conducive for you to accelerate your life at a freakish rate. I am a living, breathing example of it. You have to start your day somehow. Why not do it with a good attitude?

Another way I've learned to block out the negativity is just talking about it. In the Grant Cardone program, my mentor group would talk about our thoughts on a daily basis. It was the first time I verbalized my negative thought patterns out loud, which built new awareness of other sources of negativity in my life—like music, TV, gossiping, and so on. It had never occurred to me how much negative energy I was absorbing from all of that until I was analyzing the source of my negative thoughts out loud, with other people helping me recognize it. I learned to dial down the negativity, like turning down the volume on my old Magnavox stereo.

When you build the discipline of tuning out negativity, your eyes will be opened to the habits in your life that serve you and keep you positive, versus the areas in your life that drag you down.

READ BOOKS

Before I left Arizona, I'd been getting more exposed to the sales culture that focuses a lot on self-improvement and personal development. The other sales guys were always talking about stuff they'd learned in books, constantly recommending different titles to each other.

I didn't read books. As a kid, I loved the *Goosebumps* mysteries. But I had read my last *Goosebumps* book around age thirteen. And I basically hadn't read any books since then.

It was a point of real insecurity for me.

One night, I was drunk, talking to my mom and Shandell. I was telling them how I wanted to start cleaning myself up and be more disciplined and start reading books. When I got to the last part, I started bawling hysterically: "I want to start reading! I keep telling myself I'm going to start, but then I never pick up a book." It felt incredibly vulnerable to admit all the stuff out loud that I usually hid inside me to the two most important women in my life. I normally tried to act like I knew everything. But in that conversation, I was admitting that I was chickenshit. "I'm not keeping any promises I make to myself. I'm a bad example."

It was one of those lows that generated some fuel for change. I decided to buckle down and give it a shot. Someone had recommended *All Things Possible* by Kurt Warner. I read it—cover to cover. The book was super inspirational, and I got a lot out of it. Best of all, I felt a huge sense of accomplishment to have finished the whole thing.

But I didn't read much after that. I hadn't built in the *discipline* yet to keep it going.

The mentorship program changed that. Another one of the challenges was to read daily—just ten minutes a day. I'm a slow reader, so for me, ten minutes was sometimes only two pages. But it was a great feeling to be reading consistently.

I've read a ton of books now, and I'm constantly learning new things. That doesn't mean I've become a champion reader. My mind still wanders really easily—one concept will get me thinking about something else, and before I know it, I'll be staring at the page, wondering what I just read. I still read slowly, and I struggle with comprehension.

But I've got the *consistent* habit going now, so even with my hang-ups, I've been able to pick up a ton of new philosophies and methodologies inside of these books. It's crazy how many times it felt like a book was talking directly into my life and situation along the different points in my journey.

You're reading this book, which means you're already racking up wins in this department. Keep it going—there's a world of knowledge and inspiration out there for you to access once you start reading consistently.

> Consistent reading will give you access to a world of knowledge and inspiration.

GET YOURSELF OUT OF OBSCURITY

Another challenge that came out of the mentoring group was to get ourselves out of obscurity by posting a live Facebook video every day. Every day—five, six days a week—we'd tune in from wherever we were at, share how we were doing with the challenges, and just check in. It wasn't really geared toward "content generation" or "brand building" or anything—it was just a convenient way for us to update each other. When I hit the "Go" button, I imagined speaking right to the group of guys in the mentoring group.

But what I didn't realize until later was that *everybody* on my Facebook feed was seeing my posts. That was an accident—but it turned out to be a good thing. People who had known me as the drunk party guy were following me, watching my journey. They started posting encouragement—sometimes even sharing my videos.

It also ended up creating a record for me to look back on. I pulled up one of those videos for the mentor program the other day—I recorded it about a month after I got clean. Here's what I said:

Hey, good morning, everybody! Happy Monday. I'm just walking in to grab myself a coffee and check in with you all. Up at four o'clock, already been at the gym, wrote my goals, read about twenty pages out of my book, did my Cardone University—which, by the way, has changed my life.

But I just wanted to throw something out there. Most of us have gone through some point in our life where we got into a big change, and we had to get super uncomfortable. I've just recently gone through something similar, and it was a life-changing event. It was scary. It was crazy. It was nuts. So, I cried, and I sobbed, and I had to get over it. But I did. And I feel like I've grown because of the discomfort. And those are the moments in life that keep us moving, keep us going in the right direction.

So, don't be afraid to get uncomfortable. Don't be afraid to try something new, even if it's scary and you feel like it's just going to take everything you've got. Just do it anyway and figure the rest out later. 'Cause pushing yourself in that way may just be something that changes your life for the better. It might point you in a different direction that you may have never thought that you could accomplish, because of the pain and fear of doing something unknown.

Anyway, just wanted to throw that out there. It got real serious for a second, but, everybody—put a smile on your face today, on this beautiful Monday. 10X it! Get everything you've got and build some momentum into this week. Make 2018 the best year ever.

I look so happy in that video. I'm high on life. Those regular posts helped me track my own journey and ended up inviting other people into supporting me. In later videos, I talk about how much I'd been able to accomplish in a short period of time, sharing those wins, evolving my goals. I even talk about the income I'd produced and my income targets for the following year.

By getting myself out of obscurity with those videos, I was making commitments out loud, in a public way—for everyone to see. Because of how much I value integrity, that was a big deal for me. I wanted to do what I said I was going to do and follow through on those commitments. The habit of posting those videos kept me focused, positive, and connected to other people who were rooting me on.

That gets into the last discipline I want to talk about.

GET ACCOUNTABILITY

Maybe some people wouldn't have liked putting themselves out there in Facebook Live videos like I did. Making those commitments out loud could make you feel overwhelmed and cause you to fall back into bad habits, especially if you're not a person of high integrity. In fact, a few of the guys in the mentor program eventually went back to doing the same old shit.

But for me, I loved it. People could see what I was doing. I was building a new identity for myself—I was making a name for myself with those consistent posts. People could see how I was changing my life. I was getting responses and messages from people reaching out to tell me they cared, asking how they could partner with me. Some people said they would love to meet up if I was ever in their town.

One of my love languages is "words of affirmation," so I absolutely loved that. The positive feedback and recognition fueled my positive momentum. It also created this important close network of people holding me accountable to my commitments: my family, my friends, some of the other mentees. They were watching my steady, incremental steps toward being more disciplined, building in better daily activities and habits. They witnessed me talking about how incredible it felt to be doing something with my life.

Accountability doesn't have to come via Facebook, but the more you can surround yourself with other people who regularly see your progress, the better you'll do. Their support and encouragement will give you fuel when you're feeling tired and keep you motivated if you've slipped up. One of the most important ways to build positive momentum in your life is to get regular accountability from a community of supporters.

> The more you can surround yourself with other people
> who see and support your progress, the better you'll do.

So far in this chapter, I've mentioned the word "consistent" or "consistency" over forty times. There's a reason for that.

You're not going to accelerate your progress by doing a big thing, once. You build momentum through *consistency*—little by little, more and more, day in, day out.

People tend to want to accomplish a lot in a short period of time—you write a whole list of new habits to do before the end of the year. But when you think about trying to do all of those things at the same time, it gets overwhelming. It's easy to justify not doing *any* of it if you're trying to do ALL of it at the same time. You can't go *ALL IN* with *everything*.

Instead, go *ALL IN* with *one* thing. Take just *one* thing on your list of new habits and focus on that. For me, that was getting up a half hour earlier every day: that was the first habit I focused on. The book *Mini Habits* by Stephen Guise talks about this concept: focus on doing just one new thing for thirty days. Then, when you get one habit down, you stack on another little habit.

> Building discipline into your life starts with practicing one new habit at a time and generating consistency.

At the same time, don't let a blip derail your progress. One of the things I feel I did well in building discipline was—if I *did* have a bad day, or slept in—I wouldn't just throw in the towel. I'd get down on myself, sure, but I wouldn't let it completely derail me. Instead, I focused on keeping the streak alive. Even though I missed one day, I told myself it didn't have to turn into two. I didn't want to completely blow my streak—one day is just one day. It's just a little blip. A little blip wasn't going to throw me off track.

From what I've seen, people often go back to their bad habits or addictions because they have one day, and that turns into two, and that turns into three. Then, all the justifications and excuses lead them right back to where they were before.

That doesn't need to happen to you. If you had an off day, make a new start tomorrow. One day doesn't need to throw off your streak.

As you begin to build consistency, you're going to feel more and more confidence. There's a correlation between how you live your daily life and the energy you give off with your presence. When you keep promises to yourself and live with a high level of integrity, you show up with conviction. You feel confidence in every conversation.

The opposite is true for people who are hiding shady shit in their lives. Even if they come off as confident and outgoing, you can sense there's something off. Their energy is all wrong.

I used to experience that all the time. I'd enter a room with this subconscious insecurity that came from being addicted to drugs and alcohol. My head would be full of that negative self-talk. I'd be wondering if people could tell I was drunk or high—maybe they'd smell it on me. I felt ashamed to be hiding a bunch of shit from my wife, and going out partying all the time, always at the bar. There were all these areas of my life that didn't feel aligned with who I wanted to be. Each one caused my confidence to get dinged.

It's totally different for me now. I've got some friends who are incredibly successful—some are authors, some are leadership coaches, they have years of experience, and they're doing incredible things—but these guys I look up to, say that they look up to *me*. When I show up— even though I've only been living smart for the last five years—I've got that level of confidence that comes from consistently living a life of integrity. I walk into a room with energy and a big smile, and people are curious—they're like, "Who the hell is this guy? What has he got going on? How does he have so much energy?"

You show up differently when you live a lifestyle you can be proud of. When you can be confident in the integrity you have with yourself, it changes your entire energy. And people want to be around that.

Consistency isn't a sexy, flashy concept. But all the most important success principles are just simple concepts, repeated daily. That's what brings the highest levels of success. It's the consistency that separates people who are ultimately successful from people who remain average and ordinary. Most people *know* these principles, like read books and get up early—they just don't put them into practice.

> The most important success principles are just simple concepts, repeated daily.

Unless you're doing these positive disciplines consistently, they'll never work for you.

I've come a long way. I went from an all-time low, to doing a mentor program, to getting sober, to starting my business—all within five months. Once I had my clear focus on JKR Windows, I had something new to go *ALL IN* about. And, as I swapped out my bad habits for good habits, I gained more and more momentum.

Focus. Discipline. Consistency.

That's how I accelerated. *That's* what got me from dead last into taking the lead.

BE A BADASS

In 2011, I entered a motocross race. The course was ninety-five miles long through the desert. Motocross is one of the most physically exerting and challenging sports on the face of the planet—you've got a 250-pound motorcycle underneath you, and if you want to go really fast, you have to manipulate that thing. You've got to lean it over, put it where you want it, stand it up—you're using a *lot* of energy. Even at my fittest, my heart pumps at an average of 191 beats per minute when I'm racing. It's an incredibly intense sport.

I knew all that, in 2011. But I didn't bother to train.

ALL IN, baby.

But those were still the destructive *ALL IN* years—the driving-off-a-cliff-and-walking-barefoot-through-the-desert years. I had no discipline or focus to back up my *ALL IN* energy.

And I got my ass kicked.

Twenty people entered the race, and fifteen people finished. I managed to finish but came in dead last. Halfway through the race, I started cramping. I didn't want to quit, so I pushed past the pain and managed to make it to the finish line. As soon as I dragged my sorry ass across, I dumped my bike in the parking lot where all the trailers were and just collapsed on the ground.

I lay there for twenty minutes before anyone found me. I couldn't walk. I could barely talk. Anytime I tried to move, my body would seize up with cramps. I was half passed out, half delirious.

Finally, my family found me. They were like, "Holy shit, how long have you been out here?!" They tried helping me up, but my back spasmed and I got a Charley horse in my leg—I was in agony. Luckily, there were some paramedics there. They hooked me up to an IV to get me some fluids. That helped me come back to life.

But all in all, it was not a high point for Jefferson Rogers.

Eight years later, I'd built up some consistency getting back to the gym. I had some new confidence—and I told Shandell I wanted to do the race again. But this time, I wanted to put in the time and focus. I wanted to get *fit.*

That was in the phase of my life when my gym routine consisted of stretching on the turf and rolling on yoga balls. When I told Shandell what I wanted to do, she raised her eyebrows. "You better get a personal trainer, babe."

I looked at her and thought about it. "Yup," I agreed. "I've got to get my ass in shape." The race was four months away.

I found a personal trainer and explained the demands of the race. I told him, "This time, I want to finish top five." I knew I was going to have to start pushing myself—doing cardio, riding more, doing some strength building.

I started riding five to six days a week. At the gym, my trainer developed all these specific workouts to help me grip the bike and build up my hand and arm strength. We also worked on cardio to help me with stamina. I worked my ass off.

Three weeks before the race, I said, "You know what? Top five is out of the question. I want to go for the win." In those last three weeks, I put in an incredible amount of work. I rode more than I ever had before and pushed myself in the gym. Finally, I rested for the last couple days before the race.

On the day of, I went into that thing with so much confidence. I knew I'd put in the work. I'd put in the time. I was going ALL IN—and this time, I had the discipline and the focus to back it up.

There were three hundred guys this time. Everyone started at the same time, from a dead stop, pointed down the same straightaway. I was using an old bike—it was about fifteen years old, with a kickstart. My bike usually starts on the first or second kick, but this time, it took me three or four to get the engine revved. By the time I got my bike started, everybody was already gone.

But there were no cliffs or boulders to avoid. Everybody in front of me was funneling into this dirt path. I floored my accelerator and headed into the brush. On video, you can see it was scary, hairy, ridiculous, risky shit. I probably didn't need to jump over the things I did, or ride through piles of rocks—but I was so confident in my riding at that point, from all the work I had done—I knew there was no way I was going down. I had put in the work and damn it, I was going to ride like a bat out of hell.

I went around almost all three hundred people in the first half mile. I pushed hard that whole race. There were still some people in front of me, but I kept pushing hard, kept passing them. I had a bunch of close calls, but I wasn't about to let up. I was convinced that no one else had put in as much time or effort as I had in training. I stayed focused on that win.

Of those three hundred riders, I crossed the finish line first—twelve minutes ahead of the next guy in my class. And my body was in a completely different place than the last time. My quads cramped a little— when my mother-in-law came up to give me a hug, my leg cramped and I yelled in her ear. But other than that, I felt great.

That's what comes from focus and discipline. Confidence through the roof. Honed skills. You can spot opportunities that others don't. And you can floor the accelerator the whole fucking way, to get *exactly* where you want to go.

What's your race? What's your finish line? How do you identify exactly what to drive hard toward? We're talking about goal setting next.

ACTION STEPS

If you want to accelerate and start building momentum, then identify a clear focus and start working on your discipline. Remember: how you do anything is how you do everything.

- Think about where you want to go. Choose *one main thing* to focus on that will help you get there.
- What bad habits do you need to replace? What good habits can you replace them with?
- Identify one of the disciplines described in this chapter that you want to start incorporating into your life. For the next thirty days, try building in that discipline with consistency.
- When you show up to a room full of people, are you confident in your personal integrity? If not, look for ways to build consistency in your life. That's going to impact your confidence and energy.

Consistency isn't a sexy, flashy concept. But all the most important success principles are just simple concepts, repeated daily. Get a clear focus, work on your disciplined habits, and maintain consistency. *That's* the key to acceleration.

CHAPTER 6

Find Your Mission

HOW GOAL SETTING ACCELERATES YOUR PROGRESS

YOU WANT TO accelerate your success? Get a clear idea of what you're driving *toward*. Claim a vision for your life that you can be proud of. Write down your goals for your personal and professional life—the bigger and more seemingly impossible, the better.

I remember having a conversation with my cousin about this once. He's the CEO of a big global corporation—also, an incredible human being. I consider him a mentor. This one day, we were talking about setting goals, and he told me to close my eyes. "I'm going to tell you a little story," he said. "I want you to imagine you're driving a Ferrari down a canyon road. You're doing ninety miles an hour—and this thing is just *sticking* to the road. You're looking out over the cliffs, the ocean. You see a beautiful sunset."

"This is good so far," I commented.

He laughed. "Okay, but up ahead—you notice that you're driving into some fog. What's your first instinct when you get close to the fog?"

"To slow down," I said.

"Right, because you can't do ninety through fog on a windy canyon road. So—*that's* the situation in your life when you're foggy on your vision for where you want to go. You're trying to accelerate through thick mist. It doesn't work. But if the fog lifts and the picture is clear— you see that sunset again. You see the ocean. You can see exactly where you're *going*."

"And I can go really fast," I said. I opened my eyes.

My cousin looked at me. "You want success, Jefferson? You need a clear idea of where you want to go. You've got to clear that fog."

> When you're foggy on your vision, you slow down. You won't be able to go as fast. If you claim your vision, the picture gets clear—and that's how you can hit the gas.

He was right. Writing goals down was another element of the Grant Cardone mentorship program, and once I started consistently doing it, my success went from, like, twenty miles per hour to seventy. We were challenged to write our goals down every morning and evening, so *every* day—twice a day—I was thinking about where I wanted to go. They were just bullet points initially. This is the very first entry I made, on January 11, 2018:

- Beat the sun up
- Positive attitude
- Ten million in the bank
- I live in my dream house
- Stay busy, no white space, beware free time
- Be a maniac, crazy person, lunatic about reaching my goals and dreams

- I made one million in a year
- I'm debt free

Because it was Grant Cardone leading the goal setting, he had encouraged us to "10X" our goals—making them ten times bigger than what felt possible. The results of doing that were insane. When I was writing down these huge goals every morning and night, my ALL IN attitude kicked in and I started charging after them, hard. I put in a massive amount of activity. Within a year, I'd knocked off almost every one of my goals, most of which I thought would take me at least three to five years—and was ready to 10X my vision for the future again.

It seemed like as fast and as big as I could make them, I was achieving them. There was so much power in pointing *right* to where I wanted to go, and then hitting the gas.

When you name huge goals—write them down, then put your action and effort into achieving them—you drive your success. That's what this chapter is all about: identifying your mission. Start with your personal goals, and then determine what your professional goals should look like to support your dream life.

> When you name huge goals—write them down, then put your action and effort into achieving them—you drive your success.

GOAL SETTING: CLAIMING A VISION

Until I was enrolled in the Grant Cardone mentorship program, I didn't have a habit of writing down my goals. I *thought* I was speeding down the road—but actually, I was still moving slowly through fog. That came to light when a guy at my same company showed me up.

Early on in my sales career at ABC Windows, I started mentoring this young guy at the company. I'll call him Adam. Adam had less experience than me, so I was giving him tips, teaching him a few things, helping him practice his pitch. We traveled out of town to the same places to do sales, so we stayed together a bunch and became friends. Eventually, Adam started to close his own deals. I watched his progress and felt pretty good about myself. I figured it was my coaching that was helping him be successful.

Except one day, we were back home, and I went over to his place so we could meet up in between appointments. When I walked into Adam's kitchen, I saw this big whiteboard set up. Written in big letters next to bullet points, Adam had written his goals down: his sales targets, his income goals, the books he was reading. He saw me staring at it and grinned.

"Keeping my eyes on the prize!" he said. Then he asked me, "Do you write your goals down?"

His question immediately made me feel defensive. Back then, I didn't write my goals down. I knew I *should* write them down. I *wanted* to write them down. I just hadn't ever taken the steps to start doing it.

I felt irritated. This kid was lower than me at the company and had less experience. I was supposed to be *his* mentor. But here he was, doing things that I knew I should have been doing. I shrugged. "I write my goals down occasionally," I said. "But it doesn't really help me."

Adam looked at me, puzzled. "Huh." He looked back at the board, where he had written down a couple book titles. He grinned again. "What about books? Are you reading anything good right now?"

This was before I'd started reading consistently. I wasn't about to tell Adam that the last book I remembered reading was a *Goosebumps* novel at age thirteen. I felt even more irritated. "I'm not reading any books."

Adam must have picked up on my irritability, because he changed the subject and we started talking about work instead.

That was a moment when I felt some shame—but it was also a planted seed. This kid was supposed to be my mentee. Instead, he called me out on the things I wasn't doing. I thought about how fast he'd been progressing at work—and how focused he'd been on leveling up. I'd been patting myself on the back, thinking that was all a result of my coaching. But how much of that had to do with his clarity about his goals?

Setting goals was a principle that I'd heard about before. I listened to Tony Robbins and Esther Hicks on cassette tapes with my mom since I was six years old—they were always talking about goal setting. But I never had examples in my personal life to model what that really looked like. The beliefs and thought patterns I grew up with were very limited, and that almost became my reality. When I thought about my future, I assumed I was going to be scraping by as a carpenter.

But then, I started to *see* those success stories in my personal life. I started recognizing the power, firsthand, of what happened when people identified huge goals and went after them. Adam, my coworker, was only one example. Later, I saw it in all the guys in my 10X mentorship program. And there were also people who had a history just like me— like my friend from high school, Jeff, who I used to party with. Over the years, Jeff had cleaned up his act, then gone on to build a financial services business that was extremely successful.

I thought, "The only thing Jeff has on me is time and experience." If he could reach that level of success in that short period of time, I could too. The difference was that he *applied* the concepts I knew worked.

When I started applying the principles of goal setting, it completely changed my life. And if you do the work, it's going to change yours too.

The principles of goal setting completely changed my life.

PERSONAL VISION: LIFESTYLE DESIGN

Start your goal setting by coming up with a personal vision for the life you want to live. The vision should paint a picture of who you want to be and the lifestyle you want to provide for yourself and your family.

You can start simple. Like I said before, my personal vision started with bullet points, written down in a notebook that I kept next to my bed: "BTSU. Positive attitude. Get out of debt."

On Day 2, January 12, 2018, you can see that my personal vision was already growing and evolving. I started getting more clarity about how I was going to achieve my goals. I wrote my goals down in the past tense, as though they had already happened. Here's what I wrote down:

I made $300,000 in 2018. I make $25,000 a month. I have an abundance of money. I am debt free. I have an amazing marriage. I drive a new F350 Ford Powerstroke. I am confident in my abilities. The more people I help, the more money I make. I exercise and stretch regularly. 2018 is the year of focus.

My understanding of what it was going to take to get there was sharpening. I've got more of my core values reflected in my goals. It's almost like a clear picture is taking shape. The fog was lifting—and I started hitting the gas.

Goals without actions and plans are just daydreams. One of my favorite authors, Napoleon Hill, has helped me learn that hope, enthusiasm, and *applied* faith are a lethal combo when done together. That combination can help you accomplish incredible things, versus trying to move ahead with blind faith or passive faith. *Apply* yourself to achieve your goals, instead of waiting for things to happen to you.

If you don't claim your personal vision, then you're just drifting, not working in any specific direction. Remember the importance of focus, which I talked about in the last chapter? Writing down your goals gives you that clear focus. Without it, anything can easily take your attention away.

Goals without actions and plans are just daydreams.

Stay *focused* on working in a specific direction by taking a few simple steps:

- Focus on what you're doing that can make you a great income so that you can provide a high quality of life for your family.
- Then, ask yourself: what goals can you put together to make the highest possible income in that given field?
- List the action items and plan out the daily activities that you're going to have to execute to reach those goals.

That's basically where I started. These days, my goal setting is a little more high tech—a lot more elaborate. Shandell and I have created a **Lifestyle Design** spreadsheet for our family. It has ten categories for our personal vision: Purpose, Family, Health, Time, Finance, Business, Personal Growth, Relationships, and Experiences. I learned about creating a Lifestyle Design from my good friend Dave Allred, who had built something similar for himself and his family. He guided Shandell and me in making our own, which I'm hugely grateful for. It's been life changing.

Purpose comes first because it's what guides everything else. When I write down my purpose, I'm thinking about what motivates me, brings me joy, the lessons I've learned, the kinds of values I want to be known for, and so on. Building off Dave Allred's descriptions—in many cases, I left his own excellent wording—the document helps me capture *how* I want to live my life. Here's what I wrote down for my purpose in 2021:

JEFFERSON K. ROGERS: PURPOSE

- I am dedicated to spending my life chasing the best version of myself. I uphold commitments I've made to myself and others while being true to my core values.
- My children are my greatest legacy. I will be the superhero that my children need their dad to be.

- I will always strive to add more value than I take by focusing on helping to lift others up and inspiring them to live their best lives. I will give more to my family and friends than I take.
- My family's past does not dictate my family's future. I will uplevel my family's legacy and future posterity by raising the standard through hard work, faith, and personal example.
- I own the results of my life, recognizing that where I am is a result of the choices I made yesterday.

You get the idea. There are many more principles in my own list that collectively help me remember the truths that guide me.

On the "Family" tab, Shandell and I have written down goals for our family—like, a weekly date night, educational goals for the kids, and even stuff like "put my phone away when with family to be fully present." We've also written a list of family traditions we want to create. On the "Health" page, I've written out exercise and nutritional goals. I've also got a "Time" tab, where I've written my ideal daily schedule along with days of the week when I want certain things to happen.

I've got a "Finance" page—and this time, it's more than just a list of bullet points about my desired income. I've named some primary objectives, like, "Enjoy a great quality of life and achieve true financial freedom." But then I've also written down statements about *why* it's important to me to achieve my financial goals: "I want to provide a higher quality of life to my FAMILY. I want FREEDOM to live life on my own terms. I want to facilitate more memorable EXPERIENCES." The list goes on. At the end, I name specific financial targets and strategies. This helps me remember that—even though making lots of money is nice—it's a means to an end. My first priority will always be my family.

The spreadsheet keeps going: I've got tabs for Business, Spiritual, Personal Growth, Relationships, Experiences, and even my Dream

Home. The "Dream Home" tab was a ton of work to build—Shandell and I spent *hours* building out a list of what we wanted in our dream home. But it all paid off: there's very little on that list that didn't end up as a reality in our house.

My personal vision was simple and straightforward to start: bullet points on a notebook page. But I discovered *so much power* in naming the kind of person I wanted to be and the life I wanted to create that now, I've gone into as much detail as I possibly can.

With that Lifestyle Design worksheet, Shandell and I have a much easier time making decisions together. If an opportunity comes up but it doesn't align with our lifestyle design, we're able to turn down the opportunity with a lot of confidence. But if it *is* in direct alignment with what we have planned, we say, "Hell, yes." In other words—it's helped us hit the gas and take those canyon roads at high speed, while enjoying an incredible view.

TIPS FOR GOAL SETTING

Writing your goals doesn't have to be complicated or time consuming, but there are a few ways you can help yourself achieve them. Here are some tips I've learned about effective goal setting and execution:

- **Make big commitments.** This is the Grant Cardone "10X" mentality: set goals ten times as big as what you think seems attainable. The reason this works well is because it forces you to put an action plan in place to back it up. Most people make small, attainable goals, but they fail to put an action plan in place. Then, they don't get traction or progress. But if you've made a big, crazy-ass goal and then map out steps to make it happen—even if you come up 50 percent short, you're still going to have reached a goal that's five times bigger than what you would have done otherwise. Some people are more likely to take action with small goals. That's fine, if that works best for you. But making huge goals has been one of the biggest contributors to my own success. When I paid for the Grant Cardone mentorship course along with exposure to all the other people in the group, I decided I'd better make the most of it. I figured if I never tried to achieve these big, crazy-ass goals, I'd never know what I was really capable of. So, I just started trying. I put in the *daily activity* to make progress toward those 10X goals, and I accomplished nearly every single one within the year.

- **Write your goals as if you've already accomplished them.** It's like you're expressing gratitude for the achievement: "I am so happy and grateful that money now flows to me." When you do this, you trick your subconscious into believing in the inevitability of your goals. That's the concept described in the books *The Secret* by Rhonda Byrne and Napoleon Hill's *Think and Grow Rich*: when you put something out into the universe, the law of attraction is going to help you make those things possible, so long as you put in the work. Visualize and *believe* that your goals are possible or already happening. When you write your goals down, you start the process of manifesting these goals as a reality in your life. When I was in the Grant Cardone program, I wrote my goals down *every* morning and evening. Sometimes, I even revisited them in the middle of the day. If I ever had a bad interaction with a customer—like some guy waving a shotgun at me and telling me to get off his porch or just losing my motivation to keep going—I would get my goals back out, write them down again, and remind myself why I was doing this. That enabled me to get right back out there and push through it.

- **Use tools to increase your belief.** Shandell and I have made vision boards where we've posted pictures of ideas for our dream house, dream vacations, dream cars—some of the toys we want, and images that embody a healthy, happy family. We cut the pictures out of magazines and stuck them on a pin board. Seeing those pictures keeps us focused on our goals and motivated to keep doing the work to achieve them. Another tool that's been helpful for me is affirmations. This has been key to transforming my negative thought patterns and helping me believe in my own potential to achieve great things. I write down these affirmations by starting a sentence with "I am _____" and then write down a quality I want to build in myself: "I am abundant. I am confident. I am strong." I have some of them in my phone—I memorize some others. When you've been stuck in negative thinking for a long time, affirmations can be an important way to get yourself out of that rut and build new patterns of belief into your life.

- **Don't overplan or overanalyze.** A lot of smart people hold themselves back from going hard after their goals because they're overthinking it. If everything doesn't align just perfectly, they never take action. For example, a friend of mine has a cushy job that gives him a sense of security. He had an amazing business idea, but he wasn't willing to bet on himself that he could replace his high income in the amount of time that would be necessary for him to not have to go through all of his savings. We tried to put together a game plan—I tried to come up with every strategy, scenario, and psychological game that I could to get this guy out of his head and out of his own way. But all he wanted to do was think and analyze. Plan and strategize. He never got around to doing anything. His $90,000-a-year salary kept him from being able to make the $900,000 to a million that was possible with the business that he wanted to do. Listen: if you've got a *general* idea of the direction you want to go, the connections you'll need to make to get there, and the work you'll need to put in—then just get started. Go *execute*. You won't have everything figured out, and you may need to change some plans, but you'll be learning along the way and making progress. I have people who come to me, wanting advice that's going to help them get over their current hump. I'll ask them, "Well, what have you done so far?" They start talking about business strategies, and plans, and ideas, but when it comes down to it—it becomes obvious that they're not accelerating because they've *done absolutely nothing*. Fear and anxiety about moving forward can keep you stuck. You don't have to have all the answers first. You just need a goal, and belief in your ability to figure it out.

> Fear and anxiety about moving forward can keep you stuck. You don't have to have all the answers first. You just need a goal, and belief in your ability to figure it out.

- **Do the work.** If you asked my dad, he would tell you that the way to get successful is to just work your ass off. You will never find that guy sitting down, and if you do catch him sitting down, he'll be asleep just like that. He is nonstop—totally focused on his next project. Luckily, I picked up on some of that. Writing down huge goals is the first step—but then you need to follow that up with massive amounts of activity. It's going to take more than just having a vision for your company or your life. If there's no action, creativity, or delivery on the back side of your vision— no one's going to take you seriously. One of the things that helped me grow my company so fast is that I had a big vision, and I also backed it up with action. I was out there on the front lines, working more hours than anybody else, in order to make the vision come to reality. It's not going to be easy. Don't expect it to be. Show up for yourself and your dreams by putting in the hard work required to make it happen.
- **The Power of Accountability.** I don't think I would have had the kind of momentum I experienced reaching my goals if I hadn't been checking in every day with the other guys in the Grant Cardone mentorship program. That accountability was powerful. Those guys, plus all of the people who were following me on social media and sending me encouragement, were a huge reason to stay motivated and keep putting in the time and effort. I have even more accountability now, because I have an entire

company looking at the things I do on a day-to-day basis. I also have over 100,000 Instagram followers I'm accountable to. I want to be the guy who's willing to put in the most time because I've got a lot of people watching me. That accountability helps me operate at a consistently high level.

- **Celebrate the small wins.** Keep your positive momentum by living in a space of accomplishment. Review your wins. There's this idea in America that happiness is only achieved once you attain something—Thomas Jefferson wrote that we should have the freedom for the "pursuit of happiness." For him, happiness was something that had to be pursued and achieved, not part of the process. For generations, we've been conditioned to believe that we have to do things or accomplish things or acquire things to reach happiness. And on the flip side of that, the book *The Happiness Advantage* makes the point that there are many fulfilled, happy people out there but they're not necessarily the most successful. Listen: you can have BOTH. The people who get to the other side of all the work and agony that go into achieving their goals—while still having their lives put together—are people who enjoyed the process along the way. They celebrated their small wins. I'm still learning to do this, but I want more of it in my life.

Get that vision for who you want to be and the life you want to live. Write it down. Then, take consistent, daily action in the direction of your goals.

But there's one more crucial part in all this: you've got to live out your core values, every step of the way.

THE IMPORTANCE OF VALUES

It's not just enough to go fast. Seeing clearly down that canyon road is key—but focusing on pure speed alone isn't going to help you take those canyon turns. Pure speed alone will take you right off the cliff.

Trust me, I speak from experience.

That's where values come in. I've talked a fair amount about values already in this book, and I'm not about to shut up about them. Your values determine *how* you live and work—what you prioritize, how you do business, how you show up in a room, your reputation, and so on. You can think of values as the factor that determines your vehicle's quality: they're the difference between driving a beat-up truck with a dead battery and shitty brakes, versus a Ferrari. A lifestyle in consistent alignment with values is going to be a much smoother ride. Values also guide your progress and decision-making—helping you know when to brake, when to shift gears, when to turn—and when to floor it.

> Your values determine *how* you live and work. A lifestyle in consistent alignment with values is going to be a much smoother ride.

Goal setting was something I could sit down with a pen and write out on a piece of paper. But values are something you *live*. My personal values had been formed over a lifetime of figuring out who I did and didn't want to be. Now, I'm doing everything I can to live in alignment with my values.

In Chapter 3, I talked about how the low lows in your past have the power to help your future: your pain points teach you what really matters the most to you. Your best experiences can do the same—both the greatest and worst experiences in your life can shed light on your core values. Identifying those values can help you get unstuck. They can also help you start to accelerate toward your goals.

In an earlier chapter, I shared about an experience when a friend and I had promised a woman we would help her move, but then my friend never showed up—and he was the one with the truck. When he flaked, I was so fucking pissed. I couldn't believe he would promise to do something and then go back on his word. The fury I felt then made me realize that **integrity** was a core value for me. Breaking a promise seemed easy to him, but it infuriated me, especially because his lack of integrity made it harder for me to deliver on *my* promise to the woman.

I felt the same anger when the ABC Windows owners backed out on their partnership offer to me. In my mind, if you commit to doing something—you do it. If I tell someone I'm going to do something, I go out of my way to follow through. I also spend the extra time to do it right. In fact, I do it *better* than I was expected to do it. For some people, that doesn't matter, but in my mind, that's integrity. I want integrity to define everything I do. In fact, one of the biggest reasons I was able to stick with my new habits and disciplines was because of integrity: I wanted to keep the promises I had made to myself.

Loyalty is another core value of mine. Shandell is incredibly loyal, and it's one of the reasons I fell in love with her. When there's an obvious lack of loyalty, that's another pain point for me, like if I lose one of my sales reps to another company. That hurts. In fact, I had the opportunity to leave ABC Windows when several other companies tried to recruit me, but I never even considered leaving—even though I had some issues with my leadership. I was loyal to where I was and the guys who gave me that opportunity. Other people don't hold loyalty as a core value. If the grass looks a little greener on the other side, they jump at it without hesitation. That's not true for me—I demand loyalty out of myself, and I look for it in every person I hire.

And **commitment** is huge. Consistency and commitment separate the greats from the ordinary. Committing to do even simple things consistently helps people reach a high level. But most people struggle with consistency. Early on in my sales career, I didn't have any direction, mentorship, or coaching. The one thing I did have was commitment. The first four months, I made very little money. I used up all my credit cards. We were scraping by; I was literally putting five dollars of gas at a time in my tank just to get to appointments. But I wasn't going to quit. I ran twenty-seven appointments over six weeks before I got my first close. Most people I worked with would never make it past five or six appointments without a close before quitting. But I finally managed to get some coaching that helped me completely transform the delivery of my pitch, and suddenly, I was killing it. That only happened because I remained committed.

In the Lifestyle Design worksheet, I've written down some of my other core personal values on the "Personal Growth" page. What's funny is, the table is actually labeled "Strengths," not "Values"—but the cool thing about leaning into your values is that they actually turn into some of the defining traits of your leadership. When people know that you're a person who lives by your principles, they see you as someone with a lot to contribute. Here are some of the other values I've written down:

- Work ethic
- Ambition
- Stick to my word
- Trustworthy
- Consistent, reliable
- Focused on continual growth

Your values turn into some of the defining traits of your leadership.

These values guide me at home with my family, at work, and when I'm away on a trip. They've helped shape my reputation and guide my choices. And because I'm now living more consistently according to my values, I've leveled up. The "vehicle" I'm driving isn't some shitty truck anymore. It's more like that brand new F350 Ford Powerstroke I wrote down on my goals list years ago.

Think about your emotional patterns—the circumstances that infuriate you or excite you. There's a good chance you'll identify a core value when you think about why you feel so strongly in those moments. You might do something on a daily basis that seems normal to you but isn't normal to other people. For instance, I enjoy being able to pick up the tab for a group of people, completely unexpected. It's fun and easy and feels like second nature to me. But it turns out the reason why it never happens with other people I'm around is because it's kind of uncommon. That habit made me realize that generosity is another value I try to cultivate in my life. Your unusual tendencies or habits can alert you to your personal core values.

If you've put in the time to identify goals for yourself, return to them consistently, and then you pursue those goals in alignment with your values—you're going to start seriously picking up speed.

1 TO 100,000 TO 10 MILLION

Somewhere in my midtwenties, I taped a one-dollar bill to my ceiling directly above my bed, right where I would see it all the time. I wrote "$100,000" on it with a black Sharpie. I had just seen the movie *The Secret*, and my takeaway was that I could manifest that money if I just started visualizing and *looking* at this "$100,000" every day. Eventually, I would start making $100,000 a year.

At that point in my life, it was a huge dream to make it to six figures. The only person I knew then that made six figures was my dad, and it was only after working his ass off for twenty-five years as a fire captain. I decided to make it my goal to hit that six-figure income earlier. I started staring at that bill every night. Dreaming. Wishing.

But there's a book by Napoleon Hill called *Wishes Won't Get You Riches*, and the title alone makes a great point. I hadn't developed any discipline in my life—I wanted to manifest my goals just by visualizing them. I thought it would be enough to post that thing on my ceiling and look at it every day.

Then, over the next seven or so years, I proceeded to get drunk and high every day, smash things, get arrested, and stack up debt.

I was missing some critical components: writing down my goals, the vision boards, the affirmations, and most importantly, doing the *work* that was necessary—like taking steps in the direction of my goals in a way that would get me different results than what I had been getting.

Finally, I got clean.

Then, I got focused.

Then, I got disciplined.

And now, the goal setting got some momentum. In the beginning of the Grant Cardone program when I started writing down my goals, I wrote down an income target of $300,000 in a year. Based on my averages, I knew exactly how many doors I had to hit every day, how many appointments I needed to set, how many deals I needed to close personally, if I was going to make $300,000. So, every day when I went out, I knew how much activity I needed to do that day to stay on pace for my goal. I kept at it. I did the work.

And I ended up making a little over $300,000—just in my own personal income—that first year.

I've kept up the effort. I've kept up the activity. I've kept up my focus. And in the first year of JKR Windows, we did one million. The next year, we did two. The following year, we did *ten*. And even as I grow as a leader, I'm pushing myself to grow in all areas of my life. I'm prioritizing time with my wife and family. I'm learning to enjoy the process along the way. Our dreams are literally coming true—because there's action to back them up.

Don't leave things to chance. You've got to have a target to go for—otherwise, you're just doing wishful thinking. You're drifting through life. But when you name specific goals—even if you start small and look just six months ahead—then start revisiting them multiple times a day, you'll develop the habit of being goal oriented. Take consistent steps in the direction of those goals. Even if it feels like nothing is happening at first, just keep taking consistent steps. Little by little, you're going to start building momentum.

You've got to have that combination: your goals, your values, and the drive to make it happen. Identify that one thing you're doing that could open the doorway to a great income. If you were focused on it—how much *more* of an income could you make? Now, put together goals that will enable you to achieve the highest possible income in your given field. Get a list of action items, make a plan, and put in the daily activity that will be required to execute on reaching your goals.

In this stage of my life, it feels like I'm sticking to that canyon road, going ninety in a Ferrari. Let me tell you—the view is incredible. That's possible for you, too, if you set big, crazy-ass goals and follow them up with consistent action.

Just wait. You're going to love this drive.

ACTION STEPS

You can dramatically increase your acceleration by identifying goals for yourself that align with your values, then taking consistent action in that direction. Think about:

- What does your dream life look like? Get down some bullet-point ideas. Or, go further than that: describe your dream self and dream life in past tense, as though it's already happened.
- Try writing down your goals, both when you get up and before you go to bed. See how your thinking starts to change.
- What professional goals should you create in order to make your dream life happen?
- Identify tools that will help you achieve your goals, like vision boards, affirmations, or a group of people that will hold you accountable. Take steps to get these in place.
- What core values do you want to live by, both in your personal and professional life? Take a look at the list below and try to identify your prominent values. I look at this list often to see where I have deficiencies and where I'm strong. (The list of deficiencies is much bigger than my list of strengths!)

CORE VALUES LIST

from James Clear, author of *Atomic Habits*

Authenticity	Creativity	Justice	Recognition
Achievement	Curiosity	Kindness	Religion
Adventure	Determination	Knowledge	Reputation
Authority	Fairness	Leadership	Respect
Autonomy	Faith	Learning	Responsibility
Balance	Fame	Love	Security
Beauty	Friendships	Loyalty	Self-Respect
Boldness	Fun	Meaningful Work	Service
Compassion	Growth	Openness	Spirituality
Challenge	Happiness	Optimism	Stability
Citizenship	Honesty	Peace	Success
Community	Humor	Pleasure	Status
Competency	Influence	Poise	Trustworthiness
Contribution	Inner Harmony	Popularity	Wealth
			Wisdom

Remember: once you have a clear vision of where you want to go, you can hit the gas and enjoy the ride. That's what goal setting is all about.

PART 3

Go Further Faster

CHAPTER 7

Find Your People

GO FURTHER FASTER WITH A DREAM TEAM

THE PEOPLE YOU'RE around can make or break you—and if you hope to live a productive, prosperous life, you need to prioritize building successful relationships. I used to keep some really negative people around me. No surprise, I was a negative person. Now, I try to be deliberate about surrounding myself with positive people who inspire me. I've also learned that I have to put in the effort to keep those relationships strong.

Take the other weekend, for example. I was getting ready to leave town, but I could tell something was bothering Shandell. She was being short with me and seemed irritated.

I had a choice to make: should I take off and just ignore the fact that my wife was upset with me? Or should I rearrange my plans so that I could stay and work things out with her?

Early on in our relationship, if we were arguing, I'd get pissed off and storm out. If I had somewhere to go—to hell with her, I'd go. I told myself I didn't have time to argue, I needed to be productive.

The only problem was, I wasn't productive. Even when I tried to work, our argument was still running through my head. There was a negative energy that caused a cloud to hang over my whole day, because I had left things undone with Shandell.

Over the years, we've gotten much better at communicating and have learned healthy ways to work through arguments. We've put a lot of effort into building a good dynamic. One of the things that I've learned about my wife is that her love language is *quality time*. That means, if she's upset—one of the worst things I can possibly do is communicate I don't have time for her.

So, there we were: I've already got my bag in the truck, the engine is running, but I can tell something's upsetting Shandell. I guessed from some of the marriage work that we'd done that she was struggling over our lack of quality time.

It had been a crazy busy weekend. We'd had a great couple of days doing activities Shandell had planned with friends and family. I struggle to make the time to do those things because my list of action items feels never ending, so I rely on Shandell's help to keep those connections strong. But after a week of me being gone, traveling for work, and then our busy weekend, Shandell hadn't gotten my undivided attention at all. We hadn't gotten any alone time. Now—Sunday night—I was getting ready to leave again.

We tried hashing it out, but it was obvious we weren't going to be able to get through it all before I had to go. Part of me figured it was too late at that point to solve anything. I was ready to leave.

I weighed my options. If I left, Shandell would get over it. I knew she'd try to have a good attitude, but there would be something hanging over us—something making it hard for either one of us to be at our best.

If I stayed to work it out, I'd have to rearrange my plans for flight school the next day. I'd have to get my bag out of the truck and unpack my stuff. But I'd also be prioritizing the woman who has always been the most supportive of me—the woman whose belief in me has been a *huge* contribution to my level of accomplishment. She's given me my children, and she gives me love and encouragement every day. I could never have done any of this without her.

In the past, I undoubtedly would have pointed out the fact that she had made all the plans that made it close to impossible for us to have any time to ourselves. I would have left in a hot mess, pretending like I didn't give a shit. These days, I just want to feel loved and make her feel loved at all costs.

The right choice was obvious. I went outside, turned the truck off, then came back in and told her, "You know what? It's not worth it to me to try and leave tonight. Let's get some time together and work this out."

That night, we talked, and we connected, and we enjoyed being together. Just the fact that I made the decision to prioritize her over my travel plans helped her mood and made her feel loved. When I did leave the next day, we left things in a positive place—and I was able to function productively, from a place of good energy rather than a cloud of negativity.

If you want to go further and faster than ever before, the people around you matter. Work to strengthen your positive relationships. Be deliberate about the friends you choose and the mentors you work with. Seek out people who will help you grow, and put in the work to learn from them.

You can only go so fast if you're going alone. With a strong team around you—you're going to be unstoppable.

> If you want to live a productive, prosperous life, work at building successful relationships.

YOUR KEY PEOPLE MATTER

John C. Maxwell wrote, "Nothing of significance was ever achieved by an individual acting alone. Look below the surface and you will find that all seemingly solo acts are really team efforts." All the great success stories in the last century have powerful individuals as the headline, but if you look past the main character, there are always the organizations they built or the teams they established along the way that enabled them to achieve their success. There has never been a truly individual success that made it into the history books. Having a strong team around you is crucial if you want to develop the skills, abilities, patience, and intentionality required to become an incredible leader and communicator. If you want the opportunity to do something truly great in your life, business, and family—you can't be an island.

I could never have come as far as I have without my key people. It's because of positive relationships, productive conversations, and clear expectations that my success was made possible.

When you have positive relationships with your key people—when they're cheering you on and supporting you—you build momentum. You've got wind in your sails. If I ever need encouragement, I call Shandell and we talk for ten minutes. That's all it usually takes, just ten minutes. And there will be so much positivity and love in those ten minutes, it's all I need to get through the rest of the day. A good home life means my energy and confidence are at a high, and I'm able to accomplish what I need to do that day with incredible efficiency. Keep your key relationships in a positive place, and nothing can stop you.

But the opposite is also true. When your key relationships are consistently in a negative place, that negative energy drags you down. You can't be motivated when you're thinking about an argument from yesterday. In the past, when I left things unfinished with me and Shandell, I was way less motivated. The negative energy distracted me and weighed me down.

If you leave your key relationships in a negative place, you're going backward—personally and professionally. You can't move forward when you've got baggage dragging you down—and if you're not making progress, you're going backward. No progress can be made unless all the people around you are working in the same direction. That's true at home and at work.

> When your key relationships are in a negative place,
> you're going backward—personally and professionally.

Remember the importance of cutting out the negativity in your life, which we talked about in earlier chapters. You've got to find out which relationships are worth working on and which ones need to be cut out of your life. But even after finding positive people to be around, you need to know that every relationship is going to need work. It's rare that your relationships will all start in positive places—or stay there. That's why I'm going to talk about how to *strengthen* your positive relationships.

STRENGTHEN POSITIVE RELATIONSHIPS

Nothing beats having a team of people around you who pour positivity into your life. Sometimes I struggle to keep up my momentum. When I do, it's Shandell's encouragement and support that keeps me going. I made a point to strengthen my relationship with Shandell and keep it in a positive place. The stronger it's gotten, the more I've been able to excel in other parts of my life. I've been able to apply a lot of the lessons I've learned in my marriage to other key relationships, strengthening them across the board.

If you want to strengthen your positive relationships, try doing these four things.

BE CURIOUS AND OPEN

Just because you've always thought about a situation one way, that doesn't mean you need to continue thinking that way—or even that it's healthy to think that way. Be open to challenging your thoughts, especially when you find yourself in conflict with the people you love. Get *curious* about why other people think the way they do, and why you think the way YOU do. Instead of going right to blaming: "Why are you so sensitive?!"—and never taking any responsibility, take note of the fact that you play a part in how people respond to you. You are responsible for these interactions. So, get curious and open in trying to figure out more deeply your own responsibility.

You teach people how to treat you. The way you treat others—whether it's a key person or someone on the periphery—directly feeds into how they will respond to you. That's why I operate with the understanding that I have created every circumstance that arrives in my life. If I come home and Shandell is being defensive toward me, I ask myself, "How did my behavior teach her to do this?" She's preparing for what she thinks I'm going to do, based on how I've treated her in the past and how our relationship has gone. She's not being defensive for shits and giggles. When moments like that happen, I get curious about how I might be responsible for that moment.

I used to blame the other person, but curiosity has been more effective than blame for patching things up. Why? Because when you accuse someone, their walls go up immediately. It shuts down the whole conversation. There's tension, and tension leads to resentment, and resentment leads to more arguments, creating a cycle of negativity.

But if you're *curious*, you're able to open up the conversation between you and the other person. If I'm in a disagreement with Shandell or dealing with a miscommunication on my team, I'm curious. I ask questions. I try to encourage open conversation about how we got to this point. Once we understand how we got here, we can figure out how to get out of a negative spot and move forward.

MAKE AN EFFORT

"Just work at it"—it sounds simple. But most people don't make the effort to strengthen their relationships.

Here's an example. Typically, in a marriage, you're going to have a different love language than your spouse. (And, by the way, if you haven't read the book *The Five Love Languages* yet, by Gary Chapman... Do so, immediately.) Like I said earlier, Shandell needs a lot of quality time. It's not my love language, and it's hard to relate to another love language. I've had to work at carving out time for her and my family— and not just making time, but being fully present when I'm there. I've made it a rule that I have to put my phone away when I'm getting quality dad time with my kids.

I'm great at giving Shandell compliments, because my love language is "words of affirmation." I want her to *tell* me how good I am, and how incredible, and how strong, and how buff...Honestly, when she pumps me up with words like that, I could coast on them for the next month and never lift my head up from the grindstone. Forget about quality time— that's on the opposite end of my personal "love language" spectrum. But I've learned how important quality time is to my wife, and she's learned how to give me affirming words. She hasn't always, but she's gotten a lot better at it because she's worked at it. I have had to learn to be very tactful in the way I approach her when she needs some attention or when she thinks she is right. It is a never-ending process learning how to navigate each other's emotions and triggers. I still have a long way to go but I am happy with our progress, and we are just getting stronger.

There's a reason why so many marriages fail: people are just not committed to doing the work necessary to make a marriage thrive. Maybe at one point they were committed...But then, they just fucking quit. Listen: don't quit on your important relationships. Be 100 percent committed to always making it work. Do the small things that matter to make your partner feel loved, or you're going to end up a statistic.

Make the effort to understand the way the other person works. We assume everyone else gets their cup filled the same way we do. But that's not true. The more intentional you are about knowing what your key people's personality traits are and how they get their cup filled, the more effective you'll be at strengthening those relationships.

You can do this to optimize your professional relationships as well. In fact, Gary Chapman, the author of *The Five Love Languages,* wrote a book specifically about how to do that at the office, called *The Five Languages of Appreciation in the Workplace*. The book helps leaders build in ways of showing appreciation to their employees and recognize how they can help team members enjoy being at the workplace. You can express appreciation for your people by asking questions like, "Is there anything I can do to help you grow in this area?" A question like that can motivate improvement, more than criticism would.

ALIGN ON VISION

Aligning on vision is essential if you want your relationships to become rock solid. It helps set expectations for everyone, and ensures you're all moving forward in the same direction. Having a clear vision can also bring more key relationships into your life, because when you own your vision, other people will be drawn to it.

I remember when I was trying to convince Shandell that it was worth it to move our family from northern Utah back south, to St. George, to start up JKR Windows—and initially, that vision was a tough sell. For a long time, I had convinced Shandell that St. George was a dead end. St. George, my hometown, had been the scene of most of my petty crimes. Starting at sixteen years old, I started to get into trouble. My first week with my driver's license, I got pulled over for doing seventy-one miles per hour in a thirty-five miles per hour zone. By the time I was eighteen, I had a stack of white, pink, yellow, and green tickets that was about two inches thick: everything from traffic tickets to minor consumption of alcohol, possession of marijuana, criminal mischief, trespassing, curfew, assault, theft, and more. Most of the money I made at my first few jobs went to paying off all my tickets and fines. I told myself during those years, "If I ever leave St. George, I'm never coming back to this fucking place."

I kept those feelings with me for years after I left because I continued doing the same questionable shit with my life. In a big city, it went unnoticed, but in a small place like St. George, I wouldn't have been able to escape it—especially because it always seemed like there were a ton of cops around, just waiting to catch me doing something. Even after I started doing sales in St. George for ABC Windows, I told Shandell it was better for us to live closer to Salt Lake and I just made the commute. "St. George is way too small," I told her. "There's no potential there."

Finally, in January 2018 after getting sober for the first time in close to twenty years, I started seeing the city through clear eyes. What I saw was amazing. It's a beautiful town, a great place to raise a family. I'd lived in other places with high crime rates, sex trafficking, and run-down streets. But St. George was safe, quiet, sunny, and warm. I could see the amazing potential it had for a business and recognized what an incredible place I had grown up in—what a great place it would be to raise our kids. It also wasn't that small. The surrounding towns collectively had a market of 100,000 people, and I was the only door-to-door windows rep in the area. If I quit ABC Windows and started up my own business, I knew I could get traction fast.

Once I started thinking about the ways St. George could be used as a launch point for door-to-door sales and company growth, I realized it was exactly where we needed to be. But I had to get Shandell on board first. The first time I brought up moving to St. George and starting up my own business there, Shandell couldn't believe it. "You've been telling me for the past *eight* years that we would never consider going back there. What's changed?"

Once I fully explained the vision to Shandell, she was able to get excited. She didn't just make the move reluctantly—she was fully supportive of my goals for the business and our family, which helped me operate at the highest level and take the business to what it is now.

Getting your professional world aligned with your vision is also key. My COO shared a story with me the other day from when I first hired him. He was fresh out of school with a strong background in sales, and some experience in management and operations. He started job hunting and was doing job interviews every other day. The interview that stuck out to him the most was at JKR Windows.

It was in our early days, so JKR Windows was a tiny twelve-by-fourteen-foot office space with just one window and one door. In fact, the space was originally a closet that had been converted to an office space—that's how tiny it was. In fact, my COO still refers to the early days of JKR Windows taking place in "The Closet." Even though the company didn't look very impressive, he knew he wanted to come work for us. When he accepted the offer, he said, "I'm saying yes because of your vision for the company. I can tell your confidence and vision is going to take JKR Windows out of this tiny closet." He passed on other offers that paid more to come work for me.

Likewise, we just hired a recruiter who joined us for the same reason. He's an expert in the door-to-door industry. His skillset was so unique and highly valued that he had many, many offers for positions at other companies. But he knew me personally. He knew what I stood for and the kind of culture I had created at JKR Windows. He was aligned with my vision. "Jefferson, there's nobody else in the door-to-door industry that I would rather work for than you," he told me after accepting a position with us.

Not only will you strengthen your personal relationships with a strong, clear vision, you'll also be able to build an outstanding professional team.

BUILD TRUST

Until you can truly trust someone, your relationship won't make real progress. If there's uncertainty about whether two people can trust each other, there's never going to be full alignment or buy-in.

I had to confront my own trust issues when I realized I was sabotaging my relationships. I had trouble trusting other people—Shandell especially—because of trauma from my childhood. I saw my parents go through so many divorces, and saw other family and friends do crazy shit to one another—and I knew I was capable of plenty of my own crazy shit. I constantly thought about Shandell leaving me because of the things I had done that caused an unhealthy thought process about the way I justified my behavior. Without knowing it, I'd created a mental block to letting other people in. With the help of some coaches and counselors, I was able to start developing healthier ways of thinking about all the areas of my life and business. That's when I was able to start really strengthening my key relationships.

You won't be able to build a strong team without trust. If there's no trust, there's no team. I've seen trust make a big impact at JKR Windows—especially when teams have lacked it. Early on in business, I made the choice to hire a few people even though I had some doubts about their character. In that season, I was hiring with a scarcity mentality, trying to build as fast as I could and not being as intentional about who I brought on. Every person seemed so hard to find and retain. But in those instances when I compromised on trust, people proved my instincts right—and my hiring choices wrong. I've seen firsthand that the damage will be far greater by allowing untrustworthy people to stay on your team. Instead, you just have to come to terms with the continuous work involved with building a strong, trustworthy team. This is one area you cannot compromise on. Pay attention to those gut feelings. Trust is that important.

Your intuition about people's characters will develop with time and experience. Like wisdom, discernment is something you earn. You'll start to develop a combination of questions you can ask to suss people out. You will also learn how to listen to what they're *not* saying—watching the way people conduct themselves, picking up on whether they're out to take advantage of people. In many cases, you'll be reassured to see that someone is aligned with your values: they're interested in growth opportunities and developing their skills, they're family oriented, they want the ability to give back in some way and feel a sense of fulfillment in life. Those are the relationships worth building.

If you have trust issues like I used to, I recommend you put in the effort to work through those. Get help, mentorship, or coaching if you need it. Try to be teachable and listen to feedback from the people you love.

But when it comes to navigating someone else's trust issues, that's another story. You can't overcome someone else's trust issues—only they can. All you can do is be consistent in living according to your values so that you are someone worthy of trust. Strengthen your positive relationships by being yourself, choosing to be genuine and authentic.

YOUR DREAM TEAM

There's a saying that goes, "Show me your five closest friends, and I'll show you your future." I want people in my life who will help make my future amazing. That's why I've intentionally sought to not only strengthen my closest relationships, but to also build relationships with other people who can help me go further faster.

> There's a saying that goes, "Show me your five closest friends, and I'll show you your future." I want people in my life who will help make my future amazing.

I hang out with positive people who are going places. I bring in people who are going to help me get closer to my goals, people who support and inspire me—like a close friend of mine that I see at the gym every day. He retired in his early forties after building an incredible business with his wife through their late teens and early twenties. He now spends his days doing the things he loves and working on building a new business to continue to level up as a leader and communicator. He also cohosts a podcast with my business partner where they bring on other successful people to share their stories and give back to people who are earlier in the process. That's the kind of person I want to be around and learn from.

A strong support system is key to success. That's why you need a dream team: key people in your corner who can give you advice, motivation, support, encouragement, and accountability. When you've got a strong community and network of positive relationships, you can leverage those people's skills to help you grow and achieve great things.

So: who belongs on your dream team?

FAMILY AND CLOSE FRIENDS

You can count on your family and close friends for motivation, couches to sleep on, emotional support, you name it. And when I say "family," that may or may not refer to people you're related to by blood. If you don't have a family in place by default, you can be intentional about building a community or joining a community that provides you with the same sense of sticking by you through the ups and downs. Some people find their "family" in close friends or church groups. I'm mentoring one young guy right now who's a recovering alcoholic, and he's invited me to attend several AA meetings with him. Although my own experience with AA as an eighteen-year-old was terrible, these recent meetings have opened my eyes to the kind of community AA has built here in southern Utah for people to access positivity and growth. "Family" can be something you're born into or something you find. Either way, these are the people that will stand beside you, through thick and thin.

There were a couple years when the only person I had to lean on was my mom. My conversations with her helped me get through some tough times. "Just hang in there," she'd tell me. "You were meant to do great things." From lecturing me after she first caught me smoking weed with my brother, to talking with me on the phone every night for two weeks after I went back to school, to building me up—she was my guiding light. She helped keep me straight for the first twenty-six years of my life, and her support was a big reason I got clean and focused for a long stretch of time.

It was also family who helped me make some of the hardest but most important changes in my life. When I decided to leave Utah, I made a phone call to my aunt Margie. It was one of the most memorable and difficult phone calls I have ever made. More than anything at that point, I wanted to get out of Utah, get away from all my drinking buddies and bad habits, and start creating positive changes in my life. But I wasn't going to be able to pick up and leave Utah unless my aunt and uncle were willing to support me.

"I'm thinking about coming to Arizona to go to a Motorcycle Mechanics school," I told her. "You and Uncle Craig live forty miles away from the school...But, if you guys are willing to let me live with you, I know that I could make it work." I knew this was a big ask. I'd been kicked out of multiple homes by that point. I added, "If you guys would be willing to give me a chance."

Without any hesitation, she said yes. She didn't even ask Craig—she just made room for me. And my uncle Craig helped me stay on course too. He was incredibly influential throughout my entire life. He would have sit-down talks with me and was always trying to open my eyes to my potential, reminding me of my responsibility to my younger brothers. He showed me I could do more than smoke weed and watch movies on someone else's couch. That's the encouraging role my family has played throughout my life.

Whether your family is formed by blood or by choice, your close friends and family provide you with a foundation of support that will be key to your success.

KEY SUPPORT

You also need someone in your life who you can trust to give you validation and honest feedback: that's your key support person. It might be your spouse, parent, or a best friend. This person should be someone you trust enough to play devil's advocate, give you their true gut sense on a situation or person, and be someone you can open up to about your struggles. Ideally, you'll have a key support person in your personal life who you can be totally vulnerable with, and also someone at work who gets less of the raw truth, but can still offer support for the professional challenges.

> Your key support person is someone you can trust to give you validation and honest feedback.

Shandell is my confidentiality partner—my main support person. I can open up with her about my insecurities, my impostor syndrome—all the stuff I would never share with anyone else.

I don't open up about these issues at work—that's for me to work out on my own time. When I'm at the office, I'm leading from the front. It's my job to keep the company looking forward. But any leader still needs to rely on their team. For a season at JKR Windows, some of the key support people on my team were my own family members, and they were straightforward with me about stuff I needed to hear. One day, for example, my brother let me know that I tended to lead my team with threats: "You hold negative outcomes over the team's head, Jefferson," he told me. "You're not going to get the best out of people that way— especially not from your team."

It was gut-wrenching for me to hear that, but incredibly important too. That's why it's so important to have one or several key support people at work who can give you perspective you'll trust. Throughout your years as a leader, those people who give you honest feedback will likely change, but it's important to be intentional about surrounding yourself with candid, perceptive people. It's easier to just get rid of them—accountability isn't something that's comfortable, or that a lot of people like. But without honest feedback, you won't grow as a leader.

Whether it's your confidentiality partner or your go-to guy at work, your key support person can only support you as much as you let them. Communicate your needs, whether you're asking for more encouragement from your partner, honest feedback from a colleague, or more leadership from your managers.

BUSINESS PARTNER

A good business partnership is like a good marriage: it thrives off healthy communication and humility. If one partner always insists they're right, there will be tension and resentment in the relationship. You'll butt heads. You won't trust each other. The partnership will fall apart.

But if you're humble, you'll have a positive dynamic for the partnership. You'll be able to see how much incredible value your partner brings, and your partner will see the true value *you* offer.

A good business partnership is like a good marriage: it thrives off healthy communication and humility.

Honestly, I have a bad track record with partnerships. I've been left hung out to dry by a lot of people. I've learned I should be very careful when it comes to entering partnerships, and I'm finally working with people I have a lot of confidence in. Ideally, you should be able to trust your business partner and share a complementary skillset.

One of my business partners is a friend who built an incredibly successful financial services business that was so successful, he was able to retire before his forties and still provide a great life for his family. He's also a positive person with a lot of integrity. Ironically, even though I was finally in a solid business partnership with a guy I trusted, I started to feel impostor syndrome. I wondered, "Is this too good to be true? Am I worthy of this partnership?" Those doubts could have led me to sabotage the relationship, but I kept the partnership healthy by maintaining consistent, honest communication with him, even through my insecurities. I chose to focus on the positive, not the negative.

We also have complementary strengths. My business partner is a great speaker. He's extremely articulate, and he's also the analytical guy. He's a pro at doing PowerPoint presentations and putting together Excel spreadsheets, and he also translates dense numbers or legalese into plain language. I handle the communication side, dealing with the other parties involved in the partnership. My partner trusts me to lead in that area, keep the deal moving forward, and gets updates from me on how things are going. I also tend to set the vision for our big, crazy-ass goals, and figure out how we're going to get there.

When partners have the same strengths, the partnership usually ends up failing. If your skillsets don't complement each other, you're going to both end up trying to do the same thing, causing competition and friction. But when two partners bring different strengths to the table, you can round each other out. There's harmony.

How else can you optimize a business partnership? Get your ego out of the way. When you're dealing with strong personalities, pointing out that your partner is wrong—even if you're confident that they are—will not do any good. You could taint the entire relationship.

I remember an experience with my partner recently when we were scouting out an undeveloped area for a real estate project. We went out to the piece of land we were considering buying, but we didn't have an exact idea of where to go. This was a completely undeveloped area—just a piece of desert on a map, with no address to put into a GPS. As we drove up to this piece of land, I thought to myself, "I'm pretty sure we're in the wrong location..." Based on my interpretation of the map, I would have taken us to the opposite side of the city. Was my partner wrong? More importantly—*even if he was*, would it help anything to point it out? He's a smart guy and very confident in his opinions. I suspected that, if I suggested we were in the wrong place, he wouldn't be convinced, and it would just cause tension as we went back and forth about who knew what they were talking about. He would have felt stepped on and disrespected.

A few weeks later, the business developer showed us the plot on the map again, which was indeed on the opposite side of the city. Clarity came, and without any "I told you so's" from me. By keeping my ego out of the way, I was able to help the partnership stay healthy. Negative, prideful exchanges can tarnish relationships, one interaction at a time. That's why I'm constantly trying to improve with my communication and humility.

Funny enough, Shandell is my other business partner. So, in our case, a good business partnership literally is like a good marriage. But we've found success as business partners in the same ways: we respect and trust each other, we have complementary skillsets, and I've worked to get my ego out of the way.

NETWORK CONNECTIONS

Your network is your net worth. I've gained a ton of opportunities—both in business and investments—from just building great relationships that have come as a result of networking. You won't know the people in your network as deeply as some of the other folks on your "dream team," but there's a good chance they'll end up playing into the opportunities that come your way.

In the beginning, I was a terrible networker. I remember the first networking event that I went to. I walked into this big group of people. I was dressed a little cheap—I didn't have nice clothes yet—and everybody else was dressed nice in suits. There was a cocktail lounge and people were conversing all over the place, looking confident and sure of themselves. I was intimidated.

The only person I talked to was the bartender, to order myself a drink. And then I just kind of wandered around, not daring to talk to anybody. Finally, I just left.

Over the years, I've become a better networker. I finally learned to build the confidence to go up to someone else and initiate a conversation. That's all you really need to do. In the book *How to Win Friends and Influence People,* Dale Carnegie makes the point that if you want to be interesting, be interested in people. By being a networker and a connector of people, people will want to connect with you.

> Here's how to network: build the confidence to go up to someone else and initiate a conversation. Listen well and be curious. If you want to be interesting, be interested in people.

Here are a few other tips about how you can network well:

- **Challenge yourself to initiate a conversation.** Throughout my whole life, the things that scared me the most were exactly the things I most needed to work on. My fear of networking became a point of emphasis for me. I set up a challenge for myself: everywhere I went from then on, I *had* to introduce myself to somebody. As much as I would rather stay comfortable and just enjoy my drink in a corner of the room, I pushed myself to engage with people. I wanted to develop myself as the person everybody knew and regarded positively. Now, that's who I've become. Everywhere I go, I get compliments on that. Someone will come up to me and say, "Hey, man, I had to come introduce myself. Everybody seems to know you over here!" That only happened because I started pushing myself out of my comfort zone to go up and talk to people.

- **Be interested in other people.** Develop relationships with people by being genuinely interested in them and asking them questions. One of the big turn-offs for me at networking events is when people just want to talk about themselves the whole time. If you're at a networking event and you're constantly talking about yourself, trying to scrounge up clients, and giving away your business cards, you're going to turn people off. The impression you'll give off is that you're only focused on spreading your brand because you can't attract and develop other leaders within your business. It's a self-centered form of networking. But being interested in other people has the opposite effect. It's helped me attract high-level people into my business as well as enabled me to build lasting relationships with hundreds of people over the years, creating countless opportunities and lifelong friendships that I am incredibly grateful for. There's power in having a reputation as someone who cares about other people.

- **Learn names.** I did an interview the other day with a local news channel about how inflation was affecting the home services industry. The news channel had a bunch of stagehands working behind the scenes. By the end of it, I learned all of their names. I was even joking around with them. I caught one guy, Danny, watching the NBA finals game and gave him shit for it. "Man, you're supposed to be working over there! And you're watching the game?" We all had a good laugh about it. They weren't used to people learning their names, or even caring what they did. I started developing this trait after seeing how someone's face lights up when I ask their name. People's enthusiasm completely changes when somebody actually cares to acknowledge them. If you struggle to remember names, write them down, or come up with memory tricks. A little effort in this department goes a long way in building a network.

You should be networking with people who are operating at a higher level than you. That exposure will teach you a lot of things. It'll show you how people at a high level of success treat others, and you'll also be able to observe their presence in a room—their confidence, the clarity of their vision, and the missions they follow. You might learn a bunch of new techniques and practices you want to start doing too.

But if you continue to hang around people at your same level of success or below, you will hit a plateau of accomplishment. You'll keep doing the same things because you don't know any better. Sure, it might feel safe and comfortable—but it's not going to get you anywhere. It's definitely not going to help you go further faster.

Finding a mentor is another good way to blow past your plateau if you're stuck. A good mentor or coach is going to offer support, but also help you learn what to do and what not to do. I'll talk a lot more about mentors in a minute.

GET STARTED

Don't wait for a community to fall into your lap. Once you recognize the value of having positive relationships around you, either create your own community or plug yourself into an existing one. One of the best things I ever did was start attending meetings for Primerica Financial Services. Even though I was terrible at selling life insurance, there was still so much energy and positivity at those meetings. Everyone there was looking to level up, increase their skills, and motivate each other. They helped connect me to other highly motivated people and expose me to what might be possible to achieve in my own life.

These ready-made communities of positive people are there for you to find too. Seek people out—at the gym, at a volunteer group, in a professional network, whatever.

My regional sales director tells a story to our sales team about a time in his life, not long ago, when he was going through a tough time. He was involved in an unhealthy relationship and dealing with many other challenges with his health and current career path. As a result of those areas of dysfunction, he was experiencing all kinds of problems. One morning, he wrote down in his goals: "I want to surround myself with a group of strong, goal-oriented men to be an example to me of what it will look like to take my life to the next level." One week after writing that goal in his journal, I reached out to ask him to join JKR Windows. He has now been with me for three years and has reached incredible heights in his career and development—not just as a salesman, but also as a leader and father. He talks about how different his life would have looked, had he stayed on his previous trajectory.

His story shows that once you are ready and hungry for change in your life, the opportunities will present themselves. If he hadn't been in that particular place in his life, my message may have gone unanswered, and he wouldn't be telling the same success story.

Your community becomes your network, your support system, your safety net. You want that community to be stacked with positive players—your dream team. It might feel scary to put yourself out there and seek out a new community, but I truly believe that when you're good and hungry for a positive environment, you'll manifest that into your life. When you want it bad enough, the universe will align in your favor and present opportunities for you to take advantage of. I've seen that to be true in my life and in the lives of many people I know personally. You have to get uncomfortable enough that it becomes an urgent matter to find a more positive environment. When it does, you'll start making phone calls, asking people to mentor you, going out of your way to find groups of people that will help you, doing the hard work to get positive influences in your life. But once you start doing that, you'll be amazed at how quickly your life begins to accelerate in a positive direction.

Any dream team needs a dream coach—and that's where mentors come in. Mentors and coaches can expose you to wisdom you didn't even know you were missing. These experienced people in your corner will tell you how it really is, instead of what you might want to hear. That's why the right person, at the right time, can change your life completely for the better.

> The right person, at the right time, can change your life completely for the better.

When you seek out a mentor, it's usually with a specific goal or reason in mind. After my brother told me that I tended to lead my team at JKR Windows with threats instead of encouragement, I realized I had a problem with my leadership style. I looked for a coach to help me fix that. The coach I found, Dave Blanchard, is the author of *Today I Begin a New Life* and an expert in personal connection. He's basically my polar opposite: he's seventy years old, very calm, and an experienced leadership coach. He's an expert at being present, allowing people their own space, and helping people bring their guards down—all things I wanted to learn and work on for myself.

After working with him, I've developed to a place where I've got this calm, confident energy about me. I'm also curious all the time about how I can keep growing. Humility, curiosity, and being teachable are key to growing as a person. If I had lashed out at my brother when he gave me that feedback, I wouldn't have grown. I would've plateaued and then my team would have become resentful of my leadership style. By getting out of my own way and admitting I didn't have all the answers, there was a way for new information to get in. With the help of this coach and feedback from the people around me, I've learned how to genuinely show up for my team.

> Humility, curiosity, and being teachable are key to
> growing as a person.

You don't necessarily have to pay top dollar to meet with a good coach or mentor. One of the best ways to learn from people is through reading books. Art Williams was one of my earliest mentors, but I've never met him in person—I've just learned a ton about leadership from his book, *Pushing Up People*. Art started as a football coach. He was from the backwoods of Georgia and talked like it too. Then he went on to create a billion-dollar insurance company. His knowledge has been especially helpful in the last seven years as I've built up my own business. He accomplished extraordinary things but had a humble background. I figured, if he had done it, I could do it, too, so long as I set my mind to it. That's the power of a mentor: they help you see what you're really capable of and give you a vision of what's possible.

Advice for Finding a Mentor

Don't know where to find a mentor? Try YouTube. Or your local public library. Like I said, I didn't personally know my first mentors. I found them through their content: their books, videos, and events. I wanted to emulate the level of energy and success of guys like Art Williams and Grant Cardone.

Eventually, I decided I wanted to seek out a mentor I could meet with in person. I started trying to find ways to connect with men who were operating at a high level, guys with powerful, positive energy. It turned out to be harder than I thought. I reached out to a number of people I respected, but kept finding out that they'd moved away from Utah, or weren't coaching anymore.

I remember going to a business networking group right after starting up JKR Windows to try and find a coach or mentor. It wasn't a great experience, but there was one guy dressed sharp who looked like the real deal. He was confident and kept advertising himself as a coach and consultant. "Perfect," I thought. I asked him if he would consider coaching me, and he said he would meet with me to discuss it. I was so excited.

When we finally met, I really tried to sell myself as a client to him, and he seemed game. But as I kept asking him questions about himself, it became more and more obvious that he was inexperienced.

"One last question for you," I said. "I just started my business. I want to make three hundred thousand dollars in the first year. How much have you made this year?"

He smiled, proudly. "I'm on track to earn sixty thousand dollars this year," he said.

I paused. Was I hearing this right? "From just one of your businesses?" I asked. "Or is that going to be your entire income?"

"That'll be my entire income," he confirmed.

That was all I needed to hear. "Well, listen, man," I said. "This has been great. I appreciate you coming to meet me here at my office. But I'm on track to make three hundred thousand dollars this year. I'm not sure why I would invest in a coach that is only going to make twenty percent of what I'm going to make this year."

He tried making his case on his way out, but my mind was made up.

With all that in mind, here are a few tips when you're trying to determine if a possible mentor or coach is a worthy investment of your time.

GET MENTORED BY SOMEONE WHO:

- **Has experience.** Make sure the person you seek out has a long track record of success in the area you want to be coached. How are you going to learn from someone who hasn't learned yet themselves? If you want to learn how to fix a car, you ask a mechanic, not a chef.

- **Possesses clear integrity.** Everything that your coach advises you to do should be practices that they demonstrate in their own life. If they don't actually use the tips and techniques they recommend, they lack integrity or their approach doesn't work. Only someone who leads by example and lives according to their own recommendations will be able to motivate you to take positive action.
- **Has a life you'd want to emulate.** You want to learn from people whose lives you admire. Ask yourself: are they living a life you'd want to live? If your coach is miserable or unsuccessful, they're not going to be able to teach you anything about happiness or success. On the other hand, if you respect the way they live life and would be excited if your life followed their direction, this person might be a great person to learn from.

Always interview a potential mentor or coach *before* committing to pay them a bunch of money or investment of your time. Think about what you're hoping to learn from your mentor, and ask questions that will help you evaluate their experience in that area. Let's say I'm looking for a mentor who will guide me in running my business and eventually selling it. Here are a few example questions that I would ask to see if they're the real deal:

- How much do you make?
- What is the greatest amount of revenue one of your companies has done?
- Have you ever exited a business? How did that go?
- How much experience do you have in [this particular area]? Have you been successful in that area?

Always interview a potential mentor or coach *before* committing to pay them a bunch of money or investment of your time. Think about what you're hoping to learn from your mentor, and ask questions that will help you evaluate their experience in that area.

You've got to put yourself out there if you want to find a good mentor. After my initial failures, I had no idea how I was going to find a solid coach. I made a lot more phone calls and eventually called this guy who I knew had built a successful financial services business. I asked him if I could sit in on some of his meetings so I could see how he operated his business. "All I want to do is listen and observe," I told him. He said sure.

He still remembers that to this day. "I didn't really know you," he told me recently. "But I remember you came to *every* meeting for two or three weeks. You sat in the back and took notes every time." My desire to learn got his attention.

After that, he became more of an active mentor in my life. He watched my journey of building up my own business. He even had me on his podcast the other day to talk about our journeys. None of that would have happened if I didn't put myself out there and do my homework to find a mentor I could really learn from.

Be Coachable

Even when you find the perfect mentor, know this: they can't make progress for you. You've got to do the work. You need to be coachable and open to hearing some hard things about yourself. As hard as that stuff can be to hear, it's an important part of your growth and evolution as a leader. The sooner you can seek out people who will push you to get you out of your comfort zone, the better.

To be coachable—to be hungry for knowledge—you've got to admit you don't know everything. You've got to recognize there's room for you to grow. That can be hard for people to admit: it exposes your ego, or even worse, your lack of experience. But if you don't own that, you'll plateau and stay stuck, simply because you don't want to be vulnerable.

> Your mentor can't make progress for you. Recognize there's room for you to grow, be open to hearing some hard things about yourself, then do the work to improve.

Find a mentor you trust and can be open with. The only way you're going to make progress is if you can get past the surface level and open up about what's really going on in your head, your emotions, and your business.

Before you start looking for a mentor, ask yourself if you're ready to take one on. Are you hungry for knowledge? Are you willing to set your ego aside and be coachable? Are you ready to be vulnerable and admit what you don't know so you can learn?

If you are—then, start making some phone calls.

BE WORTH EMULATING

Recently, I finished recording a podcast with a couple of acquaintances. One of them didn't know me that well, but he'd watched my journey from following all the content I've put out on social media for the last four years. As we started packing up our stuff to go, he started commenting on some of the things he'd observed me doing.

"Jefferson," he said, "you went out of your way to have a conversation with our valet. You gave a *generous* tip to our waitress, even though she wasn't serving us very well...You're asking everyone in the podcast studio what their names are—and *remembering* them, and calling them by name."

I wasn't sure what he was getting at. He shook his head, like he was trying to figure something out.

"Jefferson, not only have you created a business that produced over thirty-five million dollars in revenue—but in the process, you've improved your relationship with your wife and kids. You've stayed physically fit. You've become a better man. And the way you go about your business isn't the way that most people do things. Everywhere we go, you treat people so good." He seemed impressed but also confused about how I'd made all that happen.

Here's the thing: in every one of those areas, I wasn't operating alone. Other people—Shandell, the team at JKR Windows, my family, my business partners, my mentors and coaches—all played a huge role in those successes. And the kind of behavior he described observing from me were all things that I picked up from surrounding myself with people who operate at a high level. I intently watched how they treated people, how they talked, how they behaved. I modeled my own life after some of these people that I look up to the most.

That's the power of finding the right people to surround yourself with. If you can set your ego aside—if you can be curious, humble, vulnerable, learn to apologize, learn where you need to improve, prioritize your key relationships—then something crazy happens. You become the person other people want to emulate. You become the leader others want to be.

ACTION STEPS

If you want to go further and faster than ever before, the people around you matter. Work to strengthen your positive relationships. Seek out people who will help you grow, and put in the work to learn from them.

- Are there any relationships you need to cut out of your life?
- What specific steps can you take to strengthen your positive relationships?

- Who are the people on your dream team? Are any players missing? Do you want to swap out some players for different ones?
- Name a specific step you can take to start to build up a stronger community for yourself.
- What is a specific area where you'd benefit from a mentor? Do you have the attitude necessary to benefit from a mentor—being coachable, humble, and curious?

You can only go so fast if you're going alone. With a strong team around you—you're going to be unstoppable.

CHAPTER 8

Do Work You're Proud Of

PRIDE OF OWNERSHIP CHANGES
THE WAY YOU SHOW UP

WHEN YOU BELIEVE wholeheartedly in your work, your conviction will inspire your team to excel and your customers to buy in. Run your business in such a way that you can be proud of what you do.

I wasn't always *ALL IN* with my level of effort. Back when I worked for my uncle Doug, repairing semis and trailers for a logistics company, I used to put in the bare minimum. I felt like they were trying to get more out of me than they were paying me for. So—even though I did good work—I found ways to waste time. I would mess around on the computer or do personal stuff at work—anything to milk time while I was on the clock.

Obviously, I had a shitty attitude for most of my time there. Maybe that's why things blew up the way they did.

On my last day of the job, I was running some parts across town when I realized I was about to miss my right turn. Without looking, I cranked the wheel hard to make a dive into the turn lane, but I didn't realize there was a big-ass truck coming up behind me. He didn't see me move over until he was right up on my bumper. We both heard that awful crunch of metal.

I managed to get out of my truck and went to check on the other driver. He'd gotten hurt— his left leg was caught between the seat and the lower dash when it caved in from the impact. I think he might have broken his leg. I started chatting with him, trying to console him a bit while we waited for an ambulance, but I didn't tell him I was the other driver. I don't think he realized it either. Finally, the medics arrived and began putting him on a gurney for the ambulance. The police arrived immediately afterward, and the cops started interviewing me to find out what happened. I began telling them a bullshit story—right in front of the other driver. That's when he realized the "nice guy" he'd been chatting with was actually the asshole who'd plowed into his lane and then lied about it.

By the time I got back to the office—feeling guilty and ashamed, with a messed-up vehicle and a ticket from the cops—I repeated my same bullshit story to my uncle Doug. I didn't own up to it. "I slowed down!" I lied. "It was the *other* guy's fault that he didn't see me." I thought I was going to get off the hook, but my uncle saw through it. He chewed me out.

"You're not taking any responsibility for this!" he accused me. "You're just trying to blame the other guy. *You* need to take some responsibility. Own up to it, for once!"

I blew up at him, yelling, "You can't treat me like that!" I wiped all the shit off his desk and swore at him, saying a whole lot of other things I regret. I kept justifying the whole thing, even though I knew I was in the wrong. But I was *not* about to give in; I was never going to admit any fault.

That lie still sticks with me. Instead of owning up to it, I lied and put it on the other guy. I felt ashamed for doing that—and that shame was why I blew up at my uncle. I knew I was justifying my own stupid actions.

The shame, the lies, the laziness, my overreactions—they were all symptoms of my bad attitude at work. I couldn't stand behind the value I was contributing. I wasn't taking responsibility, giving my best effort, or owning up to my mistakes. I felt like I deserved to be paid more—but I wasn't bringing that value, time, or commitment to the work. When push came to shove and I fucked up in this accident, I lied instead of operating with integrity.

I didn't ever want to carry that kind of shame with me ever again.

A few years later, I saw the opportunity to go *ALL IN* with a new company—and this time, I was committed to making it work. In 2014, I'd had a couple of meetings with the owner of ABC Windows. He was trying to recruit me and dangled the carrot that I would be made a partner if I committed. I signed on and started doing entry-level work—going door-to-door and setting appointments.

There wasn't a ton of direction when I learned the process. My boss and his brother gave me a seven-page script and said, "We want you to learn this, then go out and start setting appointments. Let us know when you have the first one set."

It didn't go very well at first. I didn't know how to deliver the script, and even though I was ready to put in more effort with this job, I didn't know how to operate at a high level. There was no training sequence, no system to follow. I just had to figure it out. Eventually, through a lot of trial and error, I did figure it out and started making appointments.

But then there was a new problem. After a couple of months, I started realizing that my boss was failing to show up to the appointments I'd set—usually because he was golfing or at happy hour. I started showing up to their appointments myself, to make sure at least someone from the company was keeping their promise to the customer. Half the time, it seemed, he was a no-show. Soon after, I told him, "Listen, I need to learn how to run these appointments so I can do them on my own." I wanted to take it into my own hands and start closing some of the deals myself.

He agreed to that and handed me a new script. But once again, it was on me to figure out how to run the appointments. And once again, I was pretty bad for a long time. I finally felt better about my *own* effort—but I couldn't feel proud of the work the company was delivering.

Getting a job at a different company wouldn't have solved much, in my opinion. It wasn't just ABC Windows that was failing to follow through for their employees and customers—I saw the same thing from *most* home service companies. Most of these businesses are run by technicians who become business owners. They don't often have a long-term vision for their companies, and they have high expectations for their employees but don't provide a lot of clear instructions. They also tend to put in minimal work for their clients. They'll come to collect a check from their customers but then try to avoid dealing with them again afterward. That leaves customers overcharged for work that's left undone—and this happens all over the home service industry. I'd had countless interactions with customers over the years where they told me they were wary of doing business after bad experiences with other companies. They wanted to work with someone they could trust to follow through, be fair, and deliver on their promises.

I wanted to do work for a company that I believed in, one that sent people out with the tools that enabled them to succeed at a high level. I wanted to do work I was proud of, with a company I could be proud of.

I thought about starting my own company that could do that.

Then, I'd start drinking and getting high instead.

Once I finally got clean enough to think clearly, I decided I'd had enough. I didn't want to give my all to a company I didn't believe in. I wanted to feel proud of what I was doing.

I had a belief, a conviction, that I could do better than these other companies. When I finally started JKR Windows, I was on a crusade to set us apart from everyone else. I made a commitment to not fall into the trap of treating customers like paychecks. I knew there was a power I could harness by believing wholeheartedly in my work: my conviction would inspire my team members to work at my same level and customers to buy in. JKR Windows would have an uncompromising integrity on our promise to take care of our customers. We would develop a kick-ass training process for our reps. I would take them through a well-thought-out training sequence with specific steps to follow so that their success as a door-to-door rep would be nearly guaranteed. I was going to be fully committed to learning how to be a good leader. I would provide guidance. We would build a culture of excellence for our clients.

We were going to go *ALL IN*. And that's exactly what we did.

> There's power that comes when you believe
> wholeheartedly in your work: your conviction will inspire
> your team to excel and your customers to buy in.

BELIEVE IN WHAT YOU DO

When you're doing work you feel proud of, that changes how you enter a room. There's a confidence that comes with integrity—and it's compelling. People sit up and pay attention. They want to know more about whatever you've got. If you can create an entire team or organization that feels that level of integrity and pride in their work—you're going to go even further and even faster than you thought possible.

Whether you're selling a product to a customer, or selling a vision to a team, their willingness to buy in comes down to how you sell yourself. Before you can sell at a high level, you have got to be 100 percent sold on what you're doing. How can you sell something you're not sold on? You've got to *believe* in the quality of what you're offering. When you're truly convinced of its value, you can convince others that their investment is 100 percent in their best interest—and mean every word.

This is especially important when you're shaping the vision for your team or company. A strong vision won't just help generate success for your company—it will also shape your culture and attract high-level people to your organization.

> A strong vision generates success for your company by clarifying focus, shaping your culture, and attracting high-level people to your organization.

I once knew a CEO who had risen through the ranks after starting as a janitor at his company. Now he's traveling all over the world as the CEO, but he's still so effective at growing the company and standardizing its systems. And because he's worked most of the jobs in the company, he's great at maintaining a sense of connection with the people on the ground.

"How are you so good at your job?" I asked him once.

He told me that he credited most of his success with being able to paint a picture about his vision for the company's goals, operations, and effectiveness. "And you can't just show them a PowerPoint, Jefferson," he told me. "You have to become a *master storyteller*. You need that vision to be so clearly mapped out in your own mind that you can paint a clear picture to your people. And you need to work on your delivery— just like sales reps need to work on their pitch. If you've got a choppy delivery, people aren't going to buy in. People only believe in a vision they can see in their head. So, you've got to find out how to get it out of your head and into theirs in the most effective way possible."

He grinned at me. "You have to practice. You have to get your reps in." He explained that, because he had done a majority of the jobs at his company, he could paint an especially vivid picture of how everyone could work together to bring the vision about. He fully believed in the vision he described—and it helped get everyone else on board.

That first year of JKR Windows, my vision was pretty narrow. All I could think about was catching up to ABC Windows and passing them. I put a target on their back. Maybe that professional vision was limited—but it was a vision I *believed in*. It was one I could sell to my team, and it also kept me motivated and focused. I ate, slept, and breathed JKR Windows. I was constantly pushing JKR Windows to become a better company. I never wanted my team to feel about me the way I felt back at ABC: that I was gone all the time, or that I didn't support their growth. My professional vision guided not only the company's development, but also my attitude as a leader.

> A professional vision guides the company's development and your attitude as a leader.

I got up earlier and stayed awake longer than everybody else at my company. In the first eighteen months of JKR Windows, I never missed a single meeting. I trained every single person myself. I was out in the field with the guys every single day.

When my team saw me working at that level, they started going the extra mile. I pumped up my team by telling them stories about ABC Windows—how I never got any help, and describing the lack of mentorship or training systems. People were catching the vision: they wanted JKR Windows to be a better company too. They were enthusiastic and excited. I had key people fully engulfed in projects, working all weekend on an idea they wanted to implement.

Within the first two years, we passed ABC Windows. It was sort of surprising, in fact, how quickly we surpassed them. I brushed off that chip on my shoulder and started to think bigger—way bigger.

Now, our vision is to be the biggest replacement windows company in the United States and provide an incredible lifestyle for all of our employees. We're succeeding in both areas: in the past five years, JKR

Windows has brought in over 45 million in revenue and we're working on opening twenty-seven locations. And the lives of our employees are being transformed. I've seen guys come to our company from all walks of life—restaurants, retail, the medical industry; one guy was a barber, another was a plumber. A lot of them, when they join our company, they're just getting by. Then, they start doing sales for JKR Windows and get the opportunity to make a high six-figure income. I see guys make more in one month than what they used to make in a year. That's one of the most fulfilling things in the world for me to see. They're changing their lives, and the lives of their families.

It's also a lot easier to attract top talent to your team when you have a strong vision. I've been able to recruit some very high-level individuals in the door-to-door industry by sitting down with them and painting a compelling picture of where JKR Windows is going and where it could take them. Several key new hires have told me that they turned down other offers with bigger companies because they liked the way we ran our business, and believed in the vision I was describing. They joined the team because they wanted to be part of something they could feel pride in. When you believe in your company, it inspires other people to believe in it too.

JKR Windows is the kind of company I always wanted to work for, and it's a company my people are proud to be a part of. It's one of the reasons we've been able to go so far, so fast, and it's why customers trust us. We're able to communicate a vision that draws people in—because we *all* believe in it.

When you can communicate a clear, powerful vision to your people— you get them excited. You get them motivated. You get their teamwork harmonized. And you start racking up wins.

> When you can communicate a clear, powerful vision
> to your people—you get them excited. You get them
> motivated. You get their teamwork harmonized. And you
> start racking up wins.

We also don't take shortcuts. Most businesses fail because they don't realize how much work goes into getting your product in front of customers. Shortcuts aren't going to get your product in front of your target market—only relentless activity is going to do that.

> Shortcuts aren't going to get your product in front of your target market—only relentless activity is going to do that.

The only reason JKR Windows succeeded as fast as we did was because I didn't leave any of that to chance. There are a lot of companies in the service business that don't knock on doors. But I stuck with what I knew was going to work: knocking on doors and getting in front of customers every single day.

I was 100 percent committed to making this work. I was out there with my team every day. I knew I had to take the success of my business into my own hands, so I worked every single day, even Sundays. I took one vacation in the first two years of the business. In the beginning of JKR Windows, I handled door knocking, being the salesman, following up with customers, payroll, ordering, even measurements at the clients' homes. The only thing I didn't do was the installation.

If someone asked me if I took any shortcuts with JKR Windows, I could show them the dirt and grime on my hands. No, I didn't take any shortcuts. I pounded the pavement and worked my ass off.

When I get an opportunity to speak in front of the sales team, I talk about what we stand for as a company and how we separate ourselves from the competition. I reiterate the things that we're going to do that no other company is going to even think about doing because it costs more and takes more effort. "We go above and beyond in this company," I told them in a recent meeting. "We're going to take care of our customer, no matter the cost, because we committed to them and now it's our job to follow through. And that's true, even if it comes to a point where we lose money. I've lost money on a couple jobs because I made a commitment to the customer, and then something went wrong, and the only way to get through the job with a positive outcome for the customer was to expend the extra resources to make it happen. So that's what we did. You think other companies are doing that? No. But we go the extra mile."

One of the things that we never want to lose as a company is what separates us, and that's paying attention to what's important to our customers. We go the distance for them—we're not about shortcuts. We go *ALL IN*.

FIND YOUR NICHE

Instead of looking for shortcuts—find your niche. A niche can open up market share to you that's being ignored in whatever approach is more mainstream.

When people find out I work in the window industry, I often get asked, "Do you do new construction?" There's a low barrier for entry to get involved in new construction, and you can make good money doing it. But if I was in new construction, I'd be competing with seventeen other contractors, all gunning for the same contract. The new construction market is saturated—it looks easy and has the most exposure, so it's full of contractors, all fighting over the same bids.

I had no interest in that. I wanted to avoid wherever the majority of people were flowing. Instead, I targeted a more niche market where I knew we could quickly establish a reputation as the best company to work with: replacement windows.

That's been our target clientele and our marketing strategy: we set out to make JKR Windows the best replacement window company in Utah. And our bet has paid off. Most other window companies are going after the sexy new construction—it's low-hanging fruit, high volume, and easy to install, but as a result, there's a ton of competition. And all those competing companies lower their prices to try to win the bid, because if they don't, someone else will. They have to do way more volume to be profitable at those lower prices. Replacement windows, on the other hand, are harder to install and lower volume. You're dealing with finished surfaces on the exterior and interior, so you have to be very detailed in taking the old windows out and installing new ones. But as a result, there's far less competition. We've been able to distinguish ourselves as the best in our niche and command a higher price. As a result, we make way more money off our orders than if we were in new construction, while dealing with far fewer competitors.

Find your niche. Don't be a follower and go where everyone else is trying to make money. Look for the opportunities that are *less* obvious. If you can find the smaller markets, there's more opportunity and profit because there are less competitors paying attention.

> Find your niche. Don't be a follower and go where
> everyone else is trying to make money. Look for the
> opportunities that are *less* obvious.

This is true even if you're not a business owner—you'll be more effective doing work you feel proud of if you have a niche as an individual. By choosing an area of focus where you can become an expert, you can add and achieve maximum value with your time. For example, I once coached a guy who ran a rural mail route and also had two separate side gigs. One of his side gigs was selling safes, and the other was crafting custom holsters for clients. His attention and time were split between three different areas, which limited his ability to be an expert in any of them. It was obvious where the best opportunity was—his profit selling just one safe was way higher than the money he made from the other two gigs, but the holsters and the mail route were eating up all his time. If he had targeted his focus toward becoming an expert in safes, he could easily build something big for himself. That was the niche with the greatest opportunity.

Your niche should align with your own unique skillset. Understanding what that is will come with time, experience, and awareness. For the first couple years of my business, I knew I could sell windows. But I wasn't the best at it. I could do operations, admin, and payroll, but I wasn't the best at them either—and I didn't enjoy them. Over time, I started to realize that my true skills are as a leader, visionary, and creator. I didn't need to spend my time doing operations or payroll. I needed a team around me who could take care of those things and help implement my vision. Once I understood what I excelled at, I was able to use my time in an excellent way.

I think everyone struggles with getting distracted by stuff that's not in their lane. Just the other day I walked in on my COO designing a graphic for our company's Code of Conduct poster. It was terrible. "Dude, what are you doing?" I asked him. "There are so many other important things you could be doing right now. Let's find a five-dollars-an-hour person on Upwork and pass this off." My COO is an incredible guy. He has come a long way over the past three years—incredibly coachable and consistently proactive about his personal improvements to become a better leader, communicator, and overall contributor to the business. Even so, as my *COO*, there's no way he should have been designing graphics. He should have been focused on the big-picture areas of operating our business. Thankfully, he often seeks advice and reflects on what he can do to level up. This was a moment where we could talk about the best use of his time—and I think those reflective moments are needed for all of us. As we get to higher places in our careers, we still need reminders of the important tasks that drive us forward. We need to stay focused, limit distractions, and constantly reevaluate our actions of highest impact.

The people who operate at the highest level are those people who have found their lane and they do amazing work within that lane. They're not trying to do everything. They've found their niche: their area of expertise, the area that maximizes their highest skills.

> Your niche should align with what you know best, what you could become an expert in, and where your skills are.

You've got to make the best use of your time if you want to go further faster toward your goal. Once you understand what you're the best at, you can devote your time to the niche where you excel—doing work that makes you feel proud.

IDENTIFY VALUES YOU BELIEVE IN

At the root of all of this—believing in what you do, not taking shortcuts, finding your niche—there's got to be integrity. None of this is worth shit if you're not totally committed to following through. You've got to be *ALL IN.*

Without integrity, you can't do work you're proud of. That's how I was, when working for my uncle: I believed in the company, sure. I was doing good work. I had a niche. But I wasn't conducting myself with integrity—so I still functioned with a lot of shame.

That's why values matter so much. If you don't live in alignment with your values, you won't be able to work with the kind of confidence and pride that can be so life changing. The first change I made to my own style of work was increasing my *personal* level of effort and integrity. I finally started living more in alignment with my values—and that's a step you can take, no matter where you're at in your professional career.

Later, as a business owner, I wanted to build values into my *company*. From everything I'd read, I knew that strong company culture was built on strong values. The best, most successful companies in the world have mission statements and company values that are embedded into the culture. I wanted that for JKR Windows.

The only problem was, every time I sat down to get something about our company values on paper, I got writer's block. I tried to brainstorm by researching the core values of a lot of top companies and made a list of all these sophisticated words they used in their mission statements and core values. The list was overwhelming. It didn't help.

One thing that *did* help me was bouncing ideas off people who are creative and analytical. For me, that was a combination of my brothers and my colleagues.

"What are some of the things you see in how I run this business, and how would you translate it into one word for a core value?" I asked them. Then I'd say, "What are some of the things that are important to you?"

Those conversations were super important to get clear on the core values for JKR Windows. Even still, it was difficult to get around to defining them—it took me a long time. In those early days, I easily got distracted by the day-to-day operations because they felt so urgent. Finally, I told myself, "This is important. This isn't homework. This is something that will *benefit* the company." After more processing and deliberating, we defined JKR Windows' core values as *consistency*, *dependability*, and *commitment to excellence*.

Whether you're leading a team, a company, or just doing your best to level up as an individual professional, identifying professional values will help you go further faster. Why? Because they have a direct impact on the level of pride you feel in your work.

JKR WINDOWS' VALUES

I knew—if we wanted to go as far and as fast as I wanted us to—we needed to be clear on what we stood for. Here's why. Let's say one of my sales reps is pulling decent numbers, but after he makes the sale, he flakes on the customer and won't return their calls. If I need to have a difficult conversation with that guy, but I have no core values defined for the company, the conversation becomes more difficult. He tells me, "You should be happy about my numbers!" And I'm telling him, "Yeah, but you're trashing our company's reputation." In his mind, the value should be the bottom line. In my mind, the value is dependability. But I can't hold someone to a value standard if there is no standard.

You can't hold someone to a value standard if there is no standard.

When you have core values written on the wall and you talk about them in meetings, there's clarity around expectations. My sales rep *knows* what I expect of him: I can point to the giant word "dependability" on the wall and say, "You're not upholding this core value right now, even if your sales numbers *are* good." Those core values apply to everybody in the company. They're nonnegotiable. It's part of our culture and keeps the environment positive. So, if somebody on the team doesn't align with those core values, it's going to be pretty apparent, and they won't be surprised if I ask for a sit-down.

Defining your core values will also help you attract high-performing people who align with your company culture and have similar values. In fact, your core values should be a centerpiece of every job interview. There's only a certain amount of effectiveness if you ask basic, generic interview questions. When I run an interview, a lot of my interview questions have something to do with consistency, dependability, commitment to excellence, loyalty, and integrity: all my core values.

It's also true that if you aren't intentional about what you stand for and represent, it's a lot easier to cut corners and make exceptions. I've seen a lot of people justify bad decisions to make more money—even good people will do stupid shit when it comes to money. But if you clearly define what you stand for, you won't make any exceptions or take shortcuts. That's going to make it easier for everyone in your company to do work they feel proud of—because you've made it clear you won't stand for anything less.

Here's why I finally arrived at the values that define my own company.

Consistency

Consistency makes or breaks a company. Anyone can do anything for a week or a month. Very few can do it consistently for months, that turn into years, that turn into a defining characteristic of a successful legacy.

When I started up my own company, I wanted us to be known for our consistently outstanding service to customers. No matter how long it's been, how big we've grown, and no matter what the circumstances are, that's still the attitude of JKR Windows: we will consistently offer an outstanding customer service experience. My guys know when they show up to work, their service helps maintain the consistency of quality we've become known for. We stand behind what we do with warranties and guarantees. We offer the highest quality service even *after* the sale, which is rare throughout the entire home service industry. Consistency has become part of our brand's reputation: JKR Windows is committed to helping customers.

Dependability

Once you develop a reputation for dependable service and quality, it sticks with you. But the opposite is true, and almost even more powerful: if you develop a reputation for being unreliable, then nobody's going to trust you with their money or with responsibility. That's true on an individual level and on a company one.

My mentors and sales leaders at ABC Windows were not very dependable. I would set the appointments for them, so I depended on them to show up on time, run that appointment, and execute on their part of the responsibilities. But more times than I can count, they would cancel the appointment, or not show up, or forgot to check the calendar. Why? Usually, because they were golfing. I couldn't depend on them, and as a result, ABC Windows wasn't dependable for the customers.

For the first two years of JKR Windows, I trained every single person myself. I never wanted anybody on my team to go through what I had to go through: to get their teeth kicked in and wonder if they made the right decision. I put my heart and soul into training and mentoring them. I gave them everything they needed to be successful so that we would have the most dependable salespeople out there and never miss an appointment.

That's one of the reasons JKR Windows grew so fast as a company, and why the team is so committed. If you work at JKR Windows, you have something you can be proud of while you're out doing the work. There is no company you have ever worked for or will ever work for that will stand behind their work like we do. No matter how far down the road, no matter how big or small the ask is, JKR Windows will always take care of its customers. My people know they represent a company with gold standards of dependability, and that helps them show up with pride and confidence.

Dependability is an expectation I set with all of my salespeople and operation staff at JKR Windows from day one. Our success requires us to work hand in glove, building trust and consistency between the guys making appointments, the people closing appointments, and the team responsible for fulfilling the order. We make sure everyone on our team can depend on each other—so that the customer can depend on us.

Commitment to Excellence

I don't expect my teams to be perfect—errors are going to happen. But we're never going to stop striving for excellence as a company. JKR Windows is committed to offering an excellent experience for all our customers. If something's not done right the first time, we go back and make it right.

I demonstrate that value for my company by leading from the front. I don't expect anything from my team that I don't expect of myself. That's why, in the early days of JKR Windows, I was out in the field with the guys every single day. They saw my example of what I expected of them. I also *never* missed a meeting—even when I injured my back at the gym. Shandell tried to convince me to stay home and rest. "I'm not missing a meeting," I told her. "Help me drag my ass into the car so we can make it to the office." Shandell and the girls helped make me a cane, drove me to work, and I didn't miss the meeting.

Even when I was almost completely immobile, I wanted my team to see I would show up for them, no matter what. To me, that was leading from the front. I wanted to show them I was committed to being an excellent leader, and I expected the same commitment to excellence from them.

ALL IN.

My JKR veterans know that I'm the guy who was and still is willing to do any job in the company; I'm not afraid to get my hands dirty to get the job done, whether that means I'm taking out the trash or knocking on doors. I use the same sales script I teach my guys because I know it works. Although I don't knock on doors much anymore because my responsibilities as CEO have changed, I still will. I try to lead by example in my work ethic, my personal life, leadership, communication, and personal habits. In all areas of my life, I try to model that commitment to excellence.

Alongside those high standards, there's also a focus on positivity. Getting rid of negativity in my own life created a huge change in my trajectory, and I've worked hard to create a positive culture for our team. Our environment and people have huge energy and enthusiasm for what we do. We're always talking about personal development—in fact, I regularly pay for people on my team to attend conferences with me and do other professional development. There's a strong cultural focus on being a positive presence on the team—a "plus," not a "minus." The team is committed to improving themselves, and helping improve others— they're living out the JKR Windows' Commitment to Excellence. We're committed to being the best version of ourselves.

> Be fully committed to the best version of yourself. *ALL IN*.

When you're by your team's side and teaching them the company's core values, you give them the tools to succeed. I wanted my team to understand every part of the process so they could feel proud of the work they were doing. I tried to expose them to the work as much as possible throughout training, from admin staff initiating the process through final installs. I even encourage team members to talk to customers with our windows in their homes about their experience with us. There is no better way to build belief in someone than to have them consistently run into customers who had a great experience and love our windows. Our new hires constantly hear nothing but compliments for the company.

Those three values—consistency, dependability, and commitment to excellence—came out of my own personal values and style of leadership. They've enabled my team to work together as an amazing company, and we've built an incredible culture. Our values, plus our vision, have helped us accelerate way beyond the competition. We're going further faster—and we're damn proud of what we do.

PRIDE OF OWNERSHIP

When I started feeling real pride in my work, I saw an immediate jump in my sales. The change directly impacted my bank account as my new attitude started to seriously attract customers. Grant Cardone talks about the idea of "overpromise and overdeliver." I started to *believe* in the value I could offer my customers, because I was willing to do whatever follow up was necessary to make my commitments to them happen. I overpromised because I knew I could overdeliver.

I remember the house and customer when I first started to apply that belief. I was still working for ABC Windows, knocking on doors in a neighborhood where we'd gotten some new clients. The house was a modest little brick home. The person who answered was a little old lady. When she found out I was selling windows, she mentioned that she'd gotten some bids from other companies to replace her windows.

"How many bids have you gotten?" I asked.

She eyed me, like she was trying to figure me out. "Five," she said. "But I turned them all down. I didn't like them. And besides, I don't think I'm ready to replace my windows after all." The way the conversation was going, I could tell she was working toward blowing me off like she did the other salesmen.

"Now, hang on. Why did you get five different estimates if you're not planning on doing your windows?" I asked her.

She paused. She didn't seem to really know why. "I'm just not ready yet," she finally said.

I told her, "You could buy windows at any one of these places. And there's probably half a dozen other places that you could buy windows too. Most of them are probably going to be cheaper than me—" She lifted her eyebrows. I kept going. "—But one thing that you're never going to get from any one of those companies is somebody like me, who stands behind what they do."

I pointed to my name and number on my business card. "That's my personal number. I'm *always* going to be there to pick up your phone call. I will *always* answer your questions. I will *always* make sure that you're happy—no matter how far down the road we get after your install." I looked her right in the eye. "I'm the only guy that will ever do that type of service." When I said that, I *meant* it—and she could tell.

She signed up for the installation right there.

Back then, that was a deal I normally would have walked away from. She'd already turned away five other salesmen. In the past, I would have accepted defeat. But this time, I came in with a different attitude—a different way of being. I knew I was different from the other salesmen. I believed in the work I could offer her, and I told her as much. I *over*promised, and then I overdelivered.

Before her window job was completely done, I had quit ABC Windows and started up JKR Windows. That didn't change my commitment to her one bit. I still answered the phone, every time she called. When she had a problem, I took care of it. I showed up at her installation and made sure she was happy—all of that, even though I wasn't getting paid by ABC Windows anymore. I was less concerned about getting paid, and more concerned about ensuring that my name was associated with integrity.

That was true for all of my customers I picked up in my final days at ABC Windows. After I left the company, I still spent three months fulfilling orders for them. I made sure every customer I initiated contact with was happy throughout the process. These people didn't care that they were being helped by ABC Windows. They cared that they were being helped by *Jefferson*, who stood by his word and took care of them.

That mentality started to build momentum for my own company. The next time these customers needed a windows company, they called

JKR Windows, not ABC. I've had multiple people call me back, even years later. I stay true to my word and send my own service crews to take care of them, out of pocket.

When you take pride in your work, you have a different level of energy and enthusiasm than someone who's just in it for the money—and that energy is contagious. Other people can't help but notice. The people on your team, your clients, and even other business owners—they can't help but point it out. When you're fully committed to excellence and integrity, you stand out next to people who are just going through the motions in their careers.

> When you're fully committed to excellence and integrity, you stand out next to people who are just going through the motions in their careers.

My team has seen me put in the work to hire good people and improve our systems. They've seen our consistency in hitting our targets. I want to get so good at delivering on my vision that when I talk about hitting $200 million as a company over the next eight to ten years, there's no question in anybody's mind about whether or not we're going to do that. When you've got a strong group of people aligned on the same values, who are all pumped about the direction you're going, and they're showing up fully committed to kick ass—you'll be amazed at what happens next.

That's the power of working with integrity. That's the power of overpromising, and then overdelivering. You'll see the change immediately—both in your bank account and in how you feel when you walk into a room. Do work you can be fucking proud of.

ACTION STEPS

When you believe wholeheartedly in your work, your conviction will inspire the people around you to excel and your customers to buy in. Do your work in such a way that you can be proud of what you do.

- Think of a time when you were half-assing your work. Think of a time when you gave something your all. What difference did you see in the results? What difference did you feel in your confidence?
- What's your professional vision for yourself? What steps do you need to take in order to make it happen?
- What niche can you target to establish yourself as an expert in your field and increase your market share?
- Identify the values that you want to define your own work and the culture of the people you lead.

When you operate with integrity and a high level of pride in your work—and especially if you lead a team of people who feel the same—you're going to go even further and even faster than you thought possible.

CHAPTER 9

Invest in Yourself

YOU ARE YOUR BEST RETURN ON INVESTMENT

I F YOU WANT to get to the next level of success, you need new ideas, new tools, new perspectives. All of that means you're going to have to invest in your own personal development—which will require time, money, and some serious effort on your part. But with the right attitude, that investment in yourself is going to lead to a massive rate of return.

Let me tell you what I mean. I've talked a lot about the Grant Cardone mentorship program that changed my life. Before I signed up for that program, I had to make the decision to invest in it—and more specifically, invest in myself. Even before I'd started the program, or learned discipline, or gotten clean—it was that decision to invest in myself that profoundly altered the direction of my life.

Let me back up and remind you where I was at, at that point. For six weeks after I headbutted the guy at the Florida Georgia Line concert, I felt the most shame I'd ever felt in my life. I was drinking and smoking weed every day. Things with Shandell were in a rocky place—we weren't talking much. My mom had a lot of conversations with Shandell and encouraged her to hang in there.

"He's a great man. He's just trying to figure his stuff out," she told her.

But I didn't know how to fix it. I had dug myself this hole and wasn't sure I could dig myself out. I thought about changing my behaviors and being better, but I didn't think I had the willpower to follow through. I just kept repeating the same shit over and over.

Somewhere in those six weeks, I was out working. I should have been knocking on doors. Instead, I just sat in my car, scrolling through Facebook. That's where I saw the ad for the Grant Cardone program. Grant was saying that he would personally mentor 100 people through his 10X Ambassador Program. He wanted to create success stories out of his mentees and have them share their stories onstage at the 2018 10X Growth Conference in Las Vegas.

I wanted a success story I could share onstage. *I* wanted to attend the conference. My heart was pounding—I knew I needed to sign up.

But the program wasn't cheap. The end of the ad put a number on the screen: "$1,100." I didn't even know if I had that money. Immediately, I pulled up my banking app to check our bank account. We had $1,125 left.

I swallowed hard and called Shandell.

The first thing I said to her was "Do you trust me?"

"Yes," she said, slowly.

I took a deep breath. "You know that book I just read? *The 10X Rule*, by Grant Cardone? He's doing this mentor program and it includes a ticket to the 10X Growth Conference in Vegas. He's going to personally mentor 100 people. I've got the chance right now to be one of those 100 people."

"That's great," Shandell said.

"Hang on," I told her. I paused. "It's going to cost basically all the money we have left in our bank account. It costs $1,100." She was silent on the other end.

I paused. "I think this could help me," I told her.

She didn't hesitate. "If you think it's going to help you, then absolutely," she said.

I was determined to make that $1,100 investment count—not just for me, but also for my wife and kids. I wasn't just paying for the mentorship and the conference. I was investing $1,100 in a new version of myself.

And that was the best $1,100 I've ever spent. My rate of return on that money eclipses any investment I've made since then—maybe because it cost me everything I had. I had to completely level up to make that money count.

I went *ALL IN*.

> If you want to get to the next level of success, you need to invest time, money, and effort into your own personal development. But with the right attitude, that investment in yourself is going to lead to a massive rate of return.

THE REWARDS OF INTENTIONAL SELF-INVESTMENT

Because I invested that money, I gained exposure to people operating at a high level. My perspective on what was possible in my life exponentially expanded. I started making huge progress and forming goals that were bigger than I ever could have imagined.

If you ever want things to change, you need to invest in yourself. Sometimes that's going to require money, but not always. There are a lot of ways you can invest in yourself with minimal costs: reading books, listening to podcasts, watching YouTube videos, finding a mentor, or going to free networking events. But if you want to gain exposure to people operating at a high level like I did, that typically comes with a cost.

And that's okay. When you put up a large investment—whether that's your money, time, effort, or all three—you're more determined to get something out of it. When you don't have a lot at stake, you're more likely to put in minimal effort.

> When you put up a large investment—whether that's your money, time, effort, or all three—you're more determined to get something out of it.

If you want to get the most out of investing in yourself, you have to be intentional. Go into each one of these relationships or events with an intention of a general takeaway you want to get. You may not get the exact type of nugget you imagined—but the more intentional you are, the more in tune you'll be when a relevant message comes up.

When that happens, take notes. Write it down. Don't lose the feeling. Whenever I hear something impactful, I write it down and put it in my action item list. Otherwise, I'm going to forget the fucking thing. One of the worst feelings is knowing a message could have changed your life, or your business—but you can't remember what it was.

I've had a number of people reach out to me over the years and ask what my "rate of return" has been from investing in myself. I can say things like, "It's been ridiculously huge," but really, there's no way to calculate a rate of return on mentorship or networking events—wisdom is going to serve you for the rest of your life.

> Wisdom will serve you for the rest of your life.

There are plenty of ways to invest in yourself—some are free, some are cheap, and some cost plenty. There are also plenty of ways to *waste* money, either because you blow the opportunity to learn or because you got taken in by a stupid investment. Here's some advice about ways you *do* and *don't* want to spend money on investment opportunities.

WHAT TO SPEND MONEY ON

If you are going to spend money, it's up to you to decide what's worth the cost. When I started getting involved in conferences and networking five years ago, my investment of $1,100 completely changed my life. On the other hand, I just signed up for a Mastermind group that cost $100,000. It's a hundred times more expensive—but also, the people in that group are at a completely different level. That level is a better fit for what I've grown into and, for me, it's worth that level of capital.

Whether you spend $1,100 or $100,000, it's up to you to get the value out of it. If I go to the Mastermind conference and just enjoy the festivities without building relationships, asking questions, and learning concepts to apply to my business—then I'm wasting my money. On the other hand, if I go in with real intention and curiosity, I know I'm going to maximize my investment.

> Maximize your investment by approaching each learning opportunity with intention and curiosity.

YOUR NETWORK

My last $1,100 got me plugged in with Grant Cardone and helped me develop discipline—but one of the greatest gifts it gave me was exposure to a new network of people. Building my network exposed me to success stories that gave me a new perspective about what was possible. And—other than Grant—these people weren't famous. They didn't book a private jet whenever they needed to go somewhere. These were ordinary people, dealing with real problems, doing extraordinary things. Being around them made me think, "I could achieve this too. The only thing these guys have on me is time and experience. If I put in the work—I could be where they are. Maybe even further."

That's the power of investing in your network: you're exposed to wisdom, possibilities, and opportunities you never would have encountered otherwise. I talked about networking a bit already in Chapter 7, but it's worth returning to here, in the context of investing in yourself. Remember: your network is your net worth. Networking allows you to build your personal brand and reputation through connecting with others. When you expose yourself to people operating at a high level, you get the chance to expand your perspective.

I've spent plenty of money on networking opportunities—that $1,100 was just the tip of the iceberg. But before I talk about money, I want to talk about an even greater investment required. In order to build a strong network, the most important investment is in your own *humility*.

If your ego makes you think you have all the answers, you're going to get stuck. Just recently, my mom's ex-husband—my old stepdad—came to ask me for business help. Since I'd been a kid, his business always made under $1 million in sales each year. It never got past that. For so long, he wouldn't listen to anybody else's advice about how to grow because of his ego and insecurities. But once he got older, his pride wasn't as strong as it used to be. It took some real humility for him to approach his ex-stepson for business advice, but we had a little chat. We worked together for a few months before he joined another group for help—a Grant Cardone group, actually. During the time we worked together, his company close to doubled. He is on track to have another record year in 2023.

Seek out advice early and often. If you're going to keep learning and growing your business, you've got to ask questions and seek help to get a higher outcome.

As an entrepreneur, especially early in your journey, you might feel the urge to pretend you're further along in the process than you actually are when meeting people. New entrepreneurs tend to talk all about themselves at networking events. But networking events are your opportunity to ask questions, be curious, and learn from high-level people. You are there to learn. You aren't going to learn anything if you pretend you already have all the answers.

> Networking events are your opportunity to ask questions, be curious, and learn from high-level people. You are there to learn.

I recently attended a Mastermind event in Florida where I was introduced to Kent Clothier, the CEO of Real Estate Worldwide. He's the founder of Boardroom Mastermind, the most elite real estate investor networking group in the country—and he was one of the instructors for the event. We had mutual friends, so we were hanging around the same group during the event. Instead of talking about myself and the things that I've done, I asked him questions—question after question after question. And I learned a hell of a lot! Because of some advice he gave me, I ended up making the decision to move forward on a real estate investment that is going to net me two million in profit.

Successful people want to help you with the things they've learned. They want to share their knowledge. One of the biggest mistakes you can make is only talking about yourself in front of someone who has wisdom and advice they can offer to you. Often, you don't even *need* to spend money to connect with smart, successful people—just get around the right person and be genuinely interested in what they've accomplished.

BOOKS

Books are an affordable way to invest in yourself. They can be free if you borrow physical copies or listen to audiobooks through the public library. But I prefer to pay the small amount of money to purchase them—then, I fill them with notes and highlighting.

When I first started reading books, I tried borrowing as much as possible. It hadn't clicked yet that reading books was an *investment* in myself—and worth the twenty dollars. Now, I know how valuable it is to read the wisdom other people have to share. Every book recommendation I get goes into my notes so I can buy the book later.

When I first got involved in door-to-door sales at ABC Windows, I was fucking terrible at leadership. I had very little patience. I blew a ton of people out of the water. I had a hard time training people and giving them the time they needed to learn. I didn't have the emotional regulation, communication, or empathy to lead properly. Eventually, I realized that I was lacking these necessary qualities, but I had no idea how I was going to develop any of them.

Someone recommended the book *The Five Levels of Leadership* by John Maxwell. It was an eye-opening read for me at that time in my life. In fact, it felt like a needed slap in the face. Maxwell described how the first level of leadership—the lowest one—is just having a title. As I was reading the book, I realized that was the highest level of leadership I'd reached: I expected people to listen to me because of my title. But as Maxwell's book went on, it became clear I had a ton to learn. The second and third levels were about building your communication skills and increasing your "personal production"—basically, leading from the front. The pinnacle of leadership is the fourth and fifth levels, where you start developing other leaders. That's where you can really start to make an impact with your business because you're not the only person in the company's organization who can make decisions. I remember thinking, "Holy shit. This seems like a lot of work, and I've got a long way to go, but now I've got a roadmap for my leadership journey." It was so exciting!

When I read a book, I'm not expecting to buy into every single word. I'm looking for one or two golden nuggets that I can apply to my business or my personal life. That's why I read with a pen and highlighter: I look for those nuggets, highlight the crap out of them, and then they're easy to find when I go back to the book later on.

> When you're reading a book, look for one or two golden nuggets that you can apply to your business or personal life.

With that said—if you're a couple chapters in and the book you're reading isn't speaking to you, put it down. I had somebody reach out to me on a group message one time. He asked me, "Hey man, do you think I should finish this book? I'm so bogged down with it, it's taking me forever to read." Then he told me that one of my really good friends—someone I look up to and respect—had told him to see it through and finish it. "But I don't know, I just can't get into it," he wrote. "What do you think?"

I responded, "Fuck that. If you're not feeling it and you're not getting things out of it, just put it down. I would have put it down immediately. Go find a book that you can get some energy out of and that you feel good about. Find one you're aligned with."

Your time is valuable. So don't waste valuable time on a bad book or a book that you're just not ready for yet.

COACHING, CONSULTING, MENTORING

I've already talked in previous chapters about the value of getting good coaches, consultants, and mentors in your corner. I've leveled up in areas of my *health* by working with a personal trainer and nutritionist. I've leveled up in my *leadership* by working with mentors. And I've leveled up in my *business* by bringing in experts in certain key areas that I knew would expand JKR Windows' reach. For example, we've worked with a sales consulting company that primarily partners with door-to-door companies. They build competitions and incentives for us, which makes it fun to ramp up our sales efforts. It's easy to justify what we pay them every month because of the value we get from them.

Just like my attitude with books, I'm looking for those golden nuggets from coaches, consultants, and mentors. If there is even just *one thing* that can improve the way I treat people or improve my leadership—then it's worth the money. That rate of return is enough for me.

But on that note, a word of caution: do your due diligence when it comes to high ticket items like consultants or Mastermind-type conferences. Dig up some credentials, background, or testimonials to make sure that person or group is aligned with your goals. It's up to you to get the value out of an experience—but it's also on you to make sure it offers the value you need in the first place.

I made a mistake last year of impulsively hiring a consultant. It was an expensive hire, and Shandell told me not to do it. I did it anyway. Then, I found out the guy didn't have enough experience under his belt to help me in the ways that I needed. If I had to do it all over again, I would never have spent the money on his consulting. It would have been wiser for me to invest my *time* beforehand, researching what he had to offer.

> Before investing money in a coach or consultant, invest your *time*. Research their experience, read reviews, and get a sense of how specifically they can help you. This is an area where it's important to do your due diligence.

SPECIALIZED TRAINING

If you want to achieve the next level of success, it's important to keep challenging yourself. Commit to always be learning—keep pushing yourself out of your comfort zone. One way I've done that recently is by going to flight school. The specialized training helps me continue to move the needle for myself as a business owner. Even though the training isn't directly related to my business, it opens up a lot of new opportunities. With a pilot's license, I can fly anywhere I need to at the drop of a hat. More importantly, it keeps my brain constantly alert to new information. I'm not letting myself get comfortable—I'm keeping myself on the edge of learning, which makes me more tuned-in to new ideas in my business.

There are also specialized events that can be worth investing in. Some, like the 10X Conference, are basically hyped-up personal development light shows. They're powerful because of their scale—they've got celebrity speakers, and huge audiences, and you get exposure to an entire room of 10,000 people. There's not usually a lot of education offered, but it can still be an inspiring, pivotal experience. I go to those when I want a big boost of energy and excitement.

Workshops and bootcamps tend to offer material that's more educational. You're usually with a smaller group—maybe around 100 people—and they offer training in new skills, like operating your finances, learning a new system or process, and so on. I've gone to a number of specialized training events for speaking, sales, presenting, and marketing.

SOCIAL MEDIA PRESENCE

In this day and age, it's important to build your brand. When I started posting on social media, I was just using a cell phone and posting daily content of my journey through the Grant Cardone mentoring program. That was the beginning of "building my brand" —and all it cost was some of my time and a cell bill I was already paying.

Later, I realized that building a personal brand can be a significant, long-term investment. My social media presence has a lot more polish now—I work with a videographer and a social media team. It's gotten a lot more expensive, both in terms of my time and money. I pay the social media team $6,700 a month to do two posts a day, across five different platforms. That's on top of what I pay the videographer. And the time investment is definitely more than what it used to be. But the results of that investment are growing every day. At the writing of this book, I've got over 120,000 Instagram followers and 87,000 TikTok followers. My Instagram is growing by close to 1,000 followers a week.

There's a financial motivation behind this, of course—you can monetize a personal brand, and that can start to pay off very quickly. But there's also a personal motivation. The way I got started living halfway smart was because I began following Grant Cardone on social media. This was somebody who had built a brand and was telling his story through these channels. And it changed my life.

Now, I'm living into that example. I've connected with many individuals and business owners through social media, many of whom

I've gone on to do consulting with. Between the businesses I've advised and the mentoring I do with a handful of other business owners, I have already started to see this kind of impact on people's lives and businesses.

What would it mean for you to start making an impact like this? Building a social media presence gives you the opportunity to speak into thousands of people's lives, and you can use that platform to inspire and coach. It can feel intimidating to start posting stuff on social media, but it doesn't have to be polished, especially not at first. Everyone has a unique story that holds relevance to some of the millions of people out there. By being honest and vulnerable about the journey you're on, you have the chance to positively impact thousands of people. That's worth your investment of time. It also may be worth your investment of money, down the road.

The definition of "investment" is something you pour your time and resources into, with the expectation that there's going to be a *benefit* for you on the other side. An investment in social media can have that kind of meaningful impact—both for your life and the lives of others.

> The definition of "investment" is something you pour your time and resources into, with the expectation that there's going to be a *benefit* for you on the other side.

You've got to be careful to build the brand you *want* with social media. Some people try to be authentic—they're vulnerable and share their story in a genuine way. That's closer to the direction I've tried to take. But there are other people on social media who put on a show the whole time. They act like an idiot just for the entertainment value. That's not my brand. That's not the kind of network I want to build.

Remember your core values, your lifestyle design, and your purpose. Think about your goals. Get yourself in alignment with who you want to be and where you want to go, and *then* start building your social media presence.

You can't just throw money at an investment opportunity and expect to see it pay off. Once you start making a little money, there's going to be all sorts of people trying to take advantage of you. Bullshit consultants are going to want you to hire them. Entrepreneurs want you to invest in them. And a lot of people will promise they can help you "take shortcuts," building up your passive income. But that's not the way it works. You can never just pay somebody else to make you rich. You've got to do your research to make sure your investments are going toward a valuable opportunity.

> You can never just pay somebody else to make you rich. You've got to do your research to make sure your investments are going toward a valuable opportunity.

I learned this the hard way when I got involved in a consulting platform for starting up an Amazon store. These guys said they would run an Amazon store for me, and I would pay them a percentage of the profits. They talked up how I could make a million dollars if I just let them run this Amazon store for me. It was a complete freaking scam. I spent two years paying consulting fees to these people, and they made a shitload of money. Meanwhile, I was breaking even or barely making a profit. They kept making excuses or telling me another story about how I had to "give the store more time." But it was a bunch of bullshit. Lesson learned: you've got to do your due diligence.

Avoid get-rich-quick schemes. Don't get sucked into working with unqualified coaches or consultants. Get testimonials and second opinions. Otherwise, your "investments" will just lose you money.

INVESTMENT OF TIME

You want to go further faster? If you want to operate at your best, then professional opportunities and development are just scratching the surface. Consider some of these other ways to make sure you're maximizing your potential—ones which require your investment of *time*, even more than your dollars.

PHYSICAL HEALTH

You can't operate at a high level as a business owner and leader if you're treating your body like shit. As a leader, you have to lead by example with every aspect of your life. That includes your personal health. I have a medical practitioner who helps me with bloodwork, manages my vitamins and protocols, and monitors my hormones. I also work with a personal trainer, and I pay attention to my diet and nutrition. When I show up at work or at a networking event, I've got good energy, stamina, and a presence that shows people I take care of myself. That all matters.

> As a leader, you have to lead by example with every aspect of your life. That includes your personal health.

Sleep is an important piece of the puzzle too—and that's the one area where I push my body harder than I should. I used to operate at a high level on three or four hours of sleep every night. Then I would get a twenty-four-hour sickness that I could only attribute to a lack of sleep. My immune system just couldn't keep up with the stress I was putting it through. This is an area where I still need to grow, but I'm learning that rest, recovery, and stretching are just as important as working out, dieting, and seeing my doctor regularly.

MENTAL HEALTH

I've put more emphasis on mental health in my life lately. I worked with a high-performance coach, Micheal Burt, for a little over a year who was *also* working with his own coach. He talked about his interactions with his coach in our sessions—and those conversations brought some new awareness for me. Micheal was hard on himself. He admitted that he didn't communicate with his family well. It felt like he was never making progress. Our issues were different, but they felt similar enough. It helped me realize it's unhealthy to keep going, going, going, and never celebrate the wins. If nothing's ever good enough for you, then you're chasing after something you'll never get.

Now, the next level for me is developing the calm confidence that comes from being a regulated leader—someone who is content with the things he's accomplished, but still hungry for the next level. I'm still searching for the right formula, and I know mental health is a part of it.

OUTSOURCING

One of the best ways you can invest in yourself will actually *create* more time in your schedule—more time to do all the other valuable things you want to do. That's through outsourcing tasks to people who will do the work at a lower cost. This is a way to make money, by saving money. You make time, by saving time.

I'll give you a few examples. There are some incredible people outside of the US who can operate at an extremely high level, but at a fraction of the cost of a full-time local employee. Through networking, I made a connection with a guy who runs most of his business through virtual assistants in the Philippines. I've been able to hire fairly high-level people over there at an inexpensive rate. Those assistants do some of the administrative work that is fairly straightforward but time consuming, like entering data or making spreadsheets—tasks I don't want my top people burning time on. For the price of one person's salary in the US, I have five high-level assistants.

Other staff can be hired as contractors—even some of your highest-level people. My CFO is a contracted, fractional worker for JKR Windows. He takes care of our bookkeeping and tax packages in just a few hours a week. We pay him $60,000 a year, instead of the $300,000 it would cost to keep someone of his caliber on our full-time staff.

We also outsource some things we're not good at. We use the online site Upwork for simple tasks like graphic design, or even complex tasks like data architecture. There are thousands of different genres of expertise on the site, and people from all over the world who can provide value to your team.

> Outsourcing tasks can help you save time and money, while still getting you a great result.

QUALITY TIME WITH LOVED ONES

I devote a ridiculous amount of time to work, which is why I'm so intentional about my time with my family. Just recently, I'd just gotten home after being gone for three days. My girls were waiting up for me when I got in around 11:30 p.m., ready to jump into bed as soon as I got home. They were so excited to see me and hug me. The next morning, I was doing my routine—fitting in my reading, writing my goals, meditating. I came to the last five minutes of this time slot I've set aside for my morning habits, and then I took a look at my calendar. I realized my whole day was booked out, except for one half hour.

I threw a bookmark in my book and tossed it down to go spend those last five minutes getting time with my kids. When I came in, the girls were fighting with each other. That kind of thing used to make my blood boil—I'd explode in a rage and scare them. But I don't do that anymore. I want to share *with them* the lessons I've learned from all this coaching I've received. So, I came in, used my calm voice, and within ninety seconds, I had them both calmed down. We had a cool little conversation about how we treat each other, and then they wanted to show me all the stuff they were playing with. I was reminded that the time I spend with them is so important for them to feel loved and involved in my life.

I said to them, "Hey, my day is booked pretty solid, but I've got a half hour free at 11:30 a.m. What do you girls say about getting some pool time?" They were so excited. That whole morning, while I was filming marketing content for a big event, doing work for the business—the girls were constantly peeking in, wondering if I was done yet.

Finally, I hung up my last call. "It's pool time!" I yelled. We got out to the pool and Ayva saw that I still had my phone—my kids know they're allowed to call me out if I forget to put my phone away during our time together. I've told them, "I need you girls to help me stay accountable to this. When I plan time with you, I want to be totally focused on you. I want to give you my undivided attention, and I don't want any distractions, so tell me to put my phone away. We're going to have fun—just us."

So, little Ayva—eight years old—speaks up and says, "Dad—this is our time. Put the phone away!"

I gave her a high five for calling me out, then stuck the phone back in my office. Then, I ran back outside and did a cannonball into the pool. For that next half hour, we had a blast.

There's only so much time I have to spend with my family. And the more that I spend away from them, the more I realize how big of an impact I have on their lives—and how important it is for me to make it count. So, I block out family time. That investment is part of my schedule. The most important thing to me is to have the support of my family and let them know that I love and care about them enough to put everything else aside. They deserve my undivided attention.

> The most important thing to me is to have the support of my family and let them know that I love and care about them enough to put everything else aside. They deserve my undivided attention.

And I've learned that they don't need a huge *quantity* of time—they need *quality* time. With everything I've got going on with the business, my other ventures, writing a book, putting on an event, the social media stuff—it takes a ridiculous amount of time. If I wasn't intentional about setting aside quality time for my family, I wouldn't be able to get the support from them that I need while I'm doing all that other stuff, especially because I do a lot of it from home. But because I'm intentional about investing the time—carving it out, being present with them, having conversations, letting them know how proud I am of them, giving them love—they're cheering me on.

I also look to incorporate my family into what I'm already doing, in every way possible. I regularly bring Shandell with me when I go to networking events or conferences. She's also in a lot of my Instagram and TikTok videos. I've even had my daughters appear in some videos with me. And just recently, one of my girls asked to start coming along to the gym with Shandell and me. She's waking up at 4:15 *a.m.* to go work out with us. It slows me down a little—I'm doing a lot of teaching at the gym, instead of jumping into my own workout—but it's worth it. I love seeing her absorb some of the same principles that have changed my life. I love that time with my family.

Quality time with the people who love you: that's probably the most important investment you can make in yourself.

But it's not enough to just invest in your *own* personal development. You can only have a kick-ass business if you have a kick-ass team. To have a kick-ass team, you've got to invest in them too.

INVEST IN YOUR TEAM

I heard this saying once. One business owner is talking to another business owner and says, "What if I invest all this money into my people—and they leave?"

The other, more experienced, business owner goes, "What if you *don't* invest any money into your people—and they stay?"

If you don't invest any money into your team's development, you miss out on a huge opportunity. Instead of creating a culture that people are excited to be part of, where they're constantly growing and thriving—you create a culture of stagnancy, where people are less likely to stay. Even if they do show up, they're not bringing anything close to their A game. You want a thriving team? You need to build an environment that changes people's lives.

> You want a thriving team? You need to build an
> environment that changes people's lives.

I want people to love working for JKR Windows. JKR Windows should be a place for people to feel at home, where they have opportunities to grow. I put things in place to motivate my team to keep progressing—things like creating a culture where we constantly talk about our growth and personal development, or scheduling regular performance reviews to help identify and push team members toward their life goals. The environment at our company is one that people are excited to be a part of—one where they go *ALL IN*.

PERSONAL DEVELOPMENT

If there's no expectation for your employees to complete personal development within your company, most people won't do it on their own. What's the result of that? You end up with people who have one year of experience, which they repeat over and over and over. You've got to continue to raise the bar—and raise the *value* you're offering the team to hit that bar. Otherwise, your motivating speeches about personal growth will eventually become irrelevant.

At JKR Windows, we pay over $5,000 per month for all employees to have access to Cardone University, the Grant Cardone training platform. The service offers personal development training in mindset, leadership, communication, closing, and customer service skills. It's a big investment, but we're getting our returns from a team that is always increasing their value to the company. We've also set the expectation within the company culture that we will constantly level up our training, so we all continue to improve. We also have a proprietary JKR University virtual training platform that we're constantly adding content to and evolving to become more effective and efficient in our training process. It is our goal to provide as many tools and resources as we can to help people see success.

One of the best ways you can invest in your team members is to figure out their genius and get them in a spot where their specific skills will be put to maximum effect. The Wealth Dynamics test is a simple test that helps you find out the areas where your people best excel.

I've got a team of incredible, loyal people. But, unless I really tap into what they're best at, they might feel frustration if they're not operating at the high level I hired them for. Tests like Wealth Dynamics help you find out your people's "genius," their strongest skillsets, so you can position them to produce maximum value, which will also increase their sense of fulfillment. When you know what they're good at, you're able to get a ton of productivity out of your people—and increase their level of fulfillment at the same time.

> When you know what your people are good at, you're able to get a ton of productivity out of them—and increase their level of fulfillment at the same time.

There is not always going to be a clear answer, even when you have tools like the Wealth Dynamics test. Expect that you will still need to put in some work to understand what people's strong suits are. When I started up my first company, a power washing business, way back in 2010, I started having Shandell help out with some of the tasks I didn't like, such as invoicing and filing paperwork for licensing. She had picked up balancing the checkbook from her mom growing up, and she was great at it. I had just assumed that some of these other tasks would be right up her alley. I was wrong. She *could* have been good at them, but I didn't take the time to properly teach her and coach her through those tasks. Instead, I got frustrated and angry that she couldn't just figure it out, like I had.

Over time, I realized the problem was mostly mine, and I've worked to develop the patience needed to coach the people who work for me.

I've also worked to learn the things that my team members excel at and enjoy doing, so we can avoid any challenges with unmet expectations and unfinished projects.

NO HANDOUTS

I build up my team. I talk to them about what they're capable of and communicate the expectations we have for them. But here's what I *don't* do: give arbitrary raises just because someone's been at the company for a while. We don't do handouts. Every person is expected to pull their own weight—and I view that as another kind of investment in their motivation.

JKR Windows is working on growing, and that comes with the expectation that you will put in the necessary activity and hours required to contribute to the team. Hitting high numbers can only happen if people pull their weight. You need to invest in your team—but that doesn't mean you just throw money at them. People shouldn't get more unless they're contributing a higher level of work. You have to *add* value. If you want more value, you have to contribute more value.

> If you want more value, you have to contribute more value.

I'm not a handout guy, but that doesn't mean I lead with negativity. I lead with positivity, reminding my team of what I know they're capable of. With the proper training and motivation, they're able to hit their numbers without me holding their hands the entire time.

PERSONAL TOUCH

I used to lead from a place of intimidation and fear. I had an iron fist. But I've realized that's not conducive at all for growth and loyalty. No one wants to work in those environments. Now, I understand that forming positive relationships with my people is another form of investing in my team.

I lead my company with a personal touch. I make a point to have a lot of little conversations in passing with people to show them that I care about what's going on in their lives—I want the best for everybody. We're driving numbers and pushing productivity and growth, but there's another element to what we're doing. We're a family environment where everybody cares about each other and pushes one another up. It's a growth-conducive type of culture that people want to be a part of.

THE ROCKY ROAD OF SELF-IMPROVEMENT

It's not always easy to invest in yourself and your team. Often, it means you're pushing yourself into that area where discomfort meets growth. But that's exactly where you're going to really start to pick up speed.

When I showed up at the Door-to-Door Con (D2DCon) in January 2020, I was intimidated. I had evolved a lot in the two years since my first conference, but networking still felt like a challenge. Everyone there was connected to the door-to-door home improvement industry and we all had plenty in common, but there were around 2,500 people. I felt like a shy little twelve-year-old boy with that many people around.

I was clutching my little notebook and avoided making eye contact. I kept mentally justifying why I wasn't going up to talk to people I wanted to meet: "I'm just here to learn and focus. I don't need to talk to anyone else. That's not going to benefit me."

Finally, I successfully smelled my own bullshit. I knew I was making bogus justifications—it was just me being a little bit nervous. So, I made a commitment to myself to start trying to connect with people.

I spotted a guy wearing a black-and-gold hat with a symbol that looked familiar. I went up to him and asked him, "Remind me what that symbol is? I recognize it but can't remember what it is."

The guy standing next to him said, "Hey, don't I know you?"

I said, "I get that all the time. I always look like somebody's brother or cousin or somebody."

He said, "No, no—I've got it. You're the guy that came into our office the other day."

That's when I recognized him—these two guys were the CEO and COO for another door-to-door windows business. I *had* gone into their office the other day. I was actually trying to recruit one of their salespeople. (I didn't mention that.)

The three of us ended up in the same break-out groups the rest of the day, because we were some of the only window companies at this door-to-door conference. At lunchtime, when I entered the cafeteria area, it was packed. I finally set my food down at one of the only open spots— and it just happened to be at the table where these two guys were sitting.

We talked about our businesses—what they had done, what I had done, our future goals. We talked for so long that most everybody else left the cafeteria. I was pretty proud of my two million in 2019. The owner of this other company, Jared, told me he made six million in total sales in his best year. I thought to myself, "Well, if he can do six million, I know *I* can do six million." My goal for 2020 had been four million, but instantly, I upped my goal to six.

"But," he continued, "my *new* goal for 2020 is ten million."

In my head, I thought, "Fuck it. *I'm* going to do ten million." In one day, my goal went from four million, to six million, to ten million in revenue.

"I know you want to do big things," Jared said to me. "The guy that's running this event, Sam Taggart, has some consulting that I've used in the past. If you're serious, I would talk to him about what packages he offers."

I took his recommendation seriously, even though the idea intimidated me. For the past few months, I'd watched all of Sam Taggart's social media stuff. I'd just seen him speak to an audience of 2,500 people—an audience that had all paid and gathered to come to *his* conference. This felt like a very high-level dude to me.

And I still didn't like talking to people.

That afternoon—feeling super nervous—I headed over to find Sam. He'd set up this big booth in the middle of the convention. But when I arrived, he wasn't there. That was kind of a relief. Instead, I introduced myself to one of the guys who worked for him. His name was Jake, and we hit it off. I was nervous, but he was being the nicest guy.

He handed me a brochure. "You should come back later and talk to Sam," he said.

The thought still intimidated me. The Grant Cardone mentor program had been a catalyst for my success, but consulting was a whole new thing, and I didn't have a clue how much it would cost. Besides, I hadn't magically gotten good at initiating conversations in the last two days. I thanked Jake and left, feeling like maybe it wasn't meant to be.

As I was walking away, I noticed someone wearing a bright red sports jacket. He was riding an electric Segway toward the big booth in the middle of the convention. It was Sam Taggart.

I was *this close* to not going back. But I asked myself, "Dude, what's the worst that can happen?" I could tell this was going to be an important transition in my life.

So, I went back to the booth. That same feeling of anxiety came back as I walked up to Sam.

The guy's very inviting. He saw me coming and gave me a big smile. "How are you doing?" He shook my hand warmly. "Jake said you wanted to talk. What do you have going on?"

I don't think I even told him my name. I just launched into it. "This guy, Jared, who you've been working with, recommended that I work with you. I actually own a replacement window business as well that's similar to his. And he told me about some of the work you guys have done together. He said his goal was ten million. I think I can do ten million this year. So, I'm interested in learning about what that would look like for me."

He grinned and slapped me on the back. "I hear this kind of talk all the time. But if you're serious, I can help you get to those numbers." That remark fired me up a little. His little slap on the back and the tone of his voice implied he doubted I was capable of those numbers—which, of course, made me determined to show him I was. He started showing me a couple of his consulting packages. We talked a little more and then he pointed at the brochure. "This is the one that I think would make the most sense for you."

It was $60,000.

That seemed like a huge amount of money to me. It seemed crazy. I started asking more questions about what I was going to get for that sum of money. "I'm just trying to make sense of where the value is going to come from," I said. "Sixty *thousand* dollars."

Then he said, "You told me your goal is to get from two to ten million this year. If we were to help you hit even *half* of that ten-million-dollar goal—don't you think that sixty thousand is going to pay for itself?"

He sold me. I didn't have sixty thousand on me. But I decided this was what I needed to get to the next level. He set up a payment plan and split the initial payment between two different credit cards.

Sam's training was solid—but it was up to me to get the full value of that sixty thousand. Sam Taggart's program wasn't going to magically make JKR Windows worth ten million. He gave me a blueprint to follow, and the program had account reps check in with me a few times. I went to a couple of meetups with other people in the program. But it was all on me to do the work. The program was just a catalyst, giving me tools and direction to apply to my business. Those tools made it possible for JKR Windows to start recruiting and building a team with core values and expectations, even in the middle of a pandemic. While everybody else was scared and staying home, we were shoving out any negativity and uncertainty. There was only one direction for us to go: forward.

And by the end of 2020, we had hit ten million.

There's a risk when you invest your time and your money. You might hesitate, thinking of what else you could do with those resources—and what if it doesn't pay off?

But there's a greater risk if you *don't* invest in yourself and your team: stagnation. There's only so much anyone can accomplish with their own perspective and experience. Most people live their lives, repeating the same patterns. They very rarely have any significant growth in their life.

You need outside perspective and wisdom to take yourself to the next level. Invest in opportunities, advice, and mentors through expanding your network. Invest in knowledge through books, coaches, and training. Invest in your brand by building up your social media platforms. Invest time in your health and your family. *Create* time by investing in outsourcing. Invest in your team by giving them growth opportunities and helping them find their niche.

That's how you go further faster.

And remember—with all these areas of investment: you get out what you put in. Do the work necessary to maximize every penny of your financial investment and every second of your time investment. Don't half-ass it. Go *ALL IN*.

ACTION STEPS

Growth requires your investment in new opportunities, relationships, training, and time. It also requires your investment in your team.

- What networking opportunity can you set up for yourself? How can you challenge yourself in order to make the most of that opportunity?
- Name a book you want to read, a person you want to learn from, and a training you want to plug into.
- Think about ways you can start to build your social media brand. Remember: to start with, all you need is a cell phone, a user profile, and the commitment to post regular content. If you've already started building your brand, you might be ready to invest in a social media team. Invest in your future by getting yourself out of obscurity.
- Look at your daily schedule and carve out time to work out, and time for your loved ones. When you get that quality time with your loved ones, put the fucking phone away. Get rid of all distractions so you can focus on the people who make your life great.

- Name some specific ways you want to increase your investment in your team. What first step will you take in that direction when you go into work tomorrow?

With any investment opportunity, you'll get out of it the same amount you put in. Invest *yourself*. Make the most of these chances to grow by going *ALL IN*.

CHAPTER 10

Communicate the Hard Way

SET CLEAR EXPECTATIONS AND LEAD DIFFICULT CONVERSATIONS

I F YOU WANT to be a successful leader, spouse, and parent, you've got to clearly communicate your expectations of others and clarify responsibilities. And when things get hard, your ability to succeed will be directly related to your ability to have difficult conversations and lead others toward a positive outcome. That's why effective communication is such an important accelerator for going further faster.

I was on a podcast recently, and the host, Tracy Duhs, said to me, "When I first met you, you had a smile on your face, and you were saying hi to everyone. You have an energy and a presence about you that others can feel. You can tell your mindset is 'I'm excited about this, and I'm showing up, and I'm doing it with integrity. I'm giving it my all and I'm excited to be here.' People *feel* that."

I wasn't always like that.

When I first got started in sales, I had a coach and a mentor who was helping me learn the ropes. He'd show up to the office every day and walk past me sitting in the conference room, looking over my script and study materials, getting ready to make a recruiting call. And every day, he'd see me staring down with a scowl on my face.

I was coming from being a carpenter and mechanic, smoking weed for most of my teen years, never needing to interact with people. I didn't understand the power of your facial expressions—and I always had this scowl on my face. Even when I tried to smile, it seemed awkward and forced. I was like a little kid trying to smile for a picture who didn't know how to make it look natural.

This one day, my coach came in and walked past me, looking through the big conference room window. He smiled at me—I can still see his big, cheesy smile in my head. He and his wife were always smiling—and it never seemed forced either. I wasn't used to hanging out with people who smiled all the time.

I didn't smile back. I was in the zone, focusing on work. He doubled back and poked his head into the conference room.

"What's up, man?" he asked. "Everything all right?"

I looked up from my notes. "Yeah, I'm just making some phone calls."

He stepped into the conference room and closed the door behind him. "I walked all the way by this window with a big smile on my face, trying to get a reaction out of you. But you just scowled at me the whole way by!"

I did? That was news to me. "I was just deep in thought," I said.

"You don't want people to feel like they're in trouble every time they see you, do you?" he asked. "Because when I walked by, from the look on your face—I felt like something was *wrong*." He paused, then sat down in one of the chairs and folded his hands on the table. "I know we've talked about this before, man...But you have really got to do something about your *face*."

I will never forget that line: "You have got to do something about your *face*."

My first instinct was to get pissed. I wanted to say, "Fuck you, dude, I'm in here working my ass off—and all you can say is some negative shit like that?"

But I stopped myself. I thought, "Here's something I struggle with. So, I'd better go head on with it." It became this new challenge for myself. I wanted to get good at smiling. I started observing other people who had great smiles, and realized they made me feel so welcome. That's what I wanted.

So, I did something with it. For a period of time after that day, I would turn my rearview mirror down so it was pointed right back at me, and I practiced my smile. I still do it occasionally, just to practice and make sure I've still got it dialed in.

When I first did it, it was this awkward, quarter-smile—I'd see some of my weird teeth and feel self-conscious. It was challenging in the beginning. But slowly, I started to realize how much power my smile had. Especially, when going door-to-door—if I had a scowl, people weren't likely to even open the door. When I looked pleasant, they were a lot more willing to talk to me.

It's become a lot easier to smile than it used to be. I can whip it out when I'm walking by someone at the grocery store, or when someone flips me off when they're driving—I'll just give them a smile and a thumbs-up. I smile everywhere I go now.

It's been a game changer. In fact, learning to smile has helped me make a lot of money. People tend to trust you more when you look pleasant. I'm a big, intimidating guy, so without a smile, I'm even more intimidating. When it comes to building relationships and having people warm up to me faster, I *have* to be intentional about holding my smile. I know that if I get in my head for even thirty seconds, I go from being pleasant and approachable to, "Holy shit, this guy's an asshole." I have a serious resting bitch face. But when I smile, I give off a completely different first impression, and it's changed my life. It even changes my energy—it's really hard to be in a negative headspace when you've got a smile on your face.

Learning to smile took practice for me. And that's true for communicating well in every sense. Without practicing and working at your communication, you're dealing with the equivalent of my resting bitch face. You may not even know what kind of messages you're sending, or what kind of opportunities you're missing out on.

Part of being a good leader is making people feel good. It's guiding communication in a positive direction. Two of the biggest ways you can do that are by setting clear expectations and learning how to manage difficult conversations well. These might seem like small leadership tactics—just like a smile is a small part of your entire appearance—but they'll make a world of difference in your ability to go further faster.

> Being a good leader means you guide communication in a positive direction. Learn to set clear expectations and steer difficult conversations toward a positive outcome.

SET CLEAR EXPECTATIONS

The less detailed you are about your expectations, the more disappointed you will be with the outcome. As a leader or manager, it's your responsibility to communicate expectations and responsibilities.

PROFESSIONAL EXPECTATIONS

I got my start working in construction for my dad. He wasn't a clear communicator. He just expected you to get the job done. Over time, I compiled enough knowledge and common sense to take what little direction he gave and turn out a positive outcome. I got the job done.

I carried that into my adult life: the confidence of knowing I could figure things out, even with little direction. But that doesn't translate well into running your own business. If you tell your team, "I need this project done by next week" and don't give any direction or instruction, you're setting your team up to fail.

Don't assume your team has the same capabilities as you, or will make the same decisions. The reality is that everybody has different things they're good at. If you want your team to succeed, you need to set expectations and give clear instructions.

> Don't assume your team has the same capabilities as you, or will make the same decisions. If you want your team to succeed, set clear expectations.

There are managers or leaders who communicate a low level of instruction, but have a high expectation of the outcome. This is a common management style for someone in the early stages of leadership. These managers give their team very little to work with but expect their people to do it perfectly and not let them down. As a result, they tend to nitpick the shit out of their direct reports all the way through the process. Don't be like them.

Shitty Managers belittle and ridicule team members for negative outcomes. This takes away the team member's opportunity to learn or become better next time, because all they can think about is the way the Shitty Manager made them feel. These managers are either completely unaware of their deficiency in this area, or not willing to take on the extra communication required to provide an environment where their people can improve.

That's how I did things early on when I was coming up in management in the construction industry. My style was constant belittling and negativity. There wasn't a whole lot of coaching and mentoring involved. I had an attitude of, *If you can't do this, you're no good to me.* I was a Shitty Manager, and it didn't get me very far. I didn't start going further faster until I seriously worked on my communication and made my leadership positive.

Be a Positive Leader instead. Give clear instructions and expectations. If you spell these things out in an email, you can point your team back to it as a resource. You pump your team up with confidence and give them the belief that they can get the job done. While your team is going through a project, you give them the freedom to learn some hard lessons on their own. You help them improve for next time, in a tactful but encouraging way. It took me a couple years, but that's finally the kind of leader I became.

Learning how to clearly set expectations is especially important if you want to scale. *You* need to communicate effectively so that you can teach your *managers* how to communicate effectively. I've had to learn how to help my key people properly delegate tasks. Those tasks may now be second nature to them but will take time and patience to pass off to someone else. Many mistakes can be avoided if the pass off is done properly, but if there isn't a clear understanding about how it needs to play out, people will default to making assumptions. And you'll hear your managers venting about the results of their own poor management: "I told them how to do it. I don't understand why there are so many mistakes and important aspects of this task falling through the cracks."

If you don't take the time to learn effective communication skills and train your managers to do likewise, there will always be more mistakes than necessary. Those will likely cost the company money or, even worse, build tension in those important team relationships. But by honing your own communication skills, you can help create a culture of clear direction, setting expectations, and establishing regular touch points to make sure tasks are done to the expected standards.

Even high-level people need to be reminded about your expectations for how high the bar should be set, and what their top priorities are. The reality is, most people just go through the motions, even your top people. They can easily get sucked into busywork, and then they feel too busy to keep their eyes on the most important priorities. As a leader, you need to reset the focus on your expectations for them. Call out their bullshit, if need be. Put things back into perspective about their main goals, their target numbers, and remind them that you're not interested in performing at an average, ordinary level—you've committed as an organization to do extraordinary things.

Part of improving my communication as a leader has required that we take our standard operating procedures (SOPs) seriously as a company. When we did, they became a great tool for us. SOPs have helped our people become efficient at the things we hired them for.

> SOPs are any task that's going to be repeated within the company and duplicated with other team members.

Here's how we've developed our SOPs, whether it's for payroll, operations, marketing, or anything else. When we hire someone, I sit down with the new hire and an assistant who's taking notes about the training instructions the whole time. These notes turn into a bullet-point list that becomes more detailed throughout the process, and eventually becomes the final SOP. The final SOP gets sent to the person who owns that project with as much clear instruction as possible, and it's there for any other new hires who need to do the same task.

Things go a lot smoother when you get used to this rhythm with people. That SOP becomes a resource that team members can always refer back to.

You also need to *keep* referring to the SOP, and I'll give you an example as to why this matters so much. My mom was my first employee. She had been working in the banking industry, so there was a lot of new information for her to take in. I trained her on the payroll process and ordering windows, along with a few other tasks she'd need to know for the company. I put together a handful of bullet points for a process like ordering windows.

For her to send in a contract and field work order, she had to know where the field work order would be. So, the first bullet point was:

- Give information on where all ordering resources are located.

We also had two computer screens set up at every station where somebody does window ordering so they can have everything laid out right in front of them. The second bullet point was:

- Pull up all of your resources on two screens so everything you need is right in front of you.

I would have it on the screens and on printouts in front of me. I went on and explained each next step. We created a clear SOP, and things went well for a while. My mom got the hang of it and the process became second nature for her—which meant she stopped referencing the SOP. It ended up getting lost somewhere in the deep abyss of the interweb once she got comfortable with the ordering process.

Later, we hired someone else to help my mom with some of these administrative tasks. We couldn't find the original SOP for ordering windows, so my mom trained her using more general instructions, based on her own experience. The new person wasn't great about asking questions to make sure she was on track. She also didn't have the same level of dedication my mom did to make sure each order was perfect. *And*, we also missed the mark on our regular touch points and audits over the first few months to make sure we were keeping things on track.

We started having a lot of issues. In fact, we learned a lot of very expensive lessons during this time. Mainly, it became clear that providing clear instructions in the form of a very detailed SOP was incredibly important. We needed to spell out expectations about the quality of work required, the time frame for work to be completed, and set up more coaching and mentoring early on to make sure things would go smoothly for the first several weeks while the new person became familiar with their tasks. Our SOPs evolved from a handful of bullet points to a comprehensive, detailed, step-by-step process complete with quality checks and accountability. It became clear to me that we needed *that* level of specificity in our SOPs to have consistent results.

Take the responsibility to create an SOP for every process under your direction. No matter who's doing the task, or where that person goes, or however many people you need to train—the SOP should spell out the clear best practice.

Uncertainty creates failure. That's why it's so important to set clear expectations. Even good employees won't be very productive without direction. Give them a regular sequence with emphasized priorities so that your team isn't just spinning their wheels.

> Uncertainty creates failure. An SOP can create certainty by spelling out the clear best practice.

Strong leadership will make your team efficient, and you can provide that leadership by setting expectations with a clear sequence. Redefine expectations on a regular basis to ensure everyone stays on the same page.

Setting clear expectations isn't just important at the office, though—it's equally important to do with your people at home.

PERSONAL EXPECTATIONS

Even in your personal life, you can optimize your relationships by setting clear expectations. Do this in a loving, tactful way and remember that your *own* example will speak louder than words to communicate what you expect from others. It's important for me to have high standards for myself because I ask a lot of other people. And anyone can see whether or not my actions are aligned with my words. I don't want to be the kind of leader that asks people to "Do as I say, not as I do." So, I try to embody the standard that I'm asking other people to meet.

My kids know I think it's incredibly important to be thoughtful about what we put in our bodies and to eat healthy. Especially after all my years of putting crap into my body, I've learned how critical it is to consume good fuel. My wife and I have filled the house with healthy, good foods that will nourish our kids.

In spite of that, all three of my kids have limited discipline in this area—which you might expect at their ages. The other day, I came home to find my seventeen-year-old son lying on the couch. He was wearing all black and looked pretty dirty after riding motocross all afternoon. He told me he felt lousy. I asked, "What have you eaten today?"

He shrugged. "Not a lot. I ate a Subway sandwich for lunch. That's about it."

"Have you been drinking water?" I asked.

He shook his head. "Not really."

At this point, it was around 7:30 in the evening. I shook my head. "You know better than that. If you're going to exhaust a ton of energy riding motocross, you need to put some good, solid fuel into your body so you have the energy you need to go do that at a high level. We've talked about this stuff."

He nodded. About ten minutes later, he told me he was going out. I assumed he was heading to meet up with friends, but about thirty minutes later, he came back through the door. He was holding a water cup—and a McDonald's bag.

For me, seeing a McDonald's bag in the hand of someone I love makes me want to start spouting profanities.

As tactfully as possible, I said, "Bro. You've already told me you're feeling like shit. That McDonald's burger is about the worst *possible* thing you could eat." I explained that I knew he paid attention to the things I do and what I choose to put into my body. "It's important for me to be a good example to you and your sisters because I know you're watching me. That's why you'll never see me walk into this house with McDonald's. And *you're* an example to your little sisters—they're seeing what choices *you* make about what you eat."

"I didn't know what else to eat," he said.

I walked him into the kitchen. We started looking in the fridge at some of his options. He asked me if I could help him make some bone broth and some eggs so that he could feel good enough to go take a shower and go to bed.

As we were heating up the bone broth, my daughter got home from a friend's house, carrying twelve cupcakes that she'd decorated. The cupcakes were beautiful—she was very proud of them. But as soon as she came into the kitchen, it was obvious to me that *she* felt lousy too. She was looking green and clutching her stomach.

"What have you eaten today?" I asked her.

She rattled off what they ate at her friend's house: cookies, the cupcake frosting, hot chocolate, cupcakes. I'm just shaking my head. She hadn't had *any* real food. "Honey, you know that stuff doesn't agree with you. You always feel gross when you have a lot of sugary stuff like that."

The McDonald's burger went into the trash. The twelve cupcakes—after all of us had admired them and told her what a beautiful decorating job she'd done—also went into the trash. Both kids made that decision on their own.

I sometimes get impatient to have to repeat some of these personal expectations. There are certain things I've had to tell my kids so many times, it's frustrating to have to do it again. But that's part of being a parent, and it's also true of being a leader. Expect that you're going to need to say the same shit, over and over and over. Do it in a tactful way, otherwise you're going to get more resistance and it won't sink in. But if you repeat those lessons in a tactful, loving way, then every time you restate expectations, they'll sink in a little bit more. You're planting seeds that will eventually empower them to make those positive decisions on their own. And remember—*especially* in your personal relationships where it matters the most—your own actions speak loudest about your values and expectations.

EXPECT TO DO MORE THAN OTHERS

No matter what type of partnership I'm in, and regardless how someone else shows up, I make a commitment to bring 100 percent effort to the relationship. That's true whether it's my marriage, or with my kids, or with my employees.

That doesn't mean I'm not intentional about trying to set us up for success from the get-go: I communicate as clearly as possible what each of our roles are. I lay out what our responsibilities are, and what we both bring to the table. I try to optimize the relationship by getting those things clear from the beginning.

But if my partner, employee, or wife doesn't bring their A game—that doesn't matter. I'm still going to push myself to bring *my* A game. Things are never going to go sour in a relationship because of me. I always want to be willing to be the person in the relationship who does more.

> Things are never going to go sour in a relationship because of me. I always want to be willing to be the person in the relationship who does more.

What does that look like? Let's say you haven't specified clear expectations and your partner isn't holding up their commitments, so you're feeling some resentment. Part of giving 100 percent is having *humility* when tensions come up. There's a difference between "being humble" and "having humility." The definition of being humble is thinking less of *yourself*. Having humility is thinking of *others more*.

So, if I'm in a situation where I know I'm putting in more effort, I push myself to consider where the other person might be coming from. I ask myself, "Who knows what that person has going on in their life that's limiting them from giving 100 percent effort?" I try to build up my understanding so that when we talk, I can be curious about what's going on, rather than getting defensive and making accusations. Regardless of how they're contributing, though, their effort shouldn't change my level of effort. I made this commitment, and I will give everything I have to make this work.

Resentment typically comes from people who are still learning to communicate their own expectations. If you're good at communicating, take on the responsibility to help the other person learn to communicate more clearly. Show them they're safe to be honest with you, and help them understand the benefits of being up-front with expectations. Bring them back up to the level they need to be at for this partnership to continue to work at a high level.

If your partnership is experiencing tension, recommunicate expectations. Reference any commitments you two made to each other, and review what you both said you would each bring to the partnership. Communicate in a tactful way—don't rub it in the other person's face. That's when it becomes a power play.

If you have these kinds of conversations early, then resentment and power plays never become an issue. You can avoid a lot of future challenges by simply clarifying expectations from the start. Still—if someone doesn't follow through on their end—don't get upset about them not pulling their weight "50-50." Forget about 50-50. Your expectation for yourself should be to give 100 percent effort, no matter what the other person is doing.

ALL IN.

LEADING DIFFICULT CONVERSATIONS

Pretty much across the board, your success will be directly proportionate to the amount of *value* you bring to the marketplace. Leadership is a high-value quality, and one of the most important components of leadership is having difficult conversations.

Therefore: your success will be directly proportionate to your ability to initiate difficult conversations and then steer them toward a positive outcome.

> Your success will be directly proportionate to your ability to initiate difficult conversations and then steer them toward a positive outcome.

Granted, definitions of success vary. If you're only interested in making money, you may not need to worry about leading difficult conversations in a positive direction. These days, you could make a lot of money by just playing video games. But try putting a gamer who's used to blowing shit up for eight hours a day into a team environment where difficult conversations need to happen sometimes. Yeah. They might struggle.

I consider a successful life to be a *whole* life—one with positive relationships, physical health, fulfilling work, and financial freedom. That means, as a leader, I'd better know how to initiate and lead difficult conversations.

One of the things I get the most praise for from the other CEOs I hang out with is my directness. If a difficult conversation needs to be had, I don't want to let too much time go by. Tensions don't typically get better with time, they get worse—that's why it's better to rip the Band-Aid off and confront the issue head on.

Granted, that's not easy. The majority of people are nonconfrontational. They don't want to be direct in these difficult conversations because they don't want to hurt anyone's feelings. So, they beat around the bush. Or maybe they don't initiate a conversation at all. Instead, they use sarcasm and passive-aggressive humor to communicate they want something to change.

Here's the problem with that: the person in question never gets the clarity they need to make a change. You drag out a problem that could be solved with one clear, direct conversation. And you can create *more* tension and resentment on your team because people start questioning where they stand. You foster a culture of passive-aggressive negativity, rather than honest dialogue that shows respect for the other people involved.

It's better, kinder, more productive, and healthier for everyone in the long run for you to learn how to initiate and lead difficult conversations toward a positive outcome.

Here's how I define a difficult conversation: you need to communicate hard feedback that could lead to negative emotions. And you've got to deal with these conversations tactfully because the outcome matters.

A difficult conversation is one where you need to communicate hard feedback that could lead to negative emotions, and you've got to deal with these conversations tactfully because the outcome matters.

Most people don't put thought into these conversations because they're so wrapped up in their own strong emotions. If you're not tactful or intentional, you'll enter the conversation like a bull in a china shop. You won't put a lot of thought into the outcome you want, which means things can easily get heated. Relationships get tarnished that way. Things get said that probably shouldn't have gotten said. That's why it's important to keep a cool, calm, and regulated presence in these conversations.

I used to be that person who would get fired up whenever conversations got difficult. I kept stirring the pot and saying a bunch of dumb shit. It wasn't my intention, but that's how it went because of my inexperience as a leader and my upbringing. I've had to be intentional about improving in this area—and I have. With experience and effort, I've learned to be the bigger person in the conversation and stay focused on a positive outcome.

Expect to put in a lot of reps and a lot of practice with this. It will take time for you to get comfortable leading difficult conversations, and even more time for you to feel truly confident in leading them well. Just focus on being a little bit better every time.

With experience and effort, you can learn to be the bigger person in the conversation and stay focused on a positive outcome.

I've had to navigate a lot of difficult conversations over the past four years with JKR Windows. Once I learned how to focus on achieving a positive outcome and keep myself calm and regulated, those conversations consistently ended in a good place. I usually end up shaking hands with the other person and saying, "I'm glad we had this conversation."

Those experiences taught me great lessons I want to pass on to you:

- **Take notes ahead of time.** These aren't just difficult conversations. They're also crucial. If you take ten or fifteen minutes to plan out what you're going to say, it's a lot more likely you'll say what needs to be said. Lay out the key points that you want to talk about so you don't forget half of the shit you need to address.
- **Identify the positive outcome you want.** In my preparation for these difficult conversations, I identify the outcome I hope to achieve and then figure out how I'm going to reverse engineer things to bring that outcome about. If you don't identify a target outcome, the conversation just becomes a platform to vent your emotions. That will cause the other person's walls to go up immediately, and anything you say after that is pointless. But when you identify a positive outcome, you can keep a better handle on your emotions and guide the conversation in that direction. You're bringing a productive plan to the table, which will help ensure the conversation ends in a good place.
- **Ask questions.** When I take my notes, I think through all the scenarios and possibilities of how this conversation can go. I'll realize, "Fuck, that's going to trigger him" when I think about what I could do or say. Asking questions is a way you can address issues without triggering someone else. And rather than asking a question rhetorically, like you already know the answer, ask questions *from a position of curiosity*. I wouldn't say to somebody, "You were supposed to hit 900 doors this week. What the hell happened? You only hit 300." That's going to trigger someone to get defensive and angry. Instead, I'd

ask something like, "Is there something going on that I don't know about? Is there anything I can help with?" These sorts of questions help bring someone's walls down. It lets them know that this isn't me nitpicking the shit out of them. I truly care about their personal situation and want to know if there's something going on. I want to help them get past it. And on that note...

- **Bring their walls down.** People are nervous about these kinds of conversations. They usually know when something is coming, and they want you to cut right to the chase. So, don't give them a bunch of compliments and fluffy shit first. When you lead with the fluffy stuff, and then go into all the things this person isn't doing well, it's a huge letdown. It's a ding to their confidence and makes them feel like the positive stuff you said was a bunch of bullshit. Instead, be as up-front as possible. I usually lead with something like, "We've got to talk about some difficult things today. But we're going to get a positive outcome out of this, I promise." That way, you set the stage for a productive conversation.

- **Maintain a calm, regulated presence.** In the past, whenever I got fired up, I would say a bunch of stupid shit. Now, I have a higher awareness of the negative impact these conversations can have on my relationship with another person if I don't stay regulated. It's easy to get irritated and defensive with people in these sorts of difficult conversations—and that's especially true when you're in it with someone who knows you really well, like a spouse or business partner. But those people can also help you be more self-aware. If you can sense you're starting to lose your cool—or if the other person points that out—step away and calm down. Recognize when you're no longer in a place where you can be productive. Come back to the conversation when you're regulated and start things again, focusing on reaching a positive outcome. Preparing ahead of time will also help you keep a calm, focused presence. You can also help yourself stay regulated when you...

- **Slow down your reactions.** Take a step back and count to ten. See if it's still a big deal after you count to ten. It's one of the simplest things you can do, and it sounds cliché, but it works. My mom and aunts used to tell me that a bunch when I was a kid. Back when I was really unstable and reactive, it was easy for me to blow up and say a bunch of shit I regretted. Afterward I would wonder to myself, "Why can't I just fucking chill out for a second and think about what I say?" Each time I wondered that, it got a little easier for me to slow down and become more aware of what I wanted to say.
- **Review agreed-upon commitments.** I rely a lot on my company's core values—consistency, dependability, and commitment to excellence—to have these difficult conversations. If my employee "Joe" only hit 300 of 900 doors that he was supposed to hit this month, I can point to that core value of "dependability" and ask him a question like, "Can we depend on you to hit the numbers we've agreed to?" Both of us can recognize that only meeting a third of his numbers is a sign he's not living up to these core values. If there's nothing going on behind the scenes, then there's no excuse for him to not be living up to team expectations. My job as a leader is to hold team members accountable to the expectations we've set.
- **Stay focused on a positive outcome.** Remember to keep your focus on the positive outcome you identified in your preparation. Sometimes, that evolves because I always want to include the other person in forming the solution, and the other person's perspective could be completely different. I want them to know that I'm open for discussion in achieving an outcome we both feel good about. You can also involve them in figuring out *how* to make the positive outcome a reality. In fact, you might even get some valuable feedback that can help the business as a whole. The majority of JKR Windows' systems and processes have come about as a result of these types of conversations,

combining my people's ideas with small pieces of my input to bring them to reality.

- **End well.** Let's say, in this case, you know the other person isn't going to be happy with the outcome. Maybe you're letting them go, or creating a boundary that limits their presence in your life. There's no right way to handle those situations, but there *is* a tactful and a not-so-tactful way. The *not* tactful way means you blow up and tell someone exactly how you feel, and you're all belligerent and emotional. Don't do that. If you're angry at this person, write an email and get all the angry shit off your chest— then, *delete* it. I've written a lot of those messages, but I don't ever send them. I know nothing good would come from sending the whole message—it would only harm the relationship. So: delete the whole thing, then write something a little more tactful that's going to produce a positive outcome. If you've realized some of the things in that message need to be addressed, do it in person. You don't want to burn any bridges—especially if it's a family member or a longtime business partner who will probably still have some kind of presence in your life. You want to keep the relationship in as good of a place as possible.
- **Be public with praise, and private with difficult conversations.** I heard this from a mentor of mine one time. He said, "Praise the type of behavior you want repeated. If you focus on the wrong behavior, you get the same result, so you may as well focus on the right things and handle the rest behind closed doors." I've found this to be excellent advice. When you spend meeting time talking about all the shit you're not happy with, you end up creating tensions in the group, which usually leads to more negative behavior. Only publicly recognize *the things you want more of* in a group. Handle difficult conversations behind closed doors, and do it tactfully with a focus on a positive outcome.

> In a group setting, only publicly recognize *the things you want to see more of.*

Handling difficult conversations well is something that you'll get better at over time. When I first got clean, I was so abrasive with people. I'd walk into my dad's place and see him watching some negative TV show, and I'd just grab the remote and turn it off. "This is a bunch of negative shit," I'd say. That didn't go over very well. If I saw one of my brothers smoking, I'd slap the cigarettes out of their mouths. They didn't like that either.

Be intentional about doing even just a little bit better next time. Buy into your self-improvement. Tact is something that comes with experience. With practice, you learn to create a harmony between getting the point across, keeping yourself regulated, and helping the other person stay in a positive frame of mind. You don't want someone to feel demoralized and flattened after a conversation with you. You want them to go out and deliver.

These conversations can make or break relationships. If you don't learn to do them well, you could leave a string of burned bridges behind you. But by pushing yourself to grow in this area, you can actually strengthen your relationships, recognize the positive behavior you want to see more of, and create win-win scenarios for everyone. *That's* a strategy to go further faster.

BROTHER TO BROTHER

I recently had to have a difficult conversation with my brother Jared. He was the sales manager for my northern Utah office. I had another guy, Everett, in the exact same position as him, and Everett is absolutely flourishing. He's become a great leader, his team is doing incredible, he's got great training systems and processes in place, and he's got buy-in from everybody. Meanwhile, Jared was constantly frustrated, overwhelmed, overworked, and complaining.

In the past, we'd had many conversations about how this management position was the opportunity he wanted. He wanted the ability to grow within the company. But the responsibilities and extra hours started to become a lot for him. The two of us had conversations over and over, trying to make sense of how he could be successful in this position. But the lack of results made it seem like we were just spinning our wheels. It started to seem like this wasn't a good fit. I realized we needed to have a difficult conversation about Jared moving to a different position.

And we needed to have it soon. I could see frustration and negativity building on Jared's team, and in Jared himself. I knew that a bunch of shit could happen if I didn't handle this right away. So, I told Jared I needed to chat with him.

Before the conversation, I took about fifteen minutes to get in a room by myself. I shut the door, cleared away all distractions, and got a notepad out. Then, I just thought through how I wanted the conversation to end. Once I figured that out, I reverse engineered it so that the conversation would ideally lead there. I wrote down the things that were frustrating me and the challenges for the team, then tried to think of the most tactful way to approach each one. I wanted to explain things in a way that wouldn't deteriorate our relationship at all, but just point out the importance of the move.

By the end of that prep time, I had seven bullet points. I didn't have those in front of me during the conversation—but the thought process and preparation prepared me to be calm, cool, collected, regulated, and handle it professionally. My number one focus was to get this resolved with a positive outcome.

Jared could see it coming—but even *he* was surprised by how well the conversation went. It only took us about thirty minutes. I knew what I was going to say, and I said all of it with a cool head. We decided to move him to a sales position, which is an area he's extremely good at. It would mean less responsibility but would give him the opportunity for a higher income. He felt good about that change, there was no damage done to our relationship, and it freed me up to get the right person into that management role.

I heard later from one of our other brothers that Jared was surprised by his own reaction to the conversation. He thought he was going to blow his lid and get fired up, but he said he actually felt pretty calm and collected. He told my other brother, "The way Jefferson approached it, and his calmness, and the way he explained things—it just helped me understand that this was the right decision."

I used to be the guy that blew up at people. I would yell, I would break shit—especially if I was drunk, I wouldn't give a second thought to spouting off. And even still—it's not like I enjoy difficult conversations. There's still a hesitation and uncertainty I feel before each one of these difficult interactions. There's even a level of fear. No one likes doing these.

But, as the owner of a company and as someone who wants good relationships with my family, I've pushed myself to grow in this area. Now, I've got a reputation as a strong leader and communicator—not just with people *in* my company, but also with people outside my company and across the entire home services industry. People know we have a strong culture in my company, that we've grown the company fast, and that people like working for me. I'm proud of that—because I was *not good* at my communication, at one point. I scowled instead of smiled. I made assumptions, rather than setting clear expectations. I burned bridges, rather than leading difficult conversations toward a positive outcome.

In every single one of those areas, I put in the work to *learn*. I exposed myself to other great leaders and studied how they approached communication in their leadership. I asked questions about their mentality and the preparation that went into difficult conversations.

And I didn't get defensive when someone gave me a criticism like, "You really need to do something about your *face*." Instead, I leaned into the challenge. I embraced the discomfort. I put in the work to grow and did things a lot of people would laugh at, like practicing my smile in the fucking rearview mirror.

I've gotten unstuck. I learned to accelerate. I'm going further faster.

All because I went *ALL IN*.

ACTION STEPS

Your relational health and professional success require that you learn to set clear expectations and steer difficult conversations toward a positive outcome.

- Think about the last time you asked someone to do something. How clear were you on your instructions on how it should be done? Did the person do it to your expectations? If not—could they have performed better with clearer training or expectations?
- What areas of your life or business could be improved by forming a clear "Standard Operating Procedure"?
- In your personal life, intentionally learn what other people's skills and passions are; align their areas of contribution with the stuff that lights them up.
- Make a point to regularly sit down with your key people to get on the same page about scheduling and time commitments.
- Before your next difficult conversation, prepare ahead of time. Identify the positive outcome you want to achieve; write bullets of key points you need to address. Work on becoming a more regulated, calm presence in these conversations.

Your success and ability as a leader will go further faster when you strengthen your communication skills. Do what it takes to lean into your areas of improvement, even if it makes you uncomfortable.

CONCLUSION

March 2020.

Newscasters had started getting jumpy, talking about something called "Coronavirus." I was too busy focusing on JKR Windows to give it much thought. We'd finished our second year, 2019, at 2.2 million in total revenue and we were accelerating fast. In January, we'd done over $600,000 in sales. February was even bigger. We'd already started out pretty hot in March with another 300 grand—up to 1.4 million.

We were growing fast too. In fact, I had just hired one of my good friends. He was in a rough spot—struggling to provide a quality lifestyle for his family and trying to get his marriage back together. He'd been trying to get his own business off the ground, and I had just finished convincing him that I had a better opportunity for him at JKR. "Our company is growing and expanding," I'd said. "I need your leadership. I need your help to grow this thing." I had made him all these promises about what we were going to accomplish together, painting him a vision of the lifestyle that he would be able to provide for his wife and his kids. It gave me a new weight of responsibility. This friend—and all my other employees—were counting on me to make good on those promises.

Mid-March hit and all of a sudden, I couldn't ignore the news anymore. All this stuff started coming out about the country shutting down. Everybody was going into quarantine; everybody was worried about getting sick. The stock market took a huge dive. People were freaking out about the economy. I started getting a lot of pressure from my employees—they wanted to know if we were shutting down too.

Initially, I felt some uncertainty, but I could tell they felt it even more. My employees didn't feel confident in their future anymore. People were asking me, "Jefferson, what are we going to do? Do I still have opportunities here? Am I going to lose my job?"

I thought of my friend. It was a really, really scary time.

I remember exactly where I was on March 17 when I decided to call that meeting. My friend had been working at the company for just four days. I didn't believe all the bullshit about the virus—but I was still faced with a decision about how we were going to do business. I sent a mass text out to everyone: "Emergency meeting."

When I had everyone gathered in the office, I said, "First of all, we're going to finish today out strong. I want you to go out and work until dark. Do as much as you can."

Somebody asked, "What if someone calls the cops on us?"

I said, "If you get arrested and handcuffed for knocking on doors, I'll give you a thousand-dollar bonus."

That ended up setting the tone for the rest of the meeting. I said, "Here's my opinion: they're trying to scare us out of doing what we do to make our money and support our families. We're *not* going to let them scare us. We're not going to stop supporting our families. We're going to go out there and finish the day strong." I remember everyone's eyes staring at me. I saw a lot of nodding heads.

I paused. "And I want everybody in the company at the office tomorrow morning at nine o'clock."

"So...," one of my employees asked. "We're not going to shut down?"

"Hell no, we're not shutting down," I said. I started heating up, thinking about my team, thinking about their families. "We're not slowing down. We're going to do *more* than we've ever done before. In fact, I'm going to invest in new training for everybody so that we can become better salespeople. Because it's probably going to get harder than ever before to sell. We need to be prepared to go out there, talk to people, be confident in what we do, and have great closing skills. I don't want anyone getting their teeth kicked in. So, we're not only going to be better, but we're going to work *harder*. We're going to work *longer*."

I pointed out the window. "All those other companies are shutting their doors right now. We're going to go after that market. We're not going to do what everyone else is doing. We're going *ALL IN*."

That built a ton of momentum for our team. We had started that year with the goal to do ten million, but that goal didn't become a possibility until that meeting. Before that, we'd been on track to do somewhere around six or seven million. But after that meeting, everybody bought in—we fully committed to go after it, 100 percent. We were ready to work more hours, knock on more doors, and level up the effort, more than ever before.

When people had walked into that meeting, they felt a ton of uncertainty. Some people assumed we would shut down, because that's what everybody else was doing—so we'd better do it too. Some people were speculating about how deadly the virus was going to be. Other people were asking—is this even real? And what will the consequences be?

Luckily, I was the loudest voice in the room. I wasn't worried about any of us getting sick. I was convinced that the news stories were a lot less real than my employees' livelihoods. And that confidence was what everyone needed to hear.

We went knocking on doors all over the state of Utah. We did get some pushback—and it was like nothing we had ever seen before. Some people were scared to death to see us out. They had their fucking shotguns sitting next to the front door. In some rural areas where we were knocking, people thought it was a zombie apocalypse. We got guns pulled on us, people yelled at us, a few called the cops on us.

Back at the office, I worked to give my team the mental preparation for what was going on. "Guys, this is just the beginning," I said. "We're probably going to get more guns pulled on us. But what are we going to do? Are we going to retreat and give into this? Are we going to rely on the government to take care of us? Or—are we going to go *ALL IN* and sell some fucking windows?"

No one got shot. No one got sick. No one got arrested—I'm still waiting to pay that thousand-dollar bonus.

And, as it turned out—*everybody* was at home. Zombie-apocalypse-shotgun-people aside, our door-to-door model was the best business strategy anyone could have chosen during those early months of the pandemic, and it's what we excelled at. We were in the right place, at the right time—and we had the right strategy and all the systems in place to seize the opportunity in front of us. Our numbers skyrocketed.

I've spent the better part of my lifetime ignoring the rules. A lot of times, that attitude got me into a hell of a lot of trouble. But sometimes, it fucking paid off—especially when there was discipline and focus to back it up.

People get stuck when they forget just how much ownership they have over life. It's a passive, comfortable, victim attitude that keeps you on the couch: "I'm comfortable where I'm at. I don't know anything different. I'm just going to keep sitting here and living my life the way I'm used to." It's fear that keeps us stuck—fear of the unknown, fear of discomfort. It's the same kind of fear that made a lot of businesses shut down in early 2020.

> People get stuck when they forget just how much ownership they have over life.

But I'd learned how to get unstuck. And in that moment, fear was *not* going to be our attitude. No one was going to stay on the couch. We chose to do the hard work—even if it meant taking a huge risk. We chose to go *ALL IN*.

ALL IN

Living with an *ALL IN* mentality means you're 100 percent committed to going after your goals. It can be a good thing or a bad thing, depending on what your goals are. There were periods of my life when I was *ALL IN* about stuff that was keeping me stuck. I couldn't wait for the weekend.

I had everybody's numbers on speed dial that I knew would be partying. I knew all the names of the people that would get me weed and alcohol. And that's how I went *ALL IN* for a long, long time.

But there was a shift that I made when I was ready to change my life. I recognized that my patterns were no longer serving me. *Nothing* about my stuck habits was helping me get any closer to my goals and dreams. I wanted to become the best version of myself, so I threw myself into manufacturing change in my life.

I had a couple of false starts, ones I've shared in this book. But those starts still helped me make a lot of progress, and I'm thankful for them. They helped me realize I had to *commit* to changes in my life on a completely different level than I ever had before. Once I was ready to get clean, once and for all, those prior experiences gave me fuel.

When you look at the word "decide"—there's a piece of that word, *cide*, that literally means "kill." It's the same reason we see *cide* in the word "genocide." I made the decision to put *all* those other negative habits in my life to death—all of them—so they were no longer a possibility. I decided they were completely unacceptable to me. And that's when I began to manifest the *ALL IN* lifestyle in a healthier way.

I traded one addiction in for another. I took all of that energy that I'd put into drugs and alcohol, and I refocused it on building a business. That's the thing about addictive behaviors. You can use them to drag yourself down and believe you have a sickness you'll never be able to overcome, or you can use them for positivity and growth. I had my addictive personality focused in the wrong direction for a long time. I always had these capabilities—natural skills, good genes, good energy. I just had them focused in the wrong direction. Once I focused them in a positive, productive direction, things started really cranking. I was ruthless in eliminating the negativity in my life and went after positive habits with all of my addictive energy. I held absolutely nothing back. (You can read more about how I refocused my addictive personality in the following *Deseret News* article: https://www.deseret.com /utah/2022/6/26/23160147/addiction-recovery-story-capitalism-not -alcoholism-grant-cardone-mentor).

That's the same attitude you need to get unstuck and accelerate in your own life. You have to go *ALL IN* on your potential by putting to death the negative patterns in your life. Stop believing a bullshit narrative to justify your stuck habits. Refuse to accept the unacceptable. Instead, manufacture change in your life by changing your environment and your influences.

And if you fuck up after you've started trying to live differently, don't let that suck you back into shame. *Use* your lows to help you identify what matters most to you. Make a plan to try again, in a better way. Change your thinking to get rid of all the negativity that's keeping you stuck. Remember: people are counting on you. They need you to get unstuck. Train your brain to accept positive thoughts as the truth: *you're meant to do great things with your life.*

It will be hard. I haven't tried to disguise that fact at any point in this book: it's going to be fucking hard to do the things necessary for change. Discomfort is part of it. Push through that to develop new habits in your life. Identify a clear focus about where you want to go, then develop the disciplined habits to get yourself there. Get clarity on your values and goals, then take consistent daily activity in that direction. Even if you're making small, small changes—if they're moving you closer to your goals, then every day, you're making progress. You're becoming a better version of yourself and living up to your potential. You're accelerating in the direction you want to go.

> You're making small changes, every day, and that's
> how you're making progress. You're becoming a better
> version of yourself and living up to your potential. You're
> accelerating in the direction you want to go.

Make sure you have good people around you—both to support you when things are hard, but also to help you grow and expose you to what's possible. Strengthen your positive relationships and get yourself a dream team. Find a mentor. Do work you're proud of so that you can feel the confidence that comes with integrity. Invest in opportunities for your growth. Learn to communicate your expectations clearly and lead difficult conversations toward positive outcomes. That's how you get yourself going further faster.

CHOOSE THE FUTURE YOU WANT

If you're getting to the end of this book and the message resonates—*decide* you're ready for change. Nothing is going to change unless you do. You can read all the books and surround yourself with incredible people—but unless *you* are ready to start making changes and doing the work, nothing is going to be any different.

So, start small. That's how I did it. Don't get overwhelmed by making yourself a gigantic list of things to do to reach success in a period of five years—that's too much. Just take small, little steps. The first baby step for me was getting up a little bit earlier in the morning, simple as that. Maybe that's where it starts for you: you get up a little bit earlier and now you have a little more time in your day. You do that a few days in a row, and it starts getting easier. Now, you get to choose what you're going to do with that extra time. I chose to start reading and writing my goals—that was the next baby step after getting up early. I implemented one new small step at a time, and that was what helped me make progress.

I wasn't perfect. I didn't hit my marks every single day—I still don't. But one thing that I *don't* do is get down on myself. I slept in last Saturday and got six and a half hours of sleep, which is a lot for me. But just because I sleep in one time, I'm not going to get down on myself. I'm not going to let it turn into a week or a month. Instead, I focus on keeping the streak alive. On Sunday, I woke up early, grabbed my mountain bike, and I went and broke my trail record by a minute and four seconds. So even if you miss one day—don't break the streak.

I've got so much momentum right now, and I've only just *barely* begun doing smart things. Four years ago, I was just starting the Grant

Cardone mentorship program, posting Facebook videos about the earliest steps of my progress. It's only been a year since I started really putting my story about my past out there on podcasts and Instagram, but I'm starting to hear from people who have become inspired to do great things. Just in the last year alone, I've made a ton of progress.

My story seems incredible to some, but where I'm at is just the tip of the iceberg of what's possible—both for me and for *you*. The only limitations you have are the ones you put on yourself.

MAKE A DENT IN THE UNIVERSE

Do you believe that? Maybe it's hard to buy the belief that you're meant for greatness. I was blessed with an upbringing where the people around me conditioned me, my entire life, with the message that I was meant to do great things. That upbringing helped shape and mold me. It enabled me to change my negative beliefs, thoughts, and actions into ones that served me once I was ready to make healthy changes. Their messages provided a foundation for me to become the person I am today.

But not everybody has that.

Maybe you had the exact opposite upbringing. Maybe you grew up having to fend for yourself, where you were in constant survival mode. Maybe you grew up separated from your family. Maybe you had to get through some serious shit.

But don't let that give you a victim mindset. There are *plenty* of success stories that have come from people who lived lives exactly like that. Use those pain points as fuel to help you accelerate in life. You probably learned a lot of lessons, getting through what you did. You probably had to become tough, resourceful, and resilient. Guess what? All of those skills translate really well into business.

Or maybe you were coddled as a kid. Maybe you didn't get as much attention as you wanted, but you had a cushy childhood, and you're used to being comfortable. Maybe you didn't see many examples of people building success from the ground up, and you don't believe great things are possible for you.

Whatever and *wherever* you come from, plant this seed in you right now: no matter what your upbringing or your current beliefs, *you can change*, if you're willing to put in the work. Condition yourself to believe that you don't have to stay where you are.

We were all put here to make an impact. It's your decision whether you want that impact to be small or big. It's your choices that make that impact negative or positive. Start working today on your personal belief system and self-talk. Create a positive narrative about what's possible for you, and what your life could be, and what your potential is.

You can choose to stay stuck, keep living this life on repeat. Or, you can choose to get out of your comfort zone and put yourself into circumstances that will help mold you into an incredible human being.

You can choose to be a leader. You can choose to be an amazing communicator. You can choose to make a dent in the universe.

Ready? Make the choice. You know what to do.

ALL IN.

ACKNOWLEDGMENTS

Dave Blanchard: I started meeting with you around the same time I started writing this book. I sought you out because I wanted to get better at communicating on a deeper level with people. I needed help showing empathy so I could bring down people's walls rather than causing people to put walls up. Your calm, wise presence has taught me so much. You knew what I needed to hear, and what you've taught me has changed my life and my business, in addition to impacting the message on every page of this book. Thank you.

Kane Minkus: We've been on a journey together! I originally sought you out for help launching an event. You gave me needed insight that helped me make some hard decisions about where I truly needed to focus my energy, time, and attention. Even as I made the move to cancel the event, I knew I needed to continue an advisory partnership with you. Your input at JKR Windows has led us to make a quantum leap of progress. I'm blown away by the new possibilities you've brought into my awareness—it would have taken me decades to arrive at the same place without your help. I appreciate your candor, bluntness, and friendship more than I can say.

Jeff Fieldstad: You are my oldest friend in the world! We started out as enemies in middle school, then finally became friends around age fifteen—smoking joints in our baggy clothes and sideways hats. But you had a vision for your future that you talked about with such conviction and belief—in spite of a rough background, you knew that you were going to have an amazing life. That planted seeds in my mind for what my own life could become, even though it took a lot longer for me to get there. You started in business at a young age, and your success was an inspiration to me. Your influence played a big part in helping me turn my life around. We continue to compete with each other, push each other, and challenge each other. I'm thankful for every bit of it, even though I sometimes feel like I don't deserve to have someone as incredible as you in my life. I'm thankful for all the good times we've shared together with our families. You're an inspiration.

Greta Myers: I went through two other companies and four other ghostwriters before I met you. My intuition told me right away when we met that this was going to be a great partnership, and my wife said the same thing. It's been such a great experience. You have a knack and a vision and a gift—you see an entire paragraph before I've even finished speaking it, and you know exactly where it needs to go. I'm amazed by the talent that you have.

Anna Dorfman: You had to increase your patience level with me! We had to go back and forth so many times on the cover design. Thanks for your inspiration for what turned out to be such an amazing first impression of this book. Huge appreciation for your prompt communication and artistic talent.

Brynn Strain: When I was looking for an assistant, you were described to me as "the most hard-working, disciplined, detail-oriented person." You're everything my friend described you to be and more, and you've done incredible things to help me get the final elements of this book done. I had been without an assistant for a year, but since you've come in, the possibilities for what we're going to be able to do with JKR Windows have increased exponentially, because of how you've enabled me to expand my bandwidth. Thank you. I've got a good feeling that we're going to be working together for a long, long time.

Brooks Brunson: At the end of 2019, I was looking for a logistics manager, and went through dozens and dozens of résumés. No one was even close to what I was looking for. One morning, when I arrived at "The Closet," I saw your résumé sitting on top of a stack on my desk. It was a crazy moment—like, the sun was shining through the window, making a spotlight right on your page. My mom came into the office and both of us were like, "Where did this one come from?" As soon as I saw your name on that paper, I knew you were the guy we needed. You're the longest employee we've had and the most loyal guy. I'm blown away and inspired by the progress we've witnessed in each other. I hope to count you as a close friend for the rest of my life.

JKR Windows Family: So much to say! All of the lessons I talk about in this book were learned in the context of our team, testing them on you, my people. Your loyalty amazes me. Y'all are so intent on being there for the vision and purpose of our company. You let me try out all my fucking crazy ideas, and you respond with, "I'm on it!" It's a blessing to have such an amazing group of people around me every day. You've got my back, and I hope you know that I have yours.

Mom: You always instilled in me an incredible amount of confidence. I was your firstborn, and you did everything you knew how to do to raise me the best way you could. You encouraged me to be a good example for my brothers, and to become a great man, father, and husband. Thank you for always believing in me. I love you.

Dad: I had big shoes to fill, being named after you. I've always admired your strength, work ethic, and your huge heart. Even though we didn't spend a ton of time having deep conversations, I was watching intently at everything you did. You loved your family, you paid attention to the details, and you took great pride in your work. I would not be the man I am today without your influence. You're my hero. You have been my whole life. I love you.

Hayden: I got thrown right into fatherhood when I met your mom. That night that I met her, I knew she was the girl that I wanted to marry. The next day, I found out that she had a son. I remember the first time I saw you like it was yesterday: your eyes, your amazing smile, the conversation you were already capable of at three years old. You, more than anybody else in this world, taught me to have a greater level of patience. You've become a strong, confident young man. I constantly feel so proud to be your dad. It's an honor to be someone you look to as an example, and I love you.

Lyla: There's an incredible feeling seeing your first child be born. I remember watching your heart rate as you tried to make it into the world. I can't even describe what it was like to hold you for the first time. You have a drive to do great things, be good at everything you do, and make your parents proud. Your natural ability to just figure things out blows me away. It's like nothing I've ever seen. When your mom calls me to ask me for something around the house, I ask her, "Is Lyla home? See if she can do it." And you're only eleven years old! I love you and I'm so proud of you. Thank you for loving me as powerfully as you do.

Ayva: You are the fuel to the flame: such an incredible spirit and personality. You feel everything so deeply. You're adventurous and fearless. Sometimes I get nervous seeing what you'll risk, but I'm also so excited to watch you go. It's amazing being your dad and watching you grow up. You make me feel so incredibly loved, and I love you right back. I'm proud to be your dad. You blow me away.

Shandell Rogers: I saved the best for last. You show never-ending support for my dreams and my goals and my crazy ideas. When I think about the path I was on before I met you, and where that road would have led, it's almost too painful to think about. The positive energy you bring to my life—as my wife, my partner, and the mother of my children— is miraculous. Nothing of what I love and cherish in life would have been possible without you. I'm amazed by the life we've been able to build together. Thank you for never giving up on me. I love you.

ABOUT THE AUTHOR

Jefferson K. Rogers is the founder and CEO of JKR Windows. In its first five years, JKR Windows has brought in over $45 million in revenue and is now approaching 100 employees. Jefferson achieved success after overcoming a two-decade-long struggle with alcoholism and addiction, a journey he shares candidly on his podcast, in interviews, and on Instagram. He constantly pushes himself to learn new things, living in the area where discomfort meets growth. Jefferson has trained as a pilot, won physique and motocross competitions, and is a successful real estate investor. He's also a sought-after business consultant and speaker. His greatest source of pride comes from being husband to Shandell and dad to his three stellar kids. You can connect with him on Instagram @jeffersonkrogers and at his website: jeffersonkrogers.com.

9 781544 541952